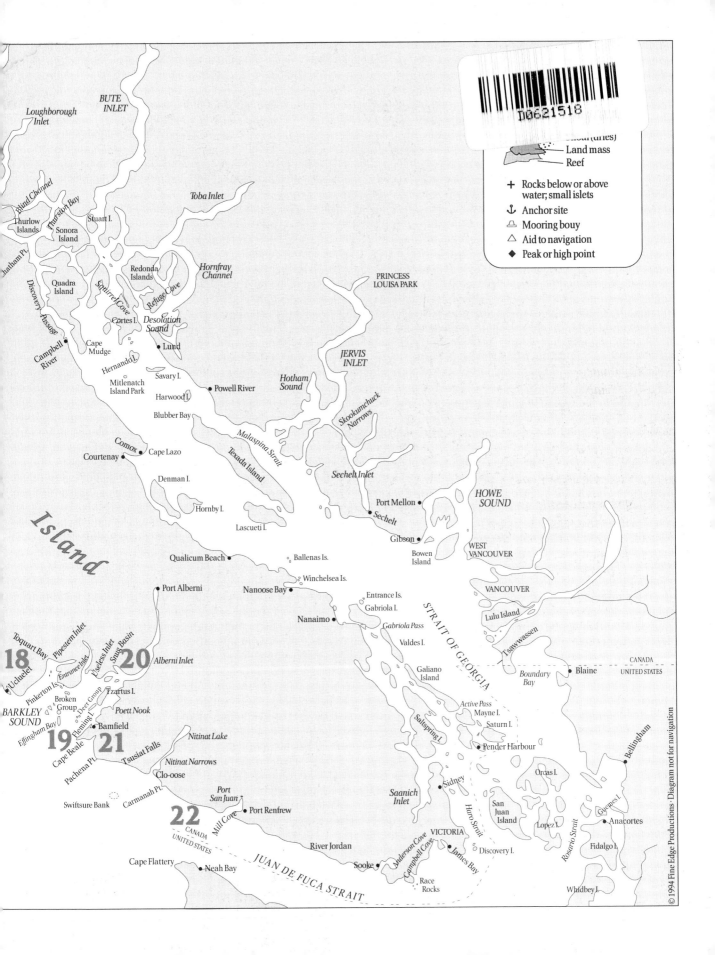

Loughborough
Inlet

BUTE
INLET

Toba Inlet

Blind Channel

Thurlow
Islands

Thurston Bay

Stuart I.

Sonora
Island

Chatham Pt.

Hornfray
Channel

PRINCESS
LOUISA PARK

Redonda
Islands

Discovery Passage

Quadra
Island

Squirrel Cove

Refuge Cove

Cortes I.

Desolation
Sound

JERVIS
INLET

Campbell
River

Cape
Mudge

Lund

Hernando I.

Hotham
Sound

Mitlenatch
Island Park

Savary I.

Harwood I.

Powell River

Skookumchuck
Narrows

Blubber Bay

Malaspina Strait

Comox

Cape Lazo

Sechelt Inlet

HOWE
SOUND

Courtenay

Texada Island

Denman I.

Port Mellon

Hornby I.

Sechelt

Lasqueti I.

Gibson

WEST
VANCOUVER

Qualicum Beach

Ballenas Is.

Bowen
Island

Island

Winchelsea Is.

VANCOUVER

Port Alberni

Nanoose Bay

Entrance Is.

Gabriola I.

Lulu Island

Nanaimo

Tsawwassen

Toquart Bay

Pipestem Inlet

Useless Inlet

Snug Basin

Gabriola Pass

Valdes I.

STRAIT OF GEORGIA

18

Entrance Inlet

20

Alberni Inlet

CANADA

Boundary
Bay

Blaine

UNITED STATES

Ucluelet

Pinkerton Is.

Galiano
Island

Broken
Group

Deer Group

Tzartus I.

Active Pass

Mayne I.

BARKLEY
SOUND

Poett Nook

Saltspring I.

Saturn I.

Effingham Bay

Fleming I.

Bamfield

Bellingham

19

21

Pender Harbour

Cape Beale

Nitinat Lake

Orcas I.

Pachena Pt.

Tsusiat Falls

Nitinat Narrows

Saanich
Inlet

Sidney

Guemes I.

Clo-oose

Swiftsure Bank

Carmanah Pt.

Port
San Juan

San
Juan
Island

Anacortes

Lopez I.

Rosario Strait

Fidalgo I.

22

Mill Cove

Port Renfrew

CANADA

UNITED STATES

Haro Strait

VICTORIA

Cape Flattery

Neah Bay

River Jordan

Sooke

Anderson Cove

Campbell Cove

James Bay

Discovery I.

JUAN DE FUCA STRAIT

Race
Rocks

Whidbey I.

© 1994 Fine Edge Productions · Diagram not for navigation

Shoal (dries)

Land mass

Reef

+ Rocks below or above
  water; small islets

⚓ Anchor site

⌂ Mooring bouy

△ Aid to navigation

◆ Peak or high point

Exploring
VANCOUVER ISLAND'S
WEST COAST
A Cruising Guide

– FIRST EDITION –

BY DON DOUGLASS

FINE EDGE
Productions
BISHOP, CALIFORNIA

Quotations from the Canadian *Sailing Directions*, Vol. 1, are used with permission of the Canadian Hydrographic Service. Reproduction of information from Canadian Hydrographic Service Sailing Directions in this publication are for illustrative purposes only, they do not meet the requirements of the Charts and Publication Regulations and are not to be used for navigation. The appropriate Sailing Directions, corrected up-to-date, and the relevant Canadian Hydrographic Service charts required under the Charts and Publications Regulations of the Canada Shipping Act must be used for navigation.

Contact the Canadian Hydrographic Service to obtain information on local dealers and available charts and publications or to order charts and publications directly:

Chart Sales and Distribution Office
Canadian Hydrographic Service
Department of Fisheries and Oceans
Institute of Ocean Sciences, Patricia Bay
9860 West Saanich Road
Sidney B.C., V8L 4B2
Telephone (604) 363-6358; FAX (604) 363-6841

Disclaimer

This book is designed to provide experienced skippers with cruising information on the West Coast of Vancouver Island. Every effort has been made to make this book as complete and accurate as possible.

There may be mistakes, both typographical and in content; therefore this book should be used only as a general guide, not as the ultimate source of information on the areas covered. Much of what is presented in this book is local knowledge based upon personal observation and is subject to human error.

The author, publisher and local authorities assume no liability for errors or omissions or for any loss or damages incurred from using this information.

Library of Congress Cataloging-in-Publication Data

Douglass, Don, 1932–
    Exploring Vancouver Island's west coast / by Don
Douglass.
        p.   cm.
    Includes bibliographical references and index.
    ISBN 0-938665-26-X
    1. Vancouver Island (B.C.)—Guidebooks. 2. Cruise ships—British
Columbia—Vancouver Island—Guidebooks. I. Title.
F1089.V3D68   1994
917.11'2044—dc20
                                                                            94-6731
                                                                            CIP

ISBN 0-938665-26-X

Dedicated to

Réanne Hemingway Douglass

Life and business partner, extraordinaire

Loyal first mate from 59° North to 54° South

Critical and patient editor
of my indecipherable rough drafts

Acknowledgments

I am indebted, first, to my crew whose patience and skill in sometimes less than ideal conditions allowed me to focus on gathering the information for this book: my wife, Réanne, and our longtime friends and fellow sailors, Bob and Anna Mae Botley.

My thanks to those in Seattle and Victoria who motivated me to undertake this project and who offered their continuing support along the way; to the Canadian Hydrographic Service for their kind permission to quote from Canadian *Sailing Directions;* to the staff of the Maritime Museum of British Columbia and the Provincial Parks for their help with research.

Meeting friendly, helpful and interesting people along the route is one of the many rewards of cruising. I count among these people the following West Coast experts who gave generously of their time to provide local knowledge as we were exploring their area, and afterwards reviewed the draft manuscript: Tom Cook, Quatsino; Steve and Martha Tyerman, Kyuquot; Dan DeVault, Nuchatlitz; Ed and Pat Kidder, Nootka Light Station; Ray Williams, Friendly Cove; Shirley Andrews and Hereditary Chiefs Jerry Jack and Larry Andrews, A'haminaquus; Hugh Clarke, Ahousat; Ken Gibson and Rod Palm, Tofino and Alan Wizinski, Nanaimo. Their knowledge, ideas and support were essential.

Many other people patiently answered endless questions; among them George Rieger and Rachel Le Mieux of Esperanza Mission; June Cameron of Vancouver; the summer residents of Julia Passage; the crew of numerous West Coast fishing and cruising vessels; the competent Canadian Coast Guard and others whose names I never was privileged to learn.

My thanks, also, to West Coast sailing companions who shared their knowledge with me and who took time to critique the manuscript: Rod Nash, skipper and fellow adventurer of *Forevergreen,* Santa Barbara Y.C; Robbie and Dolores Robinson, of *Rolling Stone,* San Francisco; and Frank and Margy Fletcher, of *Julie Ann,* Anacortes, whose years of cruising experience in the Northwest continue to amaze and inspire us.

My sincerest thanks go to the crew who helped pull it all together—Réanne Hemingway-Douglass, chief editor; Sue Irwin, book designer; Laura Patterson, cover designer; David Smith, Pat Eckart and Lorraine Schultz. Without their dedicated help there would be no book.

Contents

Edited by Réanne Douglass and Pat Eckart
Design, Layout and Typography by Sue Irwin
Cover Design by Laura Patterson
Cover Chart 3670 reprinted by permission of the Canadian Hydrographic Service
Inside Cover Map by Sue Irwin
Diagrams by Sue Irwin and Lorraine Schultz
Photography by Robert Botley and Don Douglass
Photographs on pages 88 and 90 courtesy of Tom Cook

Preface

Super, Natural British Columbia! Nowhere does the tourist motto that appears on B.C. ferries and maps come more alive than on the West Coast of Vancouver Island. In your modern cruising boat, on a two weeks' to a month's circumnavigation of Vancouver Island, you, too, can experience this feeling.

The largest island on the west coast of North America, Vancouver Island is 700 miles in circumference and 13,000 square miles in all, with over 2,000 miles of detailed coastline. Take a look at a large-scale chart of the island and you can see that all the long, deeply cut inlets are located on its West Coast. Five great sounds, 16 major inlets and over 200 islands offer a variety of wild and magnificent scenery.

Look closer at the chart, and notice the many coves and bays within these inlets. Of all "coves" mentioned in the Canadian *Sailing Directions,* Vol. 1, British Columbia Coast (South Portion), 40 percent are found on the West Coast of Vancouver Island! Add to this list the numerous additional unnamed coves documented in this book and you have over 50% of the best cruising destinations in southern British Columbia.

All these pristine and remote coves await cruising vessels willing to venture northwest from Puget Sound. Many days you won't see another cruising boat and can anchor with no one else in sight. You can see rivers of saltwater seething with rapids and observe cavorting dolphins, grey whales and orcas. You can watch sea otters poke their noses out of the water to inspect your boat, spot black bears scavenging on shore, or hear the haunting call of the loon or the scream of majestic bald eagles. You can focus your binoculars on tufted puffins, harlequin ducks, mergansers, murres and hundreds of other beautiful migratory birds.

We think exploring Vancouver Island's West Coast is a super, natural experience, and we hope it will be your cruise of a lifetime as well!

Part I
Introduction to the West Coast

1

How to Use this Book

How This Book is Organized

This book is designed to assist a small boat skipper who wants to cruise the West Coast of Vancouver Island using detailed and up-to-date information not previously available. In particular we have tried to cover the "local knowledge required" often mentioned in the Canadian *Sailing Directions* about small non-commercial coves and anchorages.

Part I provides a background about cruising along the West Coast. It presents four suggested itineraries, explains how and why certain conditions occur, and gives other important explanations and definitions of terms.

In Part II each chapter covers a separate cruising area of Vancouver Island divided into sections giving information about a specific place. Each cove or destination (shown in bold face) is followed by current chart numbers of the area. If a chart uses metric notations, this is noted. In addition to listing the chart numbers, a GPS way-point—such as a buoy, light or anchor site—is identified with its latitude and longitude specified.

Below most bold-faced place names you will find a quote in italics from the Canadian *Sailing Directions*, Vol. 1 (1990) with its page number cited. An ellipsis (three dots) indicates that we abridged a quote. If no quote is given, *Sailing Directions* does not mention the place.

Text that follows the *Sailing Directions* quotation is information (i.e. local knowledge)

we gathered while cruising these waters. An accompanying diagram illustrates route, depth and anchorage based upon our personal experience. Photographs of the entrance or prominent features are often included.

Part III, the Appendices, contains a number of references helpful for cruising the West Coast or for circumnavigating Vancouver Island: tables on distance, weather and other conditions, as well as a bibliography and place index.

It is important for the user to study this chapter as well as Weather and Cruising Considerations in Chapter 3, where information unique to Vancouver Island's West Coast is provided and important terminology and limitations are given.

Please keep in mind that this guidebook does not replace the need for large-scale Canadian charts, a copy of *Sailing Directions* and tide tables, nor does it eliminate the need for careful planning and vigilant navigation. Rather, it is designed as a "smart tool" to help navigators of the West Coast plan a trip of the area maximizing options, time, safety and comfort.

Local Knowledge

My personal observations are the main source of "local knowledge" for this guidebook, whether in text or diagrams. I have also used information gained in discussions with local skippers to verify my observations and to obtain additional details. Some of the scientific and weather information was paraphrased from the literature, and the user is invited to consult the bibliography.

Although I personally dropped my hook in all the places where the depth and type of bottom are given, collecting the information was not a scientific study on my part, nor have I made an attempt to list all potential hazards. (Please see Appendix G for procedures used in gathering the information.)

Because of the limited scope and subjective nature of these tests (frequently only one anchor test per anchor site), the information in this guidebook should be used with healthy skepticism. Prior to anchoring, any skipper should do his/her own perusal of an area, comparing depths, hazards, etc.

Diagrams and Text

Locations of anchorages, depth of the water and route information are shown in diagrammatic form. These diagrams are not representational and should not be used for navigation; they do not include all known or unknown hazards and they are only an attempt to show "local information" collected.

In the text, place names are followed by corresponding chart numbers with latitude and longitude of the site identified. Both the bottom material of an anchorage and holding power are mentioned, in addition to the kind of protection you can expect.

Some of the anchoring sites, as well as their entrances and exits, may pass nearer shore or shoals than some skippers feel comfortable with; they were chosen on a subjective basis due to their aesthetic lure and an assumption of stable weather. For more swinging room or a greater margin of safety, skippers with larger boats may wish to modify these suggested routes or anchoring sites.

The many coves explored and presented in this book were chosen in an effort to maximize alternatives for skippers seeking shelter. There are also suggestions for short lunch stops, for hikes on shore, or for bird-watching or fishing. *Because the book lists or shows a cove in a diagram does not imply that it is suitable for an overnight stay or that it is safe to leave your boat unattended.*

Although I make no representation as to this book's accuracy or suitability of use by others, I have tried to give careful attention to the collection and presentation of this "local knowledge." Every opportunity was taken to record, double-check and verify facts. Despite this care, errors and omissions may still exist in the text or diagrams, and I accept no liability for loss or damages suffered from using this book. We encourage you to evaluate and validate this "smart tool" for yourself and make your own informed personal judgment.

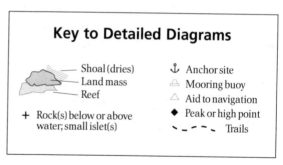

New Metric Charts and Symbols

Canada is in the process of converting all of its navigational charts from traditional British naval units to the metric system. Anyone navigating the West Coast must pay close attention to every chart used since nearly half are now metric. Each of the new charts have "Metric" printed in red in the lower right-hand corner.

These metric changes involve more than just a substitution of depth numbers—the symbols for depth and height have changed as well. For instance, $[1_3]$ on old Canadian charts and American charts means a depth of 1 fathom and 3 feet, for a total depth of 9 feet (1.5 fathoms), and an islet shown as (45) means a height of 45 feet. On the new metric charts, the symbol $[1_3]$ means 1.3 meters or about 4 feet. An islet shown as $\overline{45}$ means 45 meters (150 feet). These differences (1.5 fathoms versus 1.3 meters, 45 meters versus 45 feet) can be particularly confusing. Please obtain and study Canadian Chart 1 for all current Canadian symbols.

Conventions Used in this Book

Spelling and usage of place names follows, as closely as possible, local traditions and the lead of the Canadian *Sailing Directions.*

Because most boats that circumnavigate Vancouver Island seem to be flying the American flag, fathoms, yards, feet, degrees in Fahrenheit and other U.S. conventions are generally used. (Our Canadian friends seem to be more adept at making conversions than we Yankees are.)

Unless otherwise noted, depths listed in the text or shown on diagrams are always given in fathoms, regardless of the measurement units on the cited charts, and they are reduced to approximate zero tide. You should add the amount of tide listed in the corrected tide tables when you use these numbers. In Canada, zero tide datum is given as the lowest expected tide for the year; therefore tide tables almost always appear as a positive number rather than the frequent minus tides of the United States.

Bearings and courses, when given, are generally magnetic and identified as such. Courses are taken off the chart compass rose; they are approximate and are to be "made good." No allowances have been made for variation, deviation, or possible current or drift. When compass cardinal points are used (example NW or SE) these refer to true bearings and should be taken as approximate only.

Distances are expressed in nautical miles and speed is expressed in knots unless otherwise stated. Scales on the diagrams are expressed in yards, meters, and miles as noted and are approximate only. Time is given in four-digit 24-hour clock numbers, and all

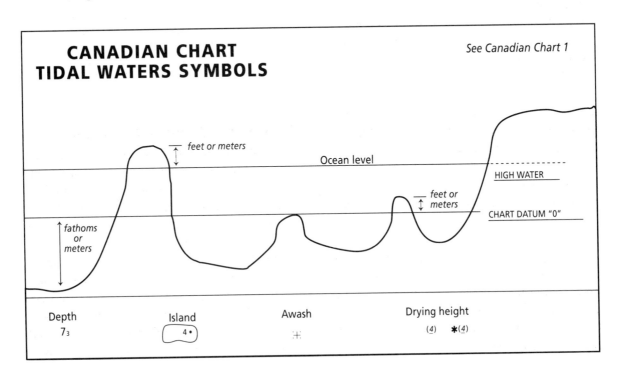

CANADIAN CHART TIDAL WATERS SYMBOLS

See Canadian Chart 1

feet or meters

Ocean level

HIGH WATER

feet or meters

CHART DATUM "0"

fathoms or meters

Depth
7₃

Island
4•

Awash

Drying height
(4)   ✱(4)

courses are given in three digits.

Latitudes and longitudes in the text are cited in degrees, minutes and decimal minutes (seconds are not used). They are taken off the largest scale chart available or from the List of Lights.

Lat/Long for anchorage sites and way-points are given to the nearest one-hundredth of a minute of latitude. West Coast charts in general are not accurate to—and many cannot be read to—one-hundredth of a degree of latitude (plus or minus 60 feet). These numbers are to be treated as approximate only.

Testing for bottom material

Routes into and out of coves and anchor sites reflect my preference for "keeping one foot on the beach" to get the feel of a place; I don't like to anchor in deep water.

Our boat, the *Baidarka*, is a 32-foot diesel trawler drawing 4 feet; when navigating tight coves, I always station at least one alert look-out on the bow. Since we have no anchor winch and we prefer nylon rode, I like to anchor close to shore where the near end of the 35-foot anchor chain comes on board before the anchor itself breaks loose (i.e. anchor in 30 feet of water or less). Skippers sailing short-handed or on larger boats will want to choose routes and anchor sites that reflect their own preferences.

Unnamed Islands and Islets

Unnamed islands and islets are referred to in the text by the height of the island enclosed in parentheses (taken from the appropriate chart). In some cases, where more than one chart covers an area, the numbers in parentheses may be either in feet or meters and may change from chart to chart.

Since this guidebook documents many small, unnamed coves and bays for the first time, we have tried to find local names and use them. Where we could find no reference to a name, we used a new one that seemed appropriate. Local names and new names are shown in quotation marks.

Updated Editions

With this publication, our intention is to update the presented local knowledge with new editions as soon as the market demand allows it.

If you have cruising details of

the West Coast which might be of interest to other skippers we would like to hear from you; in particular, we would like to receive your comments on the usefulness of the GPS way-points. Future editions of this guidebook will incorporate all appropriate information (and opinions) submitted by boat owners and skippers; acknowledgments will be made when possible.

Starting in April 1995, Fine Edge Productions will compile and make available a supplement of the prior season's observations. These supplements will be sent at no cost to any purchaser of this guide who sends a stamped, self-addressed, business-sized envelope (U.S. postage or international reply coupons).

Please send new observations, comments and SASE to Fine Edge Productions, Route 2 Box 303, Bishop, California 93514.

Other Publications

The bibliography lists a number of publications that are useful or necessary on any West Coast cruise. Canadian Hydrographic Service publications, in particular, are required by law to be carried on board any ship navigating in Canadian waters.

We recommend Don Watmough's Evergreen Pacific *Cruising Guide to the West Coast of Vancouver Island.* Originally published in 1984, this book is an excellent introduction to the West Coast. Outstanding aerial photographs by George McNutt capture the vitality and beauty of the rugged coast. (A 1993 edition printed by Evergreen Pacific is unrevised.)

History buffs may be interested in three other classics: *Vancouver Island's West Coast,* by George Nicholson (1965); *Coastal Cruising,* by Will Dawson (1959); and *British Columbia Coast Names, 1592-1909,* by Captain John T. Walbran (1971 reprint; original edition 1909).

2

Circumnavigation – Suggested Itineraries

Completing a circumnavigation of Vancouver Island is largely a matter of choosing an optimum time for each day's passage. Once you round Cape Scott, you can look forward to a series of fairly short, "outside" day-runs and quiet and secluded anchorages. The following itineraries are dependent upon time available, the average speed your vessel can maintain and equipment which allows you to travel during foggy weather.

In addition to a circumnavigation, cruising boats can head directly to Barkley and Clayoquot Sounds from Juan de Fuca Strait. Skippers who trailer their boats can reach the five major sounds of the West Coast by using dirt road access-points.

These suggested itineraries assume the popular counter-clockwise route; however, a circumnavigation is often completed in the opposite direction (clockwise) direction, particularly early in the season.

"Ultra-Marathon"
Rapid Circumnavigation of Vancouver Island
One Week (8 Days)

Total distance:
618 nautical miles (638 with add-ons)

Average daily run:
77 nautical miles (80 with add-ons)

Advantages:
For fast boats having minimal time to circumnavigate Vancouver Island

Feasibility:
Suitable for well-equipped offshore cruising boats that have a cruising speed in excess of 10 knots; good radar and GPS are mandatory

Best time:
Second half of June (longest days; least fog); requires stable weather conditions (see notes at end of chapter)

Anchoring required:
Little, if any—this route offers the possibility of staying only at marinas, government float docks or public mooring buoys (see notes at end of chapter)

Day 1 Victoria to Nanaimo		75 mi.
Day 2 Nanaimo to Campbell River		77 mi.
Day 3 Campbell River to		
Port Hardy		107 mi.
Day 4 Port Hardy to Winter Harbour		80 mi.
(Add 10 miles for route outside Hope Island)		
Day 5 Winter Harbour to Walter's Cove		54 mi.
Day 6 Walter's Cove to		
Hot Springs Cove		70 mi.
(Add 10 miles to visit Friendly Cove)		
Day 7 Hot Springs Cove to Bamfield		63 mi.
Day 8 Bamfield to Victoria		92 mi.

"The Highlights"
Fast Circumnavigation of Vancouver Island
Two weeks (15 days)

Total Distance:
671 nautical miles (684 with add-ons)

Average daily run:
45 nautical miles (46 with add-ons)

Advantages:
Gives highlights of the West Coast for those with limited time; an introduction to scenic and historical opportunities

Feasibility:
Suitable for those well-equipped cruising boats with a cruising speed of 8 knots or more; radar necessary; GPS recommended

Best time:
Early June to mid-July (long days; least fog); requires stable weather conditions (see notes at end of chapter)

Anchoring required:
Less than 50% of the time—mostly at government float docks or public mooring buoys (see notes at end of chapter)

Day 1 Victoria to Montague Harbour
     Provincial Marine Park   40 mi.
Day 2 Montague Harbour Marine Park
     to Squitty Bay Marine Park   48 mi.
Day 3 Squitty Bay Marine Park to Mitlenatch
     Island Provincial Marine Park   45 mi.
Day 4 Mitlenatch Island to Port Neville 58 mi.
Day 5 Port Neville to Port McNeil
     (or Alert Bay)   42 mi.
Day 6 Port McNeil to Bull Harbour   41 mi.
Day 7 Bull Harbour to Sea Otter Cove 38 mi.
Day 8 Sea Otter Cove to Klaskish Inlet 42 mi.
     (Add 15 miles for Winter Harbour)
Day 9 Klaskish Inlet to Columbia Cove 32 mi.
Day 10 Columbia Cove to Dixon Cove
     (Walter's Cove for fuel stop)   54 mi.
Day 11 Dixon Cove to Friendly Cove
     (via Esperanza Inlet)   51 mi.

Day 12 Friendly Cove to
     Hot Springs Cove   28 mi.
Day 13 Hot Springs Cove to
     Effingham Bay   53 mi.
Day 14 Effingham Bay to Bamfield
     (via Broken Group)   13 mi.
Day 15 Bamfield to Victoria   92 mi.

"The Classic"
Circumnavigation of Vancouver Island
Three Weeks (22 Days)

Total distance:
715 nautical miles (739 with add-ons)

Average daily run:
33 nautical miles (34 with add-ons)

Advantages:
Less hurried pace with a chance to explore some scenic and historic places; allows a wider choice of favorable times

Where freshwater meets saltwater, Bacchante Bay

Anchoring required:
About 50% of time, balance at public mooring buoys with some government float docks

Feasibility:
Suitable for well-equipped cruising boats with a cruising speed of 6 knots or more; radar recommended; GPS helpful

Best time:
Early June to mid-August (best weather, long days)

Day 1 Victoria to Montague Harbour
    Provincial Marine Park   40 mi.
Day 2 Montague Harbour to Squitty
    Bay Provincial Marine Park   48 mi.
Day 3 Squitty Bay to Squirrel Cove   53 mi.
Day 4 Squirrel Cove to Thurston Bay
    Provincial Marine Park   33 mi.
Day 5 Thurston Bay to Port Neville   34 mi.
Day 6 Port Neville to Port McNeil
    (or Alert Bay)   42 mi.
Day 7 Port McNeil to Port Hardy   23 mi.
Day 8 Port Hardy to Bull Harbour   22 mi.
Day 9 Bull Harbour to Sea Otter Cove 38 mi.
Day 10 Sea Otter Cove to Klaskish Inlet 40 mi.
    (Add 15 miles for Winter Harbour)
Day 11 Klaskish Inlet to Columbia Cove 33 mi.
Day 12 Columbia Cove to
    Scow Cove (via Battle Bay)   12 mi.
Day 13 Scow Cove to Dixon Cove
    (via Walter's Cove)   20 mi.
Day 14 Dixon Cove to Queens Cove
    (via Nuchatlitz)   27 mi.
Day 15 Queens Cove to Friendly Cove
    (via Esperanza Inlet)   30 mi.
    (Add 8 miles for Tahsis)
Day 16 Friendly Cove to
    Hot Springs Cove   28 mi.
Day 17 Hot Springs Cove to Adventure
    Cove (via Hayden Passage)   32 mi.
Day 18 Adventure Cove to Ucluelet
    (via Tofino)   30 mi.
Day 19 Ucluelet to Pinkerton Islands
    (via Broken Group)   20 mi.

Day 20 Pinkerton Islands to Bamfield (via
    Julia Passage and Deer Group) 18 mi.
Day 21 Bamfield to Mill Cove
    (Port San Juan)   42 mi.
Day 22 Mill Cove to Victoria   50 mi.

Transportation styles on the West Coast

"Dream"
Circumnavigation of Vancouver Island
Four Weeks (30 Days or More)

Total distance:
825 nautical miles (857 with add-ons)

Average daily run:
28 nautical miles (29 with add-ons)

Advantages:
Self-paced immersion trip for those who want to do the West Coast "right" with time for exploring secluded spots and major scenic and historical places; can be undertaken anytime of summer in most offshore cruising boats

Anchoring required:
Approximately 75% of the time in off-the-beaten-path coves; balance at public mooring buoys, or as desired

Feasibility:
Suitable for boats equipped for extended travel with a cruising speed of 5 knots or more; radar and/or GPS helpful

Best time:
Mid-May to early September (good weather, fewer crowds); allows time to wait out fog, weather or contrary currents

Day 1 Victoria to Montague Harbour
 Provincial Marine Park 40 mi.
Day 2 Montague Harbour to Newcastle
 Island Provincial Marine Park 28 mi.
Day 3 Newcastle Island to Lasqueti Island
 (landlocked cove NE end) 31 mi.
Day 4 Lasqueti Island to Squirrel Cove 46 mi.
Day 5 Squirrel Cove to Thurston Bay
 Provincial Marine Park 33 mi.
Day 6 Thurston Bay to Port Neville 34 mi.
Day 7 Port Neville to Port McNeil
 (or Alert Bay) 42 mi.
Day 8 Port McNeil to Port Hardy 23 mi.
Day 9 Port Hardy to Bull Harbour 22 mi.
Day 10 Bull Harbour to Sea Otter Cove 38 mi.
Day 11 Sea Otter Cove to Julian Cove 40 mi.
Day 12 Julian Cove to Pamphlet ("Quiet")
 Cove via Coal Harbour 15 mi.
Day 13 Pamphlet Cove to Klaskish Basin 34 mi.
Day 14 Klaskish Basin to Columbia Cove 33 mi.
Day 15 Columbia Cove to "Scow Cove"
 (via Battle Bay) 12 mi.
Day 16 Scow Cove to Dixon Cove
 (via Walter's Cove) 20 mi.
Day 17 Dixon Cove to Queens Cove
 (via Nuchatlitz) 27 mi.
Day 18 Queens Cove to "Critter Cove" 28 mi.
 (Add 8 miles to Tahsis)
Day 19 "Critter Cove" to Friendly Cove
 (via Resolution Cove) 11 mi.
 (Add 24 miles to Gold River)
Day 20 Friendly Cove to
 Hot Springs Cove 28 mi.
Day 21 Hot Springs Cove to West White
 Pine Cove (via Hayden Passage) 18 mi.
Day 22 West White Pine Cove to Windy Bay
 (via Matlset Narrows) 25 mi.
Day 23 Windy Bay to "Tranquilito Cove" 10 mi.
Day 24 "Tranquilito Cove" to Adventure
 Cove (via Tsapee Narrows) 15 mi.
Day 25 Adventure Cove to Ucluelet
 (via Tofino) 30 mi.
Day 26 Ucluelet to Pinkerton Islands
 (via Inner Broken Group) 20 mi.

Day 27 Pinkerton Islands to Effingham Bay
 (via Julia Passage and
 Outer Broken Group) 15 mi.
Day 28 Effingham Bay to Bamfield (via
 Outer Broken Group and
 Deer Group) 15 mi.
Day 29 Bamfield to Mill Cove
 (Port San Juan) 42 mi.
Day 30 Mill Cove to Victoria 50 mi.

"Maxi-Dream"

For boats with unlimited time, other great places to visit include Klaskino Inlet, Nasparti Inlet, Sydney Inlet, Nuchatlitz Inlet, Useless Inlet and Port Alberni.

Major Fuel and Supply Stops for Cruising Boats

Nanaimo
Comox
Lund
Campbell River
Port McNeil
Alert Bay
Port Hardy
Winter Harbour
Coal Harbour
Walter's Cove
Zeballos
Nootka Mission, Esperanza
(fuel and water only)

Tahsis
Ahousat
Tofino
Ucluelet
Bamfield
Port Alberni
Sooke
Victoria

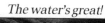
The water's great!

Notes about Circumnavigating Vancouver Island

1. A circumnavigation of Vancouver Island is a serious undertaking, and your vessel and crew should be well tested and experienced before you start. Planning ahead and using good judgment minimizes potential surprises!

2. These suggested itineraries do not include layover days for bad weather or relaxation. Your actual schedule should include time for contingencies such as fog, marginal weather, repairs or crew needs.

3. Fog is prevalent on the West Coast and may affect your schedule. Current, sea or weather conditions at Seymour Narrows, Yuculta and Dent Rapids, Johnstone Straits, Nahwitti Bar, Cape Scott and Brooks Peninsula, as well as ebb currents against a contrary wind, are major time factors that may require you to alter your schedule.

4. In marginal weather, reduced visibility or with contrary currents, certain destinations may not be viable. Have alternate anchorage(s) planned in case you need to change your route. Pre-plot your route(s) on detailed charts and calculate GPS way-points *before* you set out. (This task can take up to two hours each day en route.)

5. Vessels with planing hulls that can maintain an excess of 10 knots are less affected by the current in narrows or rapids and thus have a wider choice of transit times. Displacement vessels with a top speed of 7 knots have fewer options at narrows and rapids, especially at spring tides. When you are in doubt about whether to transit or not, observe what similar vessels with local knowledge do. To check on the magnitude of currents or optimum transit times consult *Sailing Directions* and *Canadian Current and Tide Tables.*

6. Since government docks and public mooring

Fishing in Clayoquot Sound

buoys fill up early in popular sites, have your lines and fenders ready in case you have to raft; or be prepared with adequate ground tackle in case your have to anchor nearby.

7. Carry and use up-to-date charts of the largest scale for your route as well as for alternate anchorages.

8. Long summer hours allow you to leave early, take a good rest stop en route and still have enough daylight to push on if you choose. You can sometimes accumulate layover days by jumping ahead of your schedule when it is appropriate; however, boats without radar may find themselves waiting until near noon for fog to burn off. (See Duration of Daylight, Appendix F.)

Winter Harbour

3
Weather and Cruising Considerations

In addition to outstanding beauty and solitude, Vancouver Island presents conditions that can challenge the wits of small craft skippers and keep life interesting. The list of these challenges includes frequent and fast-moving low pressure fronts; complicated and unpredictable currents, rips and whirlpools; high or confused seas caused by strong ebb currents against contrary winds; high mountain inlets with shallow bars at their entrances; and a high incidence of cloud cover or fog with frequent precipitation and low visibility. A skipper heading for the West Coast of Vancouver Island these days can prepare for such conditions and enjoy a safe and comfortable trip.

Weather

Weather plays a critical role on any West Coast cruise. Wind, which affects sea conditions, along with fog which affects visibility, are the main weather hazards. Outside passages and transits of areas with strong tidal streams should be made in times of benign weather. By taking advantage of the excellent VHF weather services available in British Columbia and the friendly help of the Coast Guard on Channel 16 (VHF) to provide updates, you can anticipate weather and thereby have a safe and comfortable trip.

Wind and fog forecasts and current conditions for all of Vancouver Island are broadcast several times a day by Environment Canada from the Pacific Weather Centre in Vancouver. These continuous VHF weather channels, through the use of repeater stations, can be monitored anywhere along the island coast with satisfactory reception in most inlets. (See Appendix B for key VHF channels.) To prepare for any changes in wind or visibility, a prudent skipper must keep a eye to windward and an ear on continuous weather forecasts, giving serious attention to significant changes in barometric pressure. You can monitor these continuous broadcasts from anywhere by dialing Victoria Marine Weather 604-656-7515 or 604-656-2714; Vancouver Marine Weather 604-270-7411. You may reach the Victoria Weather Office at 604-363-6629.

A counterclockwise circumnavigation of Vancouver Island takes you through the following forecast areas: Strait of Georgia, Johnstone Strait, Queen Charlotte Strait, West Coast Vancouver Island North, West Coast Vancouver Island South and Juan de Fuca Strait. Since different VHF channels are used for the weather repeater stations, you may need to try all weather channels to find the best reception.

The forecasts for Queen Charlotte Sound—part of North Coast forecasts—give an idea of weather approaching from the north. Likewise, forecasts for the Explorer Region cover the offshore areas of Vancouver Island, giving weather conditions as far west as 100 miles off the coast.

Semi-Annual Weather Patterns

The weather on the West Coast of Vancouver Island follows a general semi-annual pattern. In winter, there are about 10 to 15 low pressure fronts per month that affect the island. Some of these low pressure storms reach as low as 960 millibars with hurricane force winds of over 60 knots. The prevailing wind direction in winter is from the southeast with heavy precipitation.

Following late winter storms (near spring equinox, March 21), the Pacific High rebuilds off the western shore of Vancouver Island. This more or less permanent high pressure area deflects most summer lows north into the Gulf of Alaska.

During summer, low pressure storm fronts that do manage to sneak by the Pacific High to the West Coast usually occur two to six weeks apart. During these stable periods most weather stations report a high percentage of light winds with little precipitation (see Appendix D, West Coast Wind Reports).

During times of stable high pressure, the West Coast undergoes a daily pattern of diurnal micro-weather that is quite predictable until it is disturbed. The nights are usually calm and quiet over the length of the coast, with fog or low clouds moving on shore. In the afternoon, moderate northwest breezes pick up, dissipating fog and clouds and creating 1- to 3-foot chop. The evenings become calm again.

The approach of a summer low pressure storm front brings a falling barometer, a change in wind direction and intensity as well as precipitation. These lows generally last just a day or two and are well forecast.

Summer storms are not as intense as winter storms, having a low pressure center of 985 mb to 995 mb or higher, and moderate to strong winds. Wind speed of about 20 knots is common, and gale force winds (near 40 knots) are infrequent. The prevailing wind direction in the summer is northwest.

Winds in advance of a low pressure front generally arrive from the south or southwest, and they back (move counterclockwise) to southeast as the front approaches. On hearing a forecast of an approaching low pressure front a prudent skipper should seek shelter from southerly winds.

The strongest winds and highest seas generally occur just ahead of the low pressure front. With the passage of a low pressure front, the wind veers (moves clockwise) to northwest and can blow hard for a day or two.

Fall Equinox

Near the autumnal equinox (September 21), the Pacific High begins to collapse, and the first major winter low pressure front returns, bringing foul weather and more precipitation.

Surge Winds

Strong winds are occasionally generated in the summer during periods of high barometer readings (1008 mb to 1012 mb). These surge winds disturb the stable weather of the West Coast and can surprise a cruising boat. This surge of wind is caused by what is called a lee trough which forms off the coast due to prolonged thermal heating of the interior land mass. This phenomenon causes prevailing light easterlies adjacent to the coast, but a little farther offshore it can cause gale force northwesterlies, particularly off Solander Island and Brooks Peninsula. A more potentially dangerous condition called stratus surge occurs when a larger lee trough off northern California shoots north along the Oregon and Washington coast, picking up speed as it surges, bringing with it low clouds and fog. During a stratus surge, winds shift abruptly from light easterlies to southerlies of gale force or stronger. This condition can strike suddenly without much movement in the barometer, but with a sharp drop in the air temperature. Local fishermen call these winds fog winds. Other than fog or low, dark stratus from the south, there are no reliable warning of a stratus surge. When these conditions approach, they are forecast on the continuous weather broadcasts.

Wind velocities tend to be in direct proportion to the barometric pressure gradient (the rise or fall of the barometer). A falling glass (barometer) of 1 millibar per hour usually means strong winds of 20 to 30 knots. A falling glass of 2 millibars per hour means gales of 35 to 45 knots, and a 3 millibar per hour rate of change brings storm force winds of 50 to 60 knots. A rising glass of 1 millibar per hour brings strong to gale force winds of 25 to 40 knots.

The infamous Arctic outbreaks—such as the Squamish of Howe Sound or the Frazer River Arctic Outflow occur during winter when the barometer rises 2 or more millibars per hour, bringing freezing storm force winds. Small boats can monitor this pressure gradient by using a recording barograph or by recording barometric pressure in the ship's log at hourly intervals. These outbreaks are well forecast on continuous weather broadcasts.

Local Winds

Wind forecasts cover a large general area and are usually given for the highest expected wind in the area described. Local winds may be less (or rarely more) for any of the following microclimatic reasons:

Corner wind is the effect of increased wind speed when a wind blows past a headland. Winds occurring at Solander Island, just off Brooks Peninsula, are corner winds, and they are usually much stronger than those reported from either side of the peninsula.

Gap winds (or funnel winds) are increased local winds caused by funneling between islands, such as those occurring in Goletas Channel off the north end of Vancouver Island. Another example is the directional shift the wind makes to follow an inlet or channel (such as the increase in wind speed that occurs in Juan de Fuca Strait). When gap winds blow against tidal currents, they can cause dangerous, steep, breaking waves. On a hot summer day, southwesterlies can blow up Barkley Sound past Port Alberni and drop down on Qualicum Beach on the east side of the island, creating rough seas in the vicinity of Texada Island. These conditions, known as Qualicums, are gap winds.

Lee effect is a turbulent and gusty wind that occurs along a steep shoreline. Beneath cliffs, the offshore wind is usually gusty and from the opposite direction of that at the top of a cliff. Reversed eddies may be encountered with onshore winds near cliffs, along with confused and steep seas.

Sea breezes blow from sea to land during the heat of the day (usually in the afternoons) during periods of light prevailing winds. In Juan de Fuca Strait and Queen Charlotte Strait the prevailing inflow and afternoon sea breeze can combine to reach 30 to 40 knots.

Land breezes blow from land to sea during the night and can be gusty, but they usually have less velocity than a sea breeze. Both sea and land breezes die off quickly, as well as the wind chop they generate.

Anabatic winds that occur during the daytime in valleys and inlets are upslope winds caused by rising warm air.

Katabatic winds, downslope winds that occur at night, are caused by falling cool air. Sometimes known as williwaws, these winds are usually stronger than upslope winds and are the main reason to set your anchor well on an otherwise calm evening.

Wind rotation: In the Northern Hemisphere, winds flow clockwise around a high pressure cell, counterclockwise around a low pressure cell. In the Northern Hemisphere, with the wind to your back, the low pressure is on your left side while the higher pressure is on your right.

Fog

Marine fog, formed when warm Pacific air moves over relatively colder seas during the summer and early autumn, causes greatly reduced visibility a good part of the summer on the West Coast. It is a serious weather hazard to small boats. During a prolonged foggy spell, winds are usually (but not necessarily) very light and the seas are nearly flat.

Radiation fog, primarily a problem in harbors and inlets, forms over land during the early mornings on windless days and drifts with the wind out over the water. After the sun or winds come up, radiation fog generally dissipates.

Sea fog, formed when winds are moderate, may persist as winds become stronger. Sea fog

Pristine coves and beaches

may move offshore during the day and back onshore in the evening. It may last just a day or two or continue without a break for several days at a time.

During fog, visibility is reduced to 2 miles or less, and radar and GPS are required for a safe passage. Many sportfishing and commercial boats continue to fish during these foggy periods, creating hazards and stress for cruising boats near harbor entrances and fishing grounds.

Fog patches frequently form offshore and move inland in the late afternoon, remaining all night, then lifting or blowing back offshore in the late morning. The area from Estevan Point southward to Point Beale frequently has limited visibility due to fog.

Frequency of fog on the West Coast varies somewhat; Clayoquot and Barkley sounds are strongly affected in late summer. The west entrance of the Juan de Fuca Strait is also very foggy. The reader is advised to study the tables in Appendix D of the *Sailing Directions*.

Cruising boats without radar often find they have to wait until the fog burns off before they can move on. Since fog can last for several days in late summer, proper equipment such as radar and GPS are helpful, especially for boats on a tight time schedule.

In general, fog occurs with more frequency on the West Coast than it does on the east coast of the island. West Coast stations report the highest percentage of fog in their 7 a.m. observations, the least in their 4 p.m. observations. (See Appendix E, Frequency of Fog.)

Rain

To a lesser extent than fog, rain—often lasting for several hours at a time—reduces visibility and is associated with the passage of a frontal system accompanied by low, dark clouds. Drizzle (fine precipitation) also occurs with the passage of a front; however, it sometimes persists between frontal systems. While the West

Coast of Vancouver Island is in a temperate rain forest zone, rain is not nearly as pervasive in the summer as it is in the winter. Some cruising boats report little or no rain during several weeks of circumnavigation.

Rain showers cover a small area for short periods and fall from cumulus clouds, the heaviest usually occurring after a front has passed and cold northwesterly winds have set in.

Sea Conditions

Sea is defined as that segment of the wave caused by local winds and riding on top of the prevailing swell, which has its source winds outside the local region.

The Canadian marine weather forecasts use the phrase "sea state" or "combined wind wave and swell height," which refer to the significant height of the combined wind wave and swell. Significant wave height is the average height of the highest one-third of all waves present. Note that there will be waves that are half the forecast value; there will also be a maximum individual wave in a period of 3 to 4 hours that is double the forecast value. Values for sea state are given in meters. Wave height is generally in direct proportion to the distance over which the wind has been blowing (the fetch), the wind speed, and the duration of time the wind has been blowing.

Ocean swells present off the West Coast of Vancouver Island can be somewhat alarming for anyone who has sailed only on inside waters. At Cook Bank west of Hope Island on the south side of Queen Charlotte Sound, shoals cause the background swell to reach 3 or 4 meters. The swell length, however, with a 4-meter height, is generally about 100 yards; the experience, while it can be exciting, is generally not threatening.

Ocean Weather Station Papa, located 50°00' N, 145°00' W (about 600 miles west of Brooks Peninsula), reports significant wave heights ranging from 1.2 to 2 meters (4 to 7 feet), June through August.

Unless the wind is blowing, the prevailing background swells are not steep and are a long way apart. Swells build up around most headlands, and wind generated seas riding on top of these swells can be uncomfortable or even menacing to a small boat. Listen to the weather forecasts for combined wind wave and swell height. Listen, also, to the actual lighthouse reports of seas, and plan your ocean passages accordingly. On a typical morning during the summer cruising season most lighthouses report "sea rippled"—calm seas with very small wind ripples.

Steep Waves

It is the steepness of a wave that can be most dangerous. A wave becomes steeper near shore and when a current is flowing opposite to the direction of the wave. Cape Mudge, Nahwitti Bar and Cape Scott are well-known areas where a strong tidal current can create steep breaking waves. At Nahwitti Bar a 3-meter wind wave almost doubles in height against a 5-knot opposing current and steepens to the breaking point.

Fortunately the passages with significant exposure to ocean swells on a circumnavigation of Vancouver Island are of a rather short duration (a few hours in most cases). It is comforting for a crew without sea legs to know that just inside the next inlet prevailing swells and seas quickly die down and are seldom felt in any of the coves or anchorages.

Tides

Tides on the West Coast north of Port San Juan are referenced to Tofino (See *Canada Tide and Current Tables,* Vol. 6) and are corrected for secondary ports as indicated in Volume 6.

Spring tides occur every full and new moon, and the differences between high and low tides can reach 16 feet or more in Tofino.

Neap tides occur every first and last quarter of the moon, with only 2- or 3-foot differences in high and low tides in Tofino.

Currents at narrows and rapids are in proportion to the difference in adjacent high and low tides, hence spring tides have the highest velocities and neap tides the lowest. The currents for Quatsino Narrows are given in Volume 6.

Narrows and Rapids

Uncomfortable or dangerous seas can also be found in tidal narrows and rapids and across channel or inlet bars. Rips are turbulent agitation of the water caused by the interaction of currents and wind waves. In shallow water, irregular bottom rips can create short breaking waves.

Overfalls are areas of turbulent water caused by currents setting over submerged ridges or shoals. A severe overfall can produce a sharp rise or fall in water level and may even create whirlpools. Short, close-together, standing waves ("dancing waters") are also seen where currents meet. A small boat may be tossed from side to side in overfalls. Note indications of rips and overfalls on the chart and heed the warnings and instructions in the *Sailing Directions* when you transit any such area.

Currents

The clockwise-flowing Japan Current, part of which becomes the Subarctic Current, approaches the northwest coast of Vancouver Island during summer at about 50° N. About 200 to 300 miles off Brooks Peninsula the Subarctic Current divides into a north-flowing component called the Alaska Current; the south-flowing component is the California Current. The area between the bifurcation point has mild and variable currents. Currents along Vancouver Island during the summer are weak (0.1 to 0.5 knots) and generally follow the wind. Beginning in May the prevailing winds off the

Vancouver Island coast shift from southeast to northwest with a corresponding reversal in the direction of the coastal current.

Tsunamis

Tsunamis occasionally occur on the West Coast of Vancouver Island. These seismic sea waves are associated with earthquakes of magnitude 7 or higher on the Richter Scale whose epicenters are within or border the ocean floor. The largest tsunamis recorded on the Canadian west coast occurred in 1974 originating from the Anchorage, Alaska earthquake. (See Port Alberni in Chapter 20 for the effect of a tsunami.) Canadian earthquakes have not caused major tsunamis. Hazards of tsunamis to small boats come from strong currents (as much as ten times normal) that break moorings and drive boats ashore. Tsunami warnings for the Canadian west coast are disseminated by the Royal Canadian Mounted Police (RCMP) via coast radio stations. Any vessels able to do so should clear harbor and head into open waters where the effect of the waves is reduced and navigation is easier.

Coastal Navigation

Coastal navigation on the West Coast consists of selecting appropriate point-to-point routes, staying outside the reefs and rocks that are located up to a mile or more offshore. Passage between any two well-protected sounds or inlets takes a few hours and is best made in early morning hours after you have received favorable weather reports and before the prevailing wind comes up.

The West Coast lighthouses provide positive fixes and they all have powerful foghorns. (In this book, fog signal descriptions are given either in quotes from Sailing Direction or appear in the regular text.) Lighthouses report their current weather conditions to the Weather Centre in Vancouver; these reports are included in the continuous VHF weather broadcasts by place name.

Most sounds and inlets are marked with entrance buoys that make good way-points and checkpoints, and their latitude and longitude are given in each chapter. Since entrance buoys may move during storms, you should consult the latest Notice to Mariners for any changes.

Global Positioning Service (GPS)

GPS (Global Positioning Service) is revolutionizing navigation for fishing and cruising vessels. A GPS receiver will commonly read its position to one-thousandth of a minute of latitude, which equals 6 feet! While GPS is an excellent navigational tool—an essential for those on a tight time schedule—it should be used in conjunction with other means of navigation and its limitations should be allowed for. In unfamiliar territory GPS readings can give a skipper a welcome verification of position.

GPS navigation needs accurate way-points, and it takes a significant amount of time to determine those way-points and program the receiver. If you wait to program your route until you are surrounded by a fog bank, it's nerve racking. In this book, GPS way-points are given for all anchor sites and to help in rounding Cape Scott and Brooks Peninsula, etc. All anchor-site positions in this book are given to the nearest one-hundredth of a minute of latitude. The accuracy of these way-points is not as high as the resolving power of a GPS receiver, and you should maintain an adequate margin of safety.

When determining your specific West Coast GPS way-points, I would recommend that you compensate for a worst-case GPS system error by staying 200 yards on the safe side of your ideal way-point. That is, add or subtract (as the case may be) 0.1 minutes of latitude and/or 0.16 minutes of longitude to the ideal way-point as a safety factor. As an en route check, especially in limited visibility, I plot frequent GPS fixes and compare echo sounder readings against the depth indicated on the chart for the given GPS position. If they differ very much, I start asking questions and find out why.

"Selective Availability" of GPS systems (induced fuzziness in transmissions for reasons of military security) causes a random drift in Lat/Long course direction and velocity measurements. You should discount GPS readings that show unusual or erratic movement of a small nature. A correction station for Selective Availability is located near Victoria, but it requires an extra receiver for your GPS to compensate for this random error. The correction station has limited coverage on the West Coast.

Experience indicates that Selective Availability causes Lat/Long readings to vary over time, plus-or-minus 100 yards or more. GPS directional and speed information, likewise, has small random errors. Errors in speed are usually 1 or 2 knots, but they can be as high as 7 knots or more for a short time.

These systemic and random errors can be critical when you approach an important way-point. A GPS steering course is particularly susceptible to errors near a way-point. You need to be sure that your crew does not slavishly follow the GPS steering indicator but verifies steering information by checking the compass from time to time and by looking out the window!

To see the random effects of Selectivity Availability, monitor your GPS receiver when your boat is tied to a fixed object. GPS, like radar, requires that you have adequate experience in using it before you need it.

Accuracy of GPS Information

A discussion of GPS accuracy is complex. The ability of GPS to resolve short distances does not mean it is accurate to that degree. Selective Availability degrades accuracy; charts, guidebooks and other sources of positions all have small errors which add to the overall system error. My experience indicates total system error can add up to 200 yards or more in any direction. Some of these errors vary with over time, and others are static.

Each chart states the horizontal datum used in its manufacture. Set your GPS receiver to the horizontal datum shown on the chart specified for the area. Charts for the West Coast are referenced to NAD 27 or NAD 83. If you have not programmed your GPS to the datum on the specific charts, you need to make corrections by adding or subtracting the difference stated on the chart. The reference for horizontal datum of many of the West Coast charts is NAD 27. This differs from NAD 83 by about 0.011' in latitude and 0.089' in longitude, a difference of about 300 feet. Please note that the List of Lights does not indicate which chart datum—NAD 27 or NAD 83—the positions refer to.

In February 1994 the Federal Aviation Administration authorized U.S. commercial airlines to use GPS for navigation. The authorization followed Defense Department assurances that it would not turn off GPS signals or greatly degrade satellite signals without a two-days' notice. (The U.S. President can turn them off immediately without warning in "national emergency.") An FAA administrator is quoted as saying he saw no reason GPS will not become the only aircraft navigation system. Clearly, GPS will be an increasingly valuable tool for navigation, and the issue of Selective Availability may be resolved some time in the future. The inherent accuracy of GPS will challenge all providers of position information to upgrade their standards in the next few years.

GPS MOB Function

The Man Over Board (MOB) button on a GPS receiver is a useful function that can be employed easily and quickly. Besides locating the spot where someone fell overboard, this useful function can be used in other ways. When you leave an anchor site, a buoy en route or any known fixed position, push the MOB button and you can monitor your bearing and distance back to that fixed point, which is quite helpful in case the fog should roll in. By simply pushing the MOB button, you can update the fixed position you may want to return to each time you pass a known spot.

Loran

Loran-C can be useful for a trip to the West Coast for many of the same reasons as GPS. Loran-C, which depends on earthbound transmitters, has good coverage along coastal waters. Some inlets, however, have no Loran-C signals and most local boats are converting to GPS.

Cross-Border Customs Regulations

All boats entering Canada from U.S. waters must report to Canadian Customs upon entry. This is usually done by American boats in Bedwell Harbour (during summer months), at one of the marinas in the greater Sidney area—where special telephones have a direct line to Customs, or at dockside offices in the following Ports of Entry: Bamfield, Campbell River, Courtenay, Nanaimo, Port Alberni, Powell River, Sidney, Ucluelet, Vancouver, Victoria and White Rock.

Contact with land or other boats, is not allowed until this formality has been completed. Canadians do not charge a fee and are very

West Coast float house

courteous. Customs officials are concerned about guns (particularly hand guns), mace, liquor and certain vegetables. For information contact: The Regional Officer, Customs and Excise, Revenue Canada, 1001 West Pender Street, Vancouver, B.C. V6E 2M8.

American boats can obtain a U.S. Customs Service user-fee decal for re-entry into the United States. Good for a calendar year, this decal simplifies re-entry procedures. Make inquiries to the National Finance Center at (317) 298-1245 or to U.S. Customs Service, P.O. Box 198151, Atlanta, GA 30384. Decals cost $25 for US boats. Passports or visas are not required; however, some form of identification of citizenship should be carried.

Canadian Holidays
The following holidays are observed in British Columbia:
New Year's Day
Good Friday
Easter Monday
Queen's Birthday (by proclamation)
Canada Day (July 1)
Civic Holiday (first Monday in August)
Labour Day (first Monday in September)
Thanksgiving Day (by proclamation)
Remembrance Day (November 11)
Christmas Day
Boxing Day (first working day after Christmas)

Fishing Regulations
Vancouver Island is home to some of the most productive fishing waters in the world, and opportunities for quality fishing are endless when you cruise.

For current fishing regulations, request a free copy of *British Columbia Tidal Waters Sport Fishing Guide,* published by the Fisheries and Oceans. Write to: Fisheries, Ministry of the Environment, 780 Blanchard St., Victoria, B.C. V8V 1X5; telephone 800-663-9333 (24 hour) or 604-666-2268

Toxic paraplegic shellfish warnings, as well as local fishing closures/openings, are given on the continuous weather broadcasts on VHF radio.

Provincial Marine Parks Information
British Columbia has a number of outstanding Provincial Marine Parks that offer mooring and recreational sites for cruising boats. Many of these sites are mentioned in the text. A map showing the Coastal Marine Parks of British Columbia is available on all B.C. ferries and at Visitors Centers. For further information, contact:

(Southern Vancouver Island and Gulf Islands)
Ministry of Parks
District Manager
2930 Trans Canada Highway
RR 6, Victoria, B.C. V8X 3X2
Tel. 604-387-4363

(North Vancouver Island Marine Parks)
Ministry of Parks
District Manager
P.O. Box 1479
Parksville, B.C. V0R 2S0
Tel. 604-248-3931

Loading a West Coast water taxi

4

Friendly Cove – A Brief Maritime History

When you are comfortably anchored in Friendly Cove, it is fun to think back over the last 200 years of written history, to consider how events played out long ago made it possible for ships to move freely from port to port around the world.

The Freedom of the Seas Doctrine that has evolved over the last two centuries of man's exploration of the oceans and shores of the world holds that merchant ships may continue to go about their business without interference from ships of other warring nations. Key elements of that doctrine may be found in accords reached in Friendly Cove from 1790 to 1794.

Basic conflicts over who would control the lucrative fur trade led to counterclaims over Friendly Cove and its larger Alaskan and Canadian coast. A 1494 treaty between Spain and Portugal had given Spain sovereignty over the Pacific Ocean, and although her ships had plied its waters regularly between Spain, Mexico and the Philippines for over 300 years, she had shown no interest in exploring the northwest coast of America.

When rumors of Russian expansion from Siberia to the coast of Alaska reached Madrid in the 1770s, Spain became alarmed and sent two expeditions to investigate the coast. Perez sailed as far north as the Queen Charlotte Islands but did not set foot on land; Bodega y Quadra reached 58° N latitude in Alaska. Their secret reports confirmed Spanish suspicions.

Searching for a northwest passage on his third voyage of exploration in 1778, Captain James Cook discovered what is now named Nootka Sound. He spent a month in Resolution Cove and Friendly Cove making repairs to his vessels, and his journal of April 30, 1778, shows he traded for "skins of various animals...particularly the Sea Beaver [sea otter], same as is found on the coast of Kamchatka." Because Cook found the native Mowachahts particularly friendly, the cove acquired its name among visiting ships.

News of Cook's highly profitable fur trades, as well as publication of his charts and journals in 1784, fueled entrepreneurial spirits from Moscow to Boston. Basic conflicts over who would control the lucrative fur trade led to counterclaims over Friendly Cove and the larger Alaskan/Canadian coast.

In 1788 John Meares, an English venture capitalist sailing under the Portuguese flag, arrived in Nootka Sound to trade iron and copper for fur pelts. Meares had just returned from a trading trip in China. He brought with him two Chinese carpenters whom he landed in Friendly Cove, instructing them to build a ship while he left for another trading cruise. When he returned, they completed the first ship on the northwest coast of America—aptly named the *Northwest America*.

The schooner, made from timber felled at the north end of Friendly Cove, was launched

September 20, 1788. Meares found the timber to be of such excellent quality that he also made masts and spars to trade with the Portuguese in China.

Mowachaht Chief Maquinna, eager to trade with Meares, allowed him to build a house on shore at Friendly Cove. (Meares apparently intended to establish a trading post at Nootka.) In 1789 when Don Estevan Martínez sailed into the sound in an armed ship to enforce Spain's nearly 300-year claim to sovereignty, Meares claimed that Chief Maquinna had sold him Nootka Island.

Martínez quickly took possession of the port for King Carlos III , seized the "foreign" vessels, including Meares's vessels, and built a fort on the north shore in May 1789. Hostilities between England and Spain were quickly sparked. Chief Maquinna moved north to be out of the way.

Meares returned to England and published a book claiming that Maquinna had granted him land and had acknowledged British sovereignty over Nootka Sound and its islands. The English public was enraged. Great Britain, flush with victory over the French, started rattling its swords and put its fleet on maneuvers. Spain, fraught with internal difficulties, blinked. The result was a series of "Nootka Conventions" worked out in Friendly Cove.

Captain George Vancouver—at the time charting the west coast of North America for England—was commissioned to negotiate for his country; Spain was represented by Captain Juan Bodega y Quadra, an equally capable navigator and explorer. (Vancouver was so impressed by Bodega and his explorations in northwest waters that he offered to name the main island Quadra and Vancouver Island.)

Although the Spaniards under Quadra made continued efforts to hold onto their claim, they were not strongly backed by Madrid, and the English eventually prevailed. In late 1790 the ships Spain had comman-

deered were returned to their owners with damages paid. The Spanish monopoly of the Pacific Ocean was formally broken. On January 11, 1794, the two countries signed the third and final Nootka Convention. The principle of free merchant ship movement among non-warring nations was established, thus averting war, giving all parties freedom of the seas and granting Britain territorial rights to the West Coast of Vancouver Island.

Not all was sweetness and light in Friendly Cove following the demise of the Spanish influence and the ascendance of English sovereignty and language. It was one thing to mediate freedom of the seas, but quite another to work out lofty international principles on land.

Relations between traders and the indigenous population became particularly strained at Friendly Cove in 1803 over the capture of the trading ship *Boston*, the massacre of her 24 crew members, and the lengthy enslavement of two others.

The *Boston*, captained by John Slater out of Boston, Massachusetts, had sailed to England in 1802, where she was outfitted with a full complement of the latest in goods and arms calculated to take maximum advantage of the opportunities for fur trading on the West Coast of Vancouver Island. Slater knew the demand for metal goods would be very strong and outfitted the *Boston* with a special forge and the skills of 19-year-old metalworker, John Jewitt.

The *Boston* arrived in Nootka Sound March 12, 1803, and sailed some five miles past Friendly Cove to Marvinas Bay to fuel and water, and perhaps not to appear too anxious to trade. By now the natives had a better idea of what their pelts were worth on the world market and were demanding items of more value from the white man.

Chief Maquinna went aboard the *Boston* on March 13, bidding the ship a warm welcome and helping Captain Slater obtain fresh salmon and other supplies. On March 19 Slater gave the chief a gift of a double-barreled fowling piece of fine quality, which the chief used to bag several ducks for Slater. When Chief Maquinna brought the ducks, he returned the shotgun to Slater with one of its locks broken.

Slater, who took this as a gesture of contempt on Maquinna's part, called him a liar in the worst and saltiest language. Maquinna had strong leadership and language skills himself and understood all too well the captain's expressions of contempt; he seethed.

That night Maquinna and his elders held council at Friendly Cove, determined to take revenge and split the spoils. By various pretexts the chief got Slater to send nine men ashore. Maquinna signaled a quick attack, and in bloody hand-to-hand combat his warriors massacred 24 of the 26 men of the *Boston*. The *Boston* and her entire cargo had been seized, with the victims' heads severed and lined up on deck.

John Jewitt, held in great respect by Maquinna for his metalworking skills, was spared and forced into slavery along with John Thompson, who had been hiding in the bilge. Maquinna treated Jewitt well and told of his experience being aboard trader William Hanna's vessel in 1786 when 20 Indians were killed at Battle Bay in Checleset. Maquinna had escaped by diving overboard and swimming underwater until out of musket range.

The taking of the *Boston* made Chief Maquinna and his tribe the best armed, wealthiest and most powerful band on the West Coast of Vancouver Island. The *Boston* was moved to Friendly Cove, burned to the waterline and sunk. For the remainder of 1803 and into 1804 Maquinna put on magnificent potlatches—major celebrations with gift-giving and feasts for every village along the coast.

The more he gave away, the greater his esteem and the greater the allegiance of other tribes and their members to Chief Maquinna. The new wealth led to a flowering of local arts

The Governor's Totem, Friendly Cove

and crafts for the next several decades; items from this period comprise most of the Northwest artifacts seen in museums today.

Other tribes copied Maquinna's example, and several other vessels were captured and plundered by natives. This led to vessels carrying more arms, militia on board, and more precautions among the traders.

By European standards, Chief Maquinna and his tribe were never brought to justice. Captain Samuel Hill, on the brig *Lydia* out of Boston, captured him and rescued Jewitt and Thompson on July 16, 1805, after 28 months of enslavement. Hill offered to kill Maquinna, but Jewitt argued that such an act would only fuel an endless cycle of revenge, endangering future trading vessels and their crew.

Maquinna was released and his band continued to flourish, but the contacts with white men had spoiled their culture. White man's diseases, alcoholism and cultural institutions took their inevitable revenge on the First Nation's people. This cycle was repeated over and over along the coast to the great detriment of the indigenous populations. Over time, the lightly populated area and native culture was easily exploited by the technically more advanced Europeans, and English became the language of commerce.

When the sea otter population became decimated, trade fell off sharply. Fur trading became a land-based venture in the interior, but that slowly died off as well.

Borders and hegemony of Vancouver Island, Nootka Sound and Friendly Cove were further defined by the Onis-Adams Treaty with Spain in 1819. Successful British ports at Victoria and Vancouver led, in part, to the U.S.-Canadian border becoming established at the 49th parallel under the Oregon Treaty of 1846.

Evidence of Russian trading has been found in Friendly Cove, but Russia's efforts to colonize Alaska and move south failed due to lack of technology. The logistics of communication and supply were too difficult to overcome. They could not compete, and in 1869 Alaska was purchased by the United States from Russia in what was known as Seward's Folly.

Welcome to Friendly Cove. You are surrounded by some fascinating recent history.

Learning More about First Nation's People

Indigenous populations have been living on Vancouver Island for at least 10,000 years, as evidenced by archaeological findings on the West Coast. These populations had a rich oral tradition, but they had no written language; thus the writing of their history was left to white man. Unbiased accounts of native life and culture are few. Among the more interesting journals are those of Cook, Vancouver, and Jose Moziño (the botanist on Bodega y Quadra's expedition), as well as John Jewitt's account of his 28-month "enslavement." Titles can be found in this book's Bibliography.

As you visit the island, please remember that Indian Reserves (IR) and heritage sites are private, and burial sites are sacred. It is illegal to deface or remove any historic or prehistoric artifact. Permission to enter cultural sites and IR lands should be obtained at the local band office before entering. Please see Appendix for complete address and phone list of band offices.

Part II
Cruising Areas of the West Coast

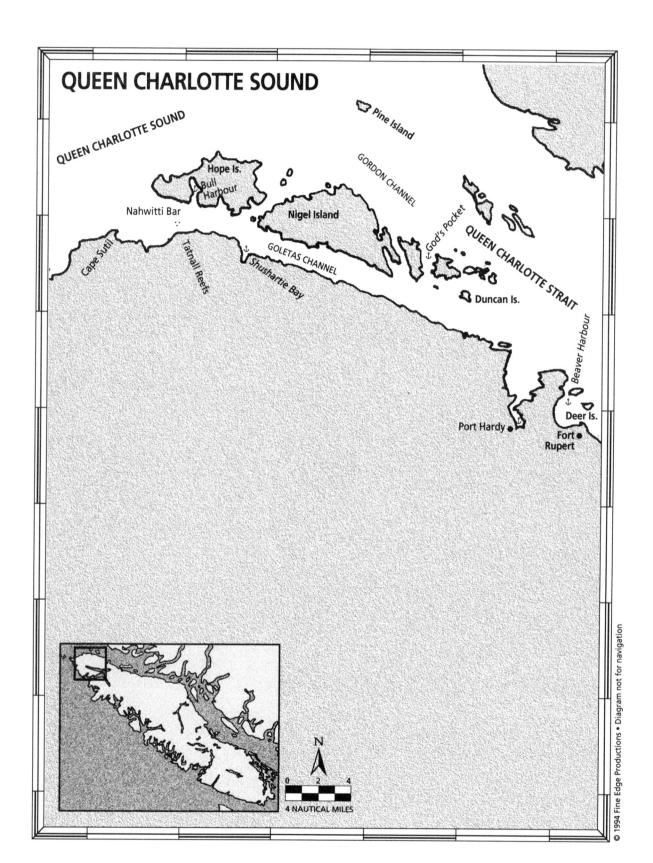

QUEEN CHARLOTTE SOUND

QUEEN CHARLOTTE SOUND

Pine Island

Hope Is.

Bull Harbour

GORDON CHANNEL

Nahwitti Bar

Nigel Island

God's Pocket

QUEEN CHARLOTTE STRAIT

Cape Sutil

Tatnall Reefs

GOLETAS CHANNEL

Shushartie Bay

Duncan Is.

Beaver Harbour

Deer Is.

Port Hardy

Fort Rupert

N

0   2   4

4 NAUTICAL MILES

5

Entering Queen Charlotte Sound

When a skipper makes the transition from Queen Charlotte Strait to Queen Charlotte Sound on the north end of Vancouver Island, the Pacific swell becomes evident, and the "outside" ocean environment comes into play. Goletas Channel is like a rifle barrel aimed and ready to fire at Queen Charlotte Sound and Cape Scott.

This area marks the beginning of the moment of truth; of exciting choices for the skipper of a small boat—choices that few cruising vessels face. Shall we take on the West Coast, making the transition from inside to outside waters, or not?

Queen Charlotte Strait to Cape Sutil
Charts 3549 metric, 3548, 3574

Queen Charlotte Strait separates the NE Side of Vancouver Island from the mainland and connects Johnstone and Broughton Straits to Queen Charlotte Sound. The seaward entrance of the strait is between Cape Sutil...on Vancouver Island and Cape Caution...on the mainland. With the exception of Goletas Channel the west part of queen Charlotte Strait is open to the Pacific Ocean and there is frequently a heavy swell.

...Gordon Channel is the usual route followed through Queen Charlotte Straits into Queen Charlotte Sound. An alternative is to follow Goletas Channel as far as Noble Islets then through Christie Passage and Gordon Channel into Queen Charlotte Sound. The route through Goletas Channel has Nahwitti Bar across its west end; in west gales heavy seas break across this bar.

Anchorages along the south side of Queen Charlotte Strait, suitable for vessels of moderate size, are in Beaver Harbour, Hardy Bay, Port Alexander and Bull Harbour. (p. 255)

Because the seas of Queen Charlotte Sound have a reputation for being rough and nasty, many cruising boats limit their northernmost activities to Johnstone Strait. While many of the stories contributing to this reputation may be true, you can assure yourself a safe and enjoyable experience if you plan and execute your crossing carefully. The secret to a successful crossing of Queen Charlotte Sound is to take advantage of the prolonged periods of benign wind and sea conditions that frequently occur in summer. The VHF continuous weather broadcasts for Pine Island and Cape Scott should be monitored and used for judging optimal transit schedules.

During summer, sea conditions along the West Coast of Vancouver Island are not that different from the U.S. coast to the south. The U.S. Navy Climatic Atlas shows the summer seas of Vancouver Island's West Coast to be the same general size and frequency as those as far south as the Southern California and Baja Coasts (see Append2ix C). Cruising across

Queen Charlotte Sound is not the same as Baja. (See Chapter 3), but a good part of the summer the seas are quite similar. These moderate conditions explain why on most summer days, except the occasional stormy ones, 1,000 small commercial fishing boats successfully troll from 1 to 10 miles off the West Coast. Because of superior fishing caused by upwelling currents, most of the fishing boats are found from Estevan Point to Cape Scott.

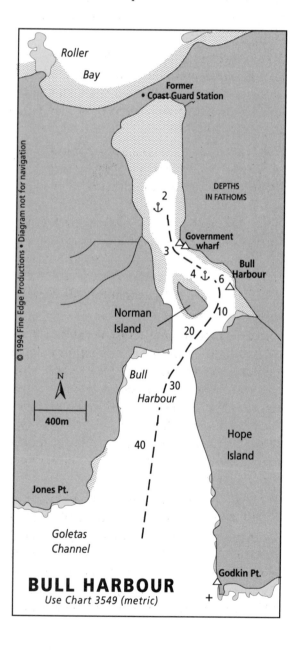

© 1994 Fine Edge Productions • Diagram not for navigation

Roller Bay

Former Coast Guard Station

DEPTHS IN FATHOMS

2

Government wharf

3

4 .6 Bull Harbour

10

Norman Island

20

N

Bull

30

Harbour

400m

40

Hope Island

Jones Pt.

Goletas Channel

Godkin Pt.

BULL HARBOUR
Use Chart 3549 (metric)

Bull Harbour
Chart 3549 metric (inset); anchor: 50°55.05' N, 127°56.13' W

> *Bull Harbour, entered between Jones and Godkin Points, is an indentation on the south side of Hope Island.... During SE gales winds gust through the harbour; when Pine Island was reporting SE winds at 70 km, measured gusts within Bull Harbour were 55 kn. West gales are generally of lower velocity within the harbour but they can blow quite strongly. Norman Island lies 0.8 mile north of Jones Point and close to the west shore; the fairway passes east of it. A drying mud and sand flat fills the head of the harbour.*
>
> *Anchorage with good holding ground in heavy mud can be obtained for small vessels in Bull Harbour. Above Norman Island anchorage is secure but with limited scope. The south part of the bay is reported to be fouled with old chain and cable; the bottom is reported to be less foul toward the head of the bay. When strong winds are forecast ensure that the anchor has adequate scope.(p. 262)*

A secure anchorage, Bull Harbour is a rendezvous point for vessels crossing Nahwitti Bar. Named for its large bull sea lions found here in the early 19th Century, this may be the place that Galiano called Valdes Harbour when he first anchored along this section of coast in 1792.

Nature is slowly reclaiming Bull Harbour. A Coast Guard station of earlier days has closed down, food and fuel supplies are no longer available, and only a few permanent residents live here now. During fishing season, when the harbour is used extensively by fishing boats, space for anchoring or tying to floats may be limited. Since some fishing vessels arrive after dark, it's a good idea to keep your anchor light on all night.

If you want to stretch your legs, you can land your dinghy on the east shore near the wharf and follow the old road across the sand spit to Roller Bay on the north side of Hope Island. The beach is covered with stones made round from incessant wave action. Since winds can kick up quite a blow across the low spit, be sure to have sufficient scope out before you leave your boat.

As you enter Bull Harbour, pass to the east of Norman Island and anchor anywhere in the center of the bay well north of the Government Wharf in 2 to 3 fathoms, good holding ground in heavy mud bottom.

Nahwitti Bar

Chart 3549 metric; entrance buoy: 50°54.15' N, 128°02.52' W

The shortest route to Cape Scott from the east is via Goletas Channel and the infamous Nahwitti Bar. The problem for skippers is that the bar is quite shallow (about 7 fathoms) with a maximum ebb current at spring tides of 5.5 knots. The prevailing northwest swell heaps up, and if wind blows at the same time, rising seas can become heavy and dangerous for small craft.

During strong westerly gales when giant eastbound rollers break over the bar, small vessels should not venture anywhere near Nahwitti. Fortunately well-sheltered Bull Harbour, less than 2 miles from the bar, gives you a chance to wait and watch for conditions to stabilize.

Most fishing boats heading out to Cape Scott use Bull Harbour as an overnight anchorage and leave early in the morning in order to cross the bar under calm water conditions. Once you have crossed to the west of the bar itself, a lighted whistle buoy "MA" in the fairway gives you a good indication of your progress. When you are abeam Cape Sutil (about 3 miles) you enter the waters of Queen Charlotte Sound and can turn southwest following the coast to Cape Scott for 16 miles in 15 fathoms.

Basic strategies for crossing Nahwitti Bar safely:

1. Cross at high water slack. Slack occurs when the water stops moving, and it is worth noting that slack varies somewhat from local high or low water according to runoff, tide levels and weather conditions. If you use this option, you limit the time it takes to push through the big swells to about 30 minutes. As you cross the bar, you experience little current. Once past the bar, you have up to 3 knots of current with you all the way to Cape Scott.

2. You can cross at low water slack, but the disadvantage to this option is that the inflowing current of 2 to 3 knots is against you all the way to Cape Scott (and perhaps around the Cape as well).

3. Follow the advice and timing of responsible local fishing boats that are similar in size and speed to your vessel. Do as they do, following at a safe distance behind them! Note: The maximum current of 5.5 knots occurs at the bar during periods of large tidal differences. It is frequently less for smaller tides. Fishing boats often try to catch the last hour or two of flood in the early morning when conditions are likely to be the smoothest.

4. In exercising any of the options above, close all port lights and stow your dinghy on deck. Towing a dinghy on any outside passage along the West Coast of Vancouver Island—especially at Nahwitti Bar—can be an extremely risky proposition. Pleasure boats frequently ignore this recommendation, and many a derelict dinghy has been found washed up on shore along the coast.

5. Arrive ahead of predicted slack time and study the conditions firsthand until you are satisfied that slack water has begun—good practice in crossing any bar. The flood at Nahwitti Bar occurs 25 minutes before low water at Alert Bay; duration of high water slack is 12 minutes. Ebb occurs 20 minutes before high

water at Alert Bay, and duration of low water slack is 17 minutes. (See Canadian Tide and Current Tables, Vol. 6, and *Sailing Directions,* Vol. 1, South Portion).

Nahwitti Bar Inner Route

Pacific Yachting (September 1992), carried an article written by June Cameron, describing a route which largely avoids the high seas sometimes found in the center of Nahwitti Bar. This routes uses the calming effect on both seas and current of the Tatnall Reefs located on the southern side of Nahwitti Bar. June ("Juno") followed a route that bears 196° magnetic for a little over 2 miles from Jones Point just outside Bull Harbour, passing the south side of Tatnall Reefs then heading west across the bar. She reported minimum depth of 18 feet, and currents and seas considerably less those in the center of Goletas Channel.

I have not personally taken this route, but it looks promising. It does not make crossing Nahwitti Bar feasible during a storm. However, it may help you to cross *after* a storm when brisk northwesterlies blow for several days. A course of 196° magnetic has to be made good in following this route. You will have to crab your boat into the current when current is running. Check your progress by making a range on Vancouver Island using a peak and lining it up against something prominent on shore. (If this

Heading out in early morning

route proves viable, we will have a diagram in our next edition.)

June is an experienced Vancouver racer and sails a 25-foot C & C sloop with outboard. She enjoyed her circumnavigation of Vancouver Island immensely and has told me that fishermen reported "hiding out" tucked up in the lee of Cape Sutil to wait for northwesterlies to die down.

Cape Sutil
Chart 3549 metric; 50°52' N, 128°03' W

> *Cape Sutil...the north tip of Vancouver Island, is a low promontory.* (p. 263)

Queen Charlotte Sound
Charts 3549 metric or 3598

If you want to avoid crossing Nahwitti Bar, altogether, you can use either Bate, Browning or Christie Passage to enter Gordon Channel and, once you pass north of Hope Island, follow the 50-fathom curve into Queen Charlotte Sound. When Pine Island bears due east, turn west and continue along the 50-fathom curve until you intersect a course-line from Egg Island to Cape Scott. At this point, you can turn southwest and cross Cook Bank in about 30 fathoms.

This route takes you about 9 miles west of Nahwitti Bar. The prevailing swells, while not menacing, are still impressive. Although about 12 miles longer, this route largely does away with the need to wait for slack water at Nahwitti Bar; you may even be able to catch the full current ebbing out of Queen Charlotte Strait. Monitor weather reports from Pine Island so you have an idea of what to expect.

Boats heading out to the West Coast on their way south from upper B.C. turn southwest at Egg Island and take a course on a direct line to Cape Scott (36 miles).

Each summer a few hardy sailboats take advantage of the brisk tail wind and cross the entire width of Queen Charlotte Sound (110 miles) on their way south from Queen Charlotte Islands.

The routes into or across Queen Charlotte Sound should be attempted only when weather forecasts call for near-calm or moderating conditions. Frequently, however, calm conditions mean bouts with fog. Monitor weather reporting stations, especially the offshore buoys, Pine and Egg islands, and have a safer alternative planned in case sea or weather conditions deteriorate. Don't be afraid to call Alert Bay Coast Guard on Channel 16 for a weather update at any time and to consult with them on possible alternatives if conditions don't appear to follow the forecasts.

During southeast gales in Queen Charlotte Strait, large pockets of kelp occasionally break loose. One summer, as we were following the Egg Island to Cape Scott route after a gale, we were obliged to change course 10 miles north of Cape Sutil to avoid patches of kelp more than a half-mile long which had blown out of the strait.

Each year many well-found small boats find that the trip around the top of Vancouver Island is a routine experience and rather anticlimactic for all the preparation and anxiety involved. Good preparation and execution can't be stressed too much—they are the keys to enjoying your passage.

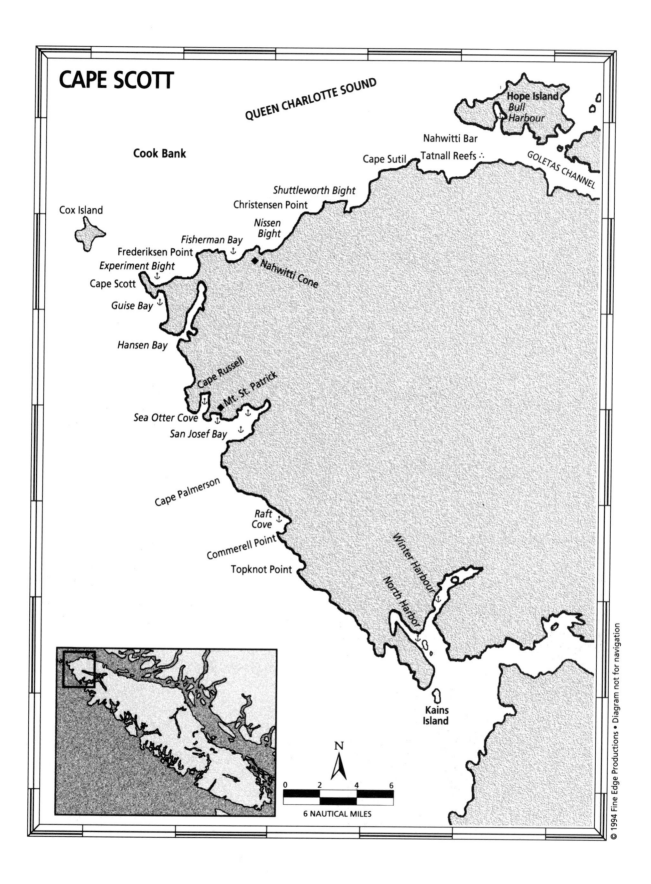

CAPE SCOTT

QUEEN CHARLOTTE SOUND

Cook Bank

Hope Island
Bull Harbour

Nahwitti Bar

Cape Sutil · Tatnall Reefs ∴

GOLETAS CHANNEL

Cox Island

Shuttleworth Bight

Christensen Point

Nissen Bight

Fisherman Bay

Frederiksen Point

Experiment Bight

◆ Nahwitti Cone

Cape Scott

Guise Bay

Hansen Bay

Cape Russell

Mt. St. Patrick

◆

Sea Otter Cove

San Josef Bay

Cape Palmerson

Raft Cove

Commerell Point

Topknot Point

Winter Harbour

North Harbor

Kains Island

0   2   4   6

6 NAUTICAL MILES

N

6
Cape Scott

Once you have crossed Nahwitti Bar without problems and your crew has started to get their sea legs, take a deep breath and relax; your boat will adapt well to the big, round Pacific swells. Although many yachtsmen push on as fast as possible to get Cape Scott behind them and start their "downhill ride" along the West Coast, the shores between Cape Sutil and Cape Scott have some beautiful spots worth exploring.

If the weather is favorable (near calm or light southerly winds), you may want to kill some time in one of the small anchorages along this section of coast in order to wait for slack tide before you round the cape. If you do, your ride will be smoother.

Remains of a double-bottom hull on shore at Fisherman Bay

Cape Sutil to Cape Scott
Charts 3598 and 3624

The coast from Cape Sutil to Cape Scott, 15 miles SW is ringed by rocks and shoals to nearly 1 mile offshore and should be given a wide berth. Strong indraughts can be encountered.(p. 270)

From Cape Sutil (50°52' N, 128°03' W), the northernmost point of Vancouver Island, the shoreline heads southwest across Cook Bank to Cape Scott.

Shuttleworth Bight
Chart 3624; entrance: 50°51.65' N, 128°08.20' W

Northwest Nipple, a 750-foot-high peak, is the prominent landmark 1.5 miles west of Cape Sutil. Shuttleworth Bight, 2 miles southwest, is the first of a series of beautiful sandy beaches. Although it is somewhat protected by fringing rocks and shoals, large surf makes landing impractical.

Nissen Bight
Charts 3598 or 3624; entrance: 50°48.50' N, 128°18.30' W

At the eastern edge of Nissen Bight 7 miles southwest of Northwest Nipple, Nahwitti Cone, a 610-foot-high peak, provides a prominent landmark for boats. The bight, itself, has a long, light-colored sand beach. Located at its far southwest end is Fisherman Bay, with a small dark sand beach.

Fisherman Bay

Charts 3598 or 3624 (same scale, better detail); anchor: 50°47.75' N, 127°53.85' W

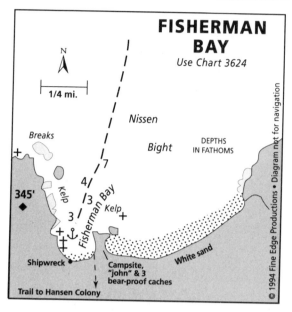

Anchorage for small craft can be obtained at the SW end of Nissen Bight, in Fisherman Bay. It is used by fishing vessels during south winds. A rock awash lies close north of the east entrance point to Fisherman Bay. (p. 270)

Fisherman Bay, a small, attractive nook that offers temporary anchorage under favorable conditions, is a good place to wait for slack water at Cape Scott. You can get ashore easily to explore part of Cape Scott Provincial Park. Since good protection can be found in southerly winds, the bay is used occasionally by fishing boats caught out in these conditions. In westerlies the summer swell is diminished in large part by offshore rocks and reefs, and the bay can be a surprisingly pleasant short-term anchorage. Little protection is afforded from heavy northwest winds or swells, however, so you need to keep a good weather eye during a stop here.

In fair weather you can land a dinghy on the dark sand-pebble beach. In the center of the beach against the brush you can examine the remains of a wooden barge. The 80-foot-long section is a piece of double-bottomed hull, common in early trading vessels that plied the rugged northwest coast. The knees (right-angle

Approaching Fisherman Bay—3 miles out

supports) were fashioned from trees specially chosen for their shape; the wooden beams were hand-finished for custom-fitted joints. The planks of the inner hull, (10 to 14 inches thick), were separated from the outer hull by a foot or so. The outer planks were 4 to 6 inches thick. All these pieces were held together with lots of iron pins. The hand craftsmanship that went into this vessel is quite amazing.

Philip Stooke (*Landmarks and Legends of the North Island*, 1978) wrote:

"...The back of the bay is strewn with the wreckage of a large wooden ship...said to have been built by the settlers, but never taken to sea. It was used only as a barge to ferry goods to or from ships anchored in the bay, but soon it was decided to use it as a breakwater near the bay's entrance. A storm threw it high onto the beach where it now lies in a dozen sections, its huge timbers tied by a forest of iron and wooden spikes a foot or more long, immensely but insufficiently strong.

"I find it hard to believe that the enormous structure seen here was built by the settlers, for though they did indeed build small ships and boats here, this great hulk surely was the product of a large shipyard."

At the east end of the beach there is another piece of double-bottomed hull about 30 feet long. In Stooke's time the hull was broken into twelve pieces; today only two remain. We have been unsuccessful in determining more of its history. Inshore from the relic, one of the Cape Scott Provincial Park trails runs to the south, offering some serious leg stretching. Another branch of the trail leads east for a short distance to a white sandy beach, a favorite camping spot for hikers. The campsite has a port-a-john and three bear-proof caches. A sign indicates drinking water is available 1,200 yards away at the northeast end of the beach.

Head slowly straight in for the small rock outcropping awash at the west end of the beach, being careful to avoid the rock off the small islet and a reef marked by kelp, which forms the eastern side of the bay. Shoals off the rocky western shore are mostly marked with kelp.

Anchor in 4 fathoms in the center of the bay close to shore over a bottom of sand and shell with good holding.

Cape Scott Provincial Park

The tip of Vancouver Island from Nahwitti Cone to San Josef Bay on the south forms the beautiful Cape Scott Provincial Park (37,238 acres). The park contains 40 miles of spectacular ocean shoreline, including nine major beaches. A rough dirt road that terminates at a parking area near San Josef Bay connects the park to Port Hardy by way of Holberg. There are over 25 miles of hiking trails and 19 primitive campsites in the park.

In the early 1900s, Fisherman Bay served as the historic landing place for most of the goods and equipment for the ill-fated Hansen Colony. Supplies for the colony were off-loaded here and had to be carried south by foot over the hiking trail at the east end of the beach to the settlement at the north end of Hansen Lagoon.

Since the deep-drafted steamers delivering their supplies were unable to use shallow Sea Otter Cove where off-loading would have been easier, goods had to be ferried ashore here. Northerly swells that prevented a permanent dock from being built in Fisherman Cove, and the lack of a good all-weather port would play a part in the eventual downfall of the colony.

When the Canadian government offered free fertile land for settlement on Vancouver Island at the end of the 19th Century, several

Fisherman Bay east rocks

dozen pioneers joined Danish founder Rasmus Hansen in establishing a colony in this wild northern land. They hoped to emulate the Norwegian colonies that had sprung up at Quatsino and Bella Coola. However, lack of a connecting road to the rest of the island (long promised by the government) as well as the lack of a port, ultimately doomed their efforts. Although the remains of the colony are being reclaimed by rain forest, evidence of their hard hand-labor—cleared meadows, decaying buildings and two sea walls—can still be seen in Hansen's Lagoon.

In *The Cape Scott Story,* Lester Peterson recalls his childhood days as a member of the colony, and the colonists' bitter struggle to obtain help from the government for the road or sea-based transportation system.

Frederiksen Point

Charts 3598 or 3624; way-point: 50°49.50' N,
128°21.50' W

Since the shore west of Fisherman Bay is foul, you must head out for at least a mile to the 12-fathom curve before turning southwest. From sea on a clear day, you can spot a large blow-hole at the south side of Frederiksen Point. When 4-meter swells are running a half-mile offshore 50-foot geysers shoot into the air through this blowhole. When lookouts on old sailing ships sighted such blowholes along the coast they would often yell, "Thar she blows," thinking they had seen a whale.

Nels Bight

Chart 3624; entrance: 50°48.03' N,
128°22.50' W

Immediately behind Frederiksen Point to the south runs the scenic mile-long white sand beach of Nels Bight. The western exposure of the beach means the surf is usually quite large and a peaceful landing is out of the question. Binoculars are the safest way for a boater to enjoy this place.

Experiment Bight

Chart 3624; anchor: 50°46.83' N, 128°24.50' W

Anchorage for small craft can be obtained in Experiment Bight, on the north side of Cape Scott. A rock, with less than 6 feet (1.8 m) over it, lies about 0.2 mile off the west side of the bight and a drying rock lies close off its south shore. (p. 270)

The bay immediately to the west of Nels Bight is Experiment Bight, situated just inside the peninsula of Cape Scott itself. The bight is named after the 100-ton *Experiment*, an East India Trading Company vessel, which arrived here just eight years after Cook had landed at Nootka. James Stuart Strange, who headed the expedition, thought he had reached the northwest corner of the North American continent;

he named the offshore islands after the patron of the expedition, David Scott, and the cape soon acquired the same name.

The beach here is a low spit that also forms the north end and beach of Guise Bay on the south side of Cape Scott. You can imagine the force of the winds that blow the sands back and forth across the spit. Along this scenic, exposed headland signs of early habitation have been discovered.

Temporary anchorage here is said to be of little difficulty in calm weather. If you go ashore keep a good eye on your boat and gauge the surf carefully; this landing spot is not as well protected from swells as is Fisherman Bay.

Anchor in 5 fathoms in the center of the bay. Be careful to avoid the charted rock with 6 feet over it at low tide located on the western shore in 7 fathoms, as well as a rock awash on the southeast side close to shore.

Cape Scott

Chart 3624; way-point: 50°47.80' N,
128°31.30' W

Cape Scott...is connected to the NW end of Vancouver Island by a low sandy isthmus. (p. 270)

Cape Scott is the most westerly point of Vancouver Island, and the high rugged promontory, which looks like a detached island from a distance, is barely connected to the island by the sand spit to the east.

The lighthouse is a welcome sight for mariners plying these waters. The light is shown from a short square tower 229 feet above sea level. The light, which flashes every 10 seconds, can be seen from a distance of 21 miles. The fog signal consists of three blasts on a horn every minute. High water occurs at 7 minutes after high water at Tofino, and low water occurs 9 minutes after high water at Tofino (see Volume 6, Canadian Tide and Current Tables).

The weather and sea conditions of this

View of Cape Scott from 1 mile northeast

great cape are infamous. As the southern promontory of Queen Charlotte Sound, Cape Scott receives a pounding from both northwest and southwest winds and waves. The wind can quickly change in direction as well as severity, and squalls can blow up or die down in an hour or less. Because of this tendency, weather reports from Cape Scott often are given after the fact and may not reflect current conditions. Have alternate locations to the east or south in mind in case alternate plans are required.

Many sailing schooners and whaling and sealing vessels have gone down off the cape with all hands lost, due undoubtedly to strong currents, fickle winds and a rocky shoreline. This is not a place to be caught when you are uncertain of your position, or if you loose steerage for any reason!

The notorious reputation of Cape Scott is not based on weather alone. (The winds are not as strong on the average as those off Cape Saint James on the south end of Queen Charlotte Island.) Its reputation may have more to do with the strong and somewhat unpredictable currents that merge here. The resultant tide rips and leaping seas, as well as the many rocks and islets between Cape Scott and Triangle Island, made old-time navigation hazardous. A lighthouse built on perilous Triangle Island in 1910 proved so difficult to maintain it was abandoned 10 years later. The current lighthouse on Cape Scott dates from 1960.

The Queen Charlotte Sound flood generally flows up the coast from the southeast, and when it meets a fresh contrary wind it can create a confused sea. This condition can occur on the ebb as well.

Dangerous rocks extend half a mile off the west-facing shore at the cape, and a cautious navigator stays outside the 20-fathom curve. Because of the geometry of the cape and offshore islands, converging currents create their own particular rips; these include short 2- to 3-foot leaping waves that break for no apparent reason during completely calm weather. Timing a passage to round the cape at slack water maximizes the comfort of both crew and vessel.

Scott Channel, between Cape Scott and Cox Island 5.5 miles to the west, is clear of obstructions and 30 to 40 fathoms deep. Flood and ebb currents flow through here at about 3 knots.

For perspective, remember that you are not alone out here; you will frequently see one or more fishing boats trolling back and forth a mile or two offshore in these fertile waters.

As you bring the lighthouse abeam, the seas quickly settle down; you can pick up a following northwest swell and cruise southeast, enjoying a great view of the coast.

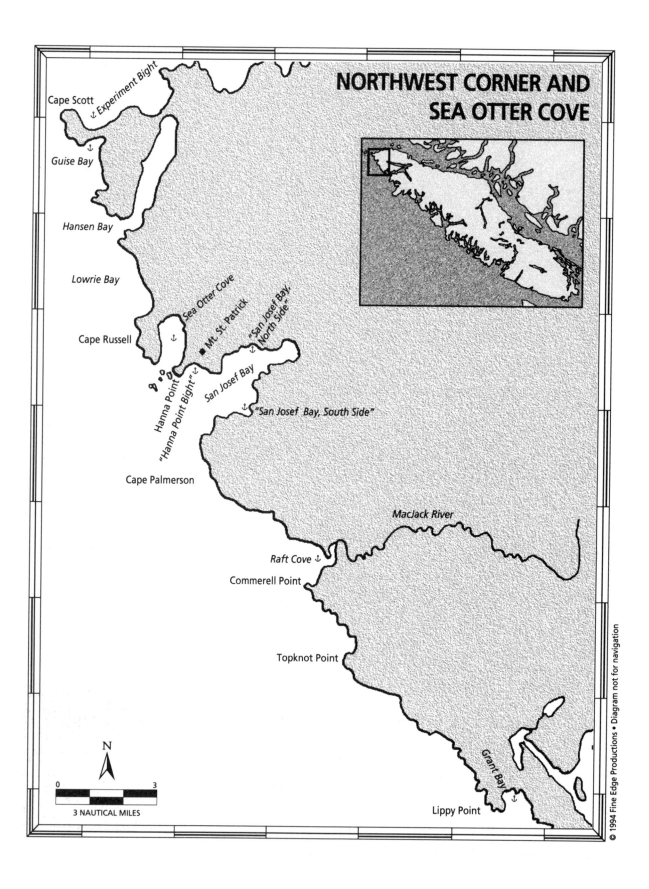

NORTHWEST CORNER AND SEA OTTER COVE

Cape Scott

Experiment Bight

Guise Bay

Hansen Bay

Lowrie Bay

Sea Otter Cove

Cape Russell

Mt. St. Patrick

"San Josef Bay, North Side"

Hanna Point

"Hanna Point Bight"

San Josef Bay

"San Josef Bay, South Side"

Cape Palmerson

MacJack River

Raft Cove

Commerell Point

Topknot Point

Grant Bay

Lippy Point

N

0   3

3 NAUTICAL MILES

7

Northwest Corner and Sea Otter Cove

Rounding Cape Scott is a major accomplishment for small boat skippers, and the ride southeast with the wind and swell behind you is a glorious feeling.

Cook Bank extends 20 miles north of the Scott Islands and southward along the north end of Vancouver Island with depths of less than 50 fathoms. This area is used by many commercial fisherman. The currents reaching Cook Bank and the continental shelf, as well as the banks on the south end of the island, are rich in nutrients (as much as 1,000 times the ocean normal). The upwellings of these currents create some of the most productive fisheries in the world.

Cape Scott to Lippy Point
Chart 3624

The northwest corner of Vancouver Island is extensively fished during the summer by small trollers from the Nanaimo and Vancouver areas. Their usual fishing grounds range from Brooks Peninsula (Solander Island) up to and including the Scott Islands. Fishing boats frequently troll along parallel loran lines in depths of 50 to 100 fathoms. While they fish, trollers normally use autopilot and do not always keep a sharp lookout. Give them a wide berth when you are heading down the West Coast. At night they seek shelter in places like Sea Otter Cove, San Josef Bay or Quatsino Sound. A friendly bunch, they readily share lo-

cal knowledge with you. In most cases these men and women commute from the inside passage around Cape Scott once or more during fishing season and seldom venture farther south than Checleset Bay.

Some publications say that a small craft is safe along the West Coast of Vancouver Island as long as it follows the 20-fathom curve. Boats and crew that can tolerate a lot of white water and foam sometimes follow the 10-fathom curve. While this may work for most of the coastline, there are many rocks found a mile or more from shore that rise abruptly. Under foul weather or poor visibility you will be perilously close to the breakers. The 30-fathom curve is a better choice unless visibility is good, seas are regular and your position is accurately known at all times.

Trollers inside Sea Otter cove

Scott Islands

Chart 3625

The Scott Islands, which extend 26 miles west of Cape Scott, consist of five named and several smaller unnamed islets and reefs. Chart 3001 indicates that there are dangerous tide rips and overfalls in the vicinity of these islands. The waters around the Scott Islands are very productive fishing grounds.

Cox Island

Chart 3624; position: 50°48' N, 128°36' W

Cox Island, 1,025 feet high, and Lanz Island, its western neighbor at 695 feet high, can be seen for a great distance. The water close ashore is relatively shallow; the 20-fathom line is generally a mile or more offshore and is filled with islets, rocks and reefs. *Sailing Directions* states that anchorage can be taken on the northwest side of Cox Island and off the northeast side of Lanz Island. This area, however, appears to offer protection only from southerly winds, and even then the prevailing northwest swell is likely to make the anchorage uncomfortable. Furthermore, *Sailing Directions* states that tidal streams set strongly between the passages of the islands, and during the strength of the stream there are strong tide rips that are particularly dangerous to small craft.

Triangle Island

Chart 3625; position: 50°52' N, 129°05' W

Triangle Island is the most westerly of the Scott Islands and is 26 miles west-northwest of Cape Scott. It is 690 feet high, precipitous and bare of trees. At the turn of the century a lighthouse was constructed here with some difficulty, but the winds proved to be too much. After a major storm in 1912 the station was abandoned.

One of the stories about Triangle Island relates that winter winds blew a couple of chickens, and even one cow, into the ocean.

Guise Bay

Chart 3624; anchor: 50°46.15' N, 128°24.50' W

Guise Bay...affords anchorage but has rocks in its approach and should not be entered without local knowledge. (p. 270)

Located 1 mile south of Cape Scott light, Guise Bay has a beautiful crescent-shaped sand beach reported to have beachcombing as good as Experiment Bight, when you can get ashore.

Temporary anchorage is offered close to shore in northerlies, but Guise Bay is no place to be in a southerly! During periods of sizeable northwest swells, all of the many offlying rocks—including 12-foot-high Strange Rock at the south end of the entrance—are masses of white foam, and it takes a strong heart to enter these waters for a closer look.

Hansen Bay

Chart 3624; entrance: 50°44.04' N, 128°23.62' W

Hansen Bay affords no shelter. (p. 271)

Hansen Bay is a half-mile-deep indentation in the coast 3 miles south of Guise Bay. It has a major rocky reef jutting out from the south shore and is wide open to westerlies. Sailing schooners anchored here in the early 20th Century during favorable weather. Some were even said to enter the lower part of the lagoon, which heads northeast for nearly 3 miles. *Sailing Directions* states that Hansen Bay affords no shelter and current local knowledge has been difficult to obtain.

The geometry and history of the lagoon call for exploration. The failure of the Hansen Colony was due in large part to an inability to use the bay as a dependable anchorage for their supply ships.

Lowrie Bay

Chart 3624; entrance: 50°41.91' N, 128°21.10' W

Lowrie Bay affords no shelter. (p. 271)

Lowrie Bay, immediately south of Hansen Bay, is long and shallow. It offers no shelter to small craft except during rare easterlies. The beach at the south end collects many relics from northwest storms. A primitive trail leading to this beach from the head of Sea Otter Cove is the destination of many campers who visit Cape Scott Provincial Park.

Sea Otter Cove

Chart 3624 (insert); anchor: 50°40.74' N, 128°20.94' W

> *Sea Otter Cove...offers indifferent shelter and is used by sail craft during summer months.* (p. 271)

Sea Otter Cove, located just west of Cape Russell, the conspicuous headland 7 miles south of Cape Scott, is a convenient anchorage for small to moderate-sized boats in favorable weather. It is undeveloped except for eight public buoys. It seems to be avoided by most yacht skippers who opt for the better protection and services of Winter Harbour. The sea breaks heavily on the islets, which form the southwest side of Sea Otter Cove.

The most commonly used entrance to Sea Otter Cove is located between Hanna Point and Helen Islands. On the far west shoulder of Mount St. Patrick, a half-mile due north of Hanna Point, an earth slide about 700 feet long gives a good visual target from seaward. Use a

Approaching Sea Otter Cove—Mount St. Patrick mark on right

slow approach (following the insert on Chart 3624) and keep a sharp lookout; both the entrance and bay have shoal water and a number of rocks.

Once you are in the lee of the southernmost Helen Island, kelp beds flatten the northwest seas, and the entrance and bay become perfectly calm.

The fairway has a minimum of 21 feet until you bring your starboard almost abeam the flashing light. From here on, the fairway has about 9 feet minimum and appears to be a flat, soft mud bottom with only the few rocks marked on the chart. The water in the bay is

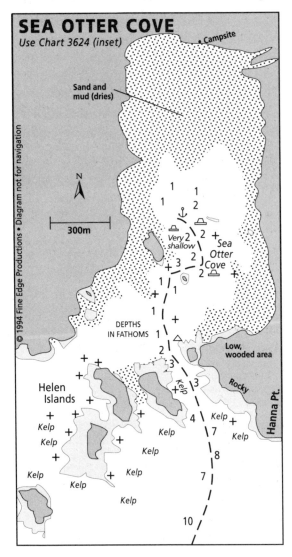

murky and it is easy to run aground before you see the bottom.

The head of this well-protected, large bay dries at low water. When you are well anchored inside you heave a welcome sigh of relief. The prevailing wind blows down the bay from the north with little effect, and heavy surf pounding the beach at Lowrie Bay 1.5 miles away can be heard most of the time.

Because Sea Otter Cove has a worse reputation than it deserves, it is frequently avoided. In northwest winds with a heavy swell running, a thick white foam blows to leeward off Winifred Islands all the way to Hanna Point. Although this makes the entrance look foul and dangerous, it is quite easy to enter in northwest winds.

During southerly storms, the entrance may break. In talking with fishermen, we learned that when a southerly swell enters the bay, it creates an uncomfortable surge.

All in all the eight hurricane-duty buoys placed by the Department of Fisheries seem bombproof. At normal tides there is plenty of anchoring and swinging room. In summer Sea Otter Cove has a lot going for it.

Note: If your boat draws 6 feet or more, it is important that you monitor tide levels carefully and avoid the outside mooring buoys during low water levels. Follow the suggested route, carefully passing through the center of the north line of buoys. There is adequate room for many boats to anchor just north of the northernmost mooring buoys.

You can explore Sea Otter Cove by dinghy or on foot. Colorful tents and campfires can often be seen at the head of the bay in summer, and visitors usually hike down the western shore to check out the wildlife and views. A

Above: Inside the entrance to Sea Otter Cove looking aft. Below: Inner Light, Sea Otter Cove

Above: Inner mark, Sea Otter Cove Below: West shore, Sea Otter Cove

primitive trail leads from the low point at the northwest head of the bay to the beautifully rugged Lowrie Bay beach on the outside coast. You can use Sea Otter Cove as a secure anchorage to explore the two coves to the north and Raft Cove to the south.

Sea Otter Cove was named by Captain James Hanna in 1786 after his vessel of the same name. Hanna was one of the early explorers involved in the sea otter trade.

Anchor in 1 to 2 fathoms, close north of the buoys, over a mud-sand bottom with good holding.

San Josef Bay

Chart 3624

> *San Josef Bay, entered south of Hanna point, affords no shelter except from north winds.... San Josef River, at the head of the bay, can be entered at HW and small craft can obtain shelter.* (p. 271)

San Josef Bay has three anchorage sites that cruising boats can use during good summer weather—Hanna Point Bight and San Josef Bay, north and south sides. Small boats can cross the bar and enter San Josef River at high tide. A campsite is located 2 to 3 miles up the river at the end of the dirt road.

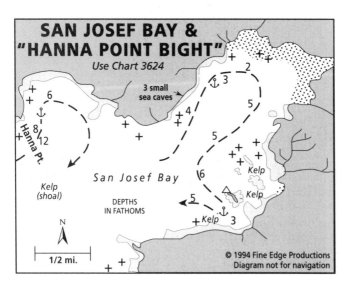

"Hanna Point Bight"

"Hanna Point Bight"

Chart 3624; anchor: 50°40.13' N, 128°20.18' W

In northerly winds, the unnamed Hanna Point Bight, close northeast of Hanna Point, is a favorite temporary anchorage for fishing boats. It is close to the fishing grounds and has easy access, but it is somewhat rolly with an undetermined but largely flat bottom.

Anchor in 6 fathoms in the center of the bight, close in, keeping an eye for the uncharted rocks awash next to shore.

San Josef Inner Bay, North Side

Chart 3624; anchor: 50°40.30' N, 128°17.80' W

The offlying charted rock southeast of Mount St. Patrick knocks down most of the remaining northwest swell and affords a quiet and scenic place where you can relax in fair weather. The steep, rocky shore has several small sea caves; the center cave is actually a land bridge with a pebble beach behind it. Although the inner bay is subject to southwest swells, for the most part it remains flat in fair weather.

The outlet of San Josef River, obvious for its large, flat sandy beach and drying flats, lies to the east. *Sailing Directions* says the river can be entered at high water and small craft can obtain shelter. We could find no local knowledge of this.

Anchor in 3 fathoms close off the north shore. The flat bottom is sand and shells with good holding power.

Northeast cove, San Josef Bay

San Josef Inner Bay, South Side

Chart 3624; anchor: 50°39.10' N, 128°17.80' W

Some protection can be found on the south side of San Josef Bay. Upwards of 70 fishing boats crowd into the bay during summer southerlies. The south side, out of the direct line of fire, is subject to a heavy surge with a southwest swell. At such times, fishing boats sometimes badly chaff their anchor rode.

This is a picturesque temporary anchorage where you can study the bountiful bird life that includes groups of tufted puffin and Cassin's auklet.

Anchor in 3 fathoms in a small pocket just west of the small islet in the center off the south shore. The bottom is mixed with rocks, gravel-sand and sea grass. Holding is fair.

Raft Cove

Chart 3624; anchor north side: 50°35.30' N, 128°14.90' W

Raft Cove...offers no shelter. (p. 271)

Raft Cove, five miles south of San Josef Bay, is a shallow but scenic cove with a wild, exciting aspect all its own and many features to explore. The big sandy beach, a favorite of kayakers, makes an excellent place to hike or camp. A trail extends northeast from this beach to a logging roadhead—about a 40-minute hike.

The Macjack River flows into the southern part of the cove, and the lagoon behind the sand spit can be explored by kayak or inflat-

able boat for some distance. Wildlife abounds here. Note, however, that swells sometimes break over the river outlet.

This cove is in the realm of the sea kayaker, hence its name. Only the diehard sport fisherman or lagoon explorer will find this place worth the risk as an anchorage.

There is room to anchor behind the large kelp patch marking the shoal just south of the rocks on the north side of the beach. The kelp and rocks break the serious part of the northwest swell, but you need a bow and stern anchor to keep your boat facing into the small residual swell and prevent it from rolling wildly.

This anchorage offers only minimal protection. It is useful for fishing or exploring the Macjack River outlet.

Anchor in 5 to 6 fathoms. The bottom is rocky and kelp-covered, and it is difficult to set an anchor. Test the anchor with a power pull-down to be sure it is set. The beach to the east is a bad lee shore, not a good place to leave your boat unattended.

Above: Raft Cove, 1 mile out
Below: North anchorage, Raft Cove

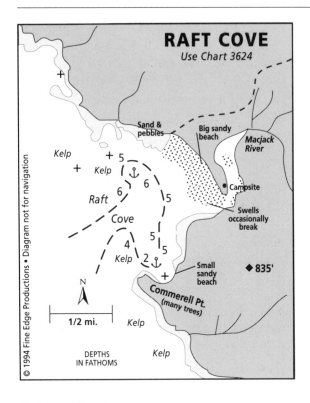

Commerell Point

Chart 3624; anchor: 50°34.47' N, 128°14.47' W

Commerell Point has many trees growing to its outer edge. Kayakers can land and camp on the small beach behind Commerell Point on the south side of the river's outlet.

Two miles south of Commerell Point is a sandy beach with an unusual 40-foot-high, south-facing, grassy knoll on its north side. A small creek empties between the beach and the grassy knoll—perhaps a good campsite.

Topknot Point is on the south side of this beach. When you are approaching from the north close to shore, the point looks like a small tree-covered island, hence its name. Six miles southeast of Topknot Point, Lippy Point marks the northern boundary of Quatsino Sound.

Anchor in 2 fathoms in the small nook behind the point, but only for a short time in relatively calm weather.

Raft Cove, looking west

South end of Raft Cove—Commerell Point

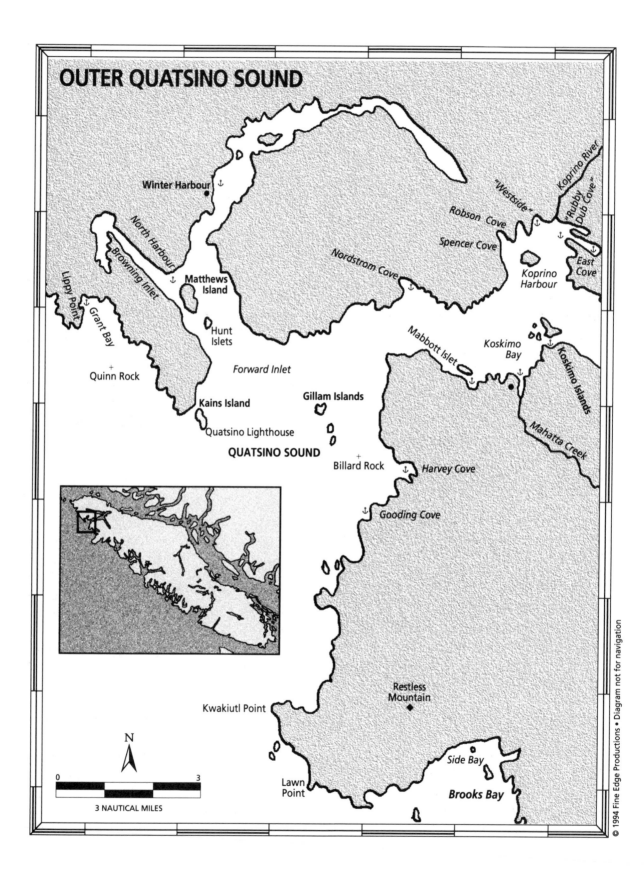

OUTER QUATSINO SOUND

Winter Harbour

North Harbour

"Westside"

Koprino River

"Ruby Dub Cove"

Robson Cove

Spencer Cove

Nordstrom Cove

East Cove

Koprino Harbour

Browning Inlet

Lippy Point

Matthews Island

Grant Bay

Hunt Islets

Mabbott Islet

Koskimo Bay

Koskimo Islands

Forward Inlet

Quinn Rock

Mahatta Creek

Kains Island

Gillam Islands

Quatsino Lighthouse

QUATSINO SOUND

Billard Rock

Harvey Cove

Gooding Cove

Restless Mountain

Kwakiutl Point

Side Bay

Lawn Point

Brooks Bay

N

0   3

3 NAUTICAL MILES

© 1994 Fine Edge Productions • Diagram not for navigation

8

Outer Quatsino Sound

As you head south, Quatsino Sound is the first of the five major sounds you come to on the West Coast. Many secure, protected anchorages are found in the sound, as well as access to supply centers and the island road system. At its extreme eastern end Quatsino Sound comes within 8 miles of Port Hardy.

The sound—home of the once-powerful Kwakiutl tribe—has an interesting history and offers over a hundred miles of calm cruising waters.

Grant Bay—ruins of cabin

Lippy Point to Kwakiutl Point
Charts 3624, 3679 metric

As you approach Quatsino Sound from the north, Lippy Point (a dark, flat point on the shoulder of Mount Kains) and Restless Mountain can be seen to the southeast.

Restless Mountain—whose 2,240-foot peak, one of the highest along the western shore, marks the southern extreme of Quatsino—can be seen from 25 miles away. Kwakiutl Point lies at the end of a flat apron on the flanks of the mountain. On a clear day, Brooks Peninsula with its long, tall range that extends westerly is visible over 30 miles away to the south.

Quatsino Sound
Charts 3679 metric, 3686 metric, 3681 metric

Quatsino Sound has four major arms: Forward Inlet to the north, with Winter Harbour just inside its entrance; Neroutsos Inlet, which turns south toward the mill town of Port Alice; Holberg Inlet to the north with its Coal Harbour; Rupert Inlet to the east, where the giant Utah Copper Mine is located.

If you need easy access to supplies or transportation, Coal Harbour, 25 miles inside the sound, is just a 20-minute drive to Port Hardy over paved road. Despite its heavy industrial sites, Quatsino Sound offers good cruising within its protected waters even when the weather outside is nasty. Like the other sounds to the south, Quatsino has its own microclimate; summer nights are usually calm despite winds that continue to blow on the outside.

If your destination is Winter Harbour, stay close to shore (avoiding Quinn and Parkins rocks), take Quatsino lighthouse on Kains Island close to port and round north into the 6-mile-long Forward Inlet. If you are heading deeper into the sound, stay clear of Robson Rock (swells break) and then head for the buoy marking Brown Rock to the east.

For a somewhat safer route, continue southeast from Parkins Rock until you sight the green buoy on Billard Rock, and clear South Danger Rock (swells break heavily). As soon as you are behind Gillam Islands, the swells diminish.

Grant Bay, just a few hours south of Sea Otter Cove, has one of the more attractive beaches along this section of coast that makes an excellent lunch stop, as well as an easy overnighter during stable conditions.

Quatsino is an adaptation of Koskimo, the name for the once numerous and powerful natives who lived here. A branch of the Kwakiutl, these people summered on exposed beaches at the south entrance of the sound near Restless Bight, feasting on rich marine life. Protected by numerous rocks and reefs, these locations made excellent landing spots for canoes. During the winter these people retreated to more protected inland coves.

Although Quatsino Sound was shown unnamed on the original charts of 1792, the name first appeared as Quatsinough Harbour on the 1849 Admiralty chart. Following surveys by Captain Richards in *H.M.S. Plumper* and *Hecate* from 1860 to 1862, it acquired its present spelling.

Beach—Grant Bay

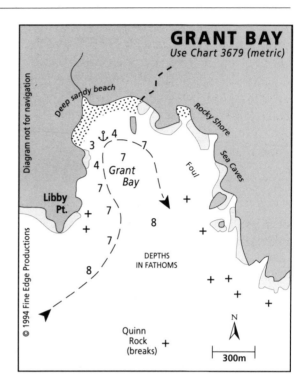

Grant Bay

Chart 3679 metric; anchor: 50°28.65' N, 128°05.83' W

> *Grant Bay is exposed to all winds, but anchorage in fine weather can be obtained near the middle of the bay in 11 meters (26 ft).* (p. 271)

Tucked in just east of Lippy Point, Grant Bay with its beautiful light-colored sandy beach offers shelter in stable northwest winds. Winds that whistle through trees overhanging the steep rocky shores are of no consequence. Lippy Point prevents the large swells that run outside from reaching the northwest corner of the bay. In any kind of southerly blow or southwest swells the bay has a dangerous lee shore and should be vacated.

Don't miss the chance to stretch your legs ashore. There is easy dinghy access at the far west side of the beach; the calmest spot for landing dinghies is west of the rocky area. The beach is covered with an impressive collection of driftwood, including trees up to 6 feet in diameter that choke the creek as far upstream as 500 feet! If you hike about 50 yards east of the creek outlet among ferns and moss, you can spot a crude cabin. Two sea caves on the eastern shore are worth checking out by dinghy. Sea kayakers can find excellent spots for hauling out and camping. Browning Inlet is just a 30-minute hike over a trail from the east side of the beach.

Sport fishermen out of Winter Harbour like to fish Grant Bay; commercial fishing boats sometimes use it as an overnight anchorage in stable weather.

As you enter or leave Grant Bay, give wide berth to Quinn and Parkin Rocks, both noted on the chart. Since swells break over them only occasionally in calm seas, you may have no advance warning of their location.

Small boats can anchor off the outlet to the creek at the west end of the beach in 3 to 4 fathoms; the bottom is clear and sandy with good holding. Farther off the beach, the bottom is flat at 7 to 8 fathoms, and there is plenty of swinging room for a number of boats. Use caution near the rocks on the eastern shore, where the bottom turns foul.

Drift logs, Grant Bay

Above: Lippy Point entrance to Grant Bay
Below: West corner, Grant Bay beach

Forward Inlet
Chart 3686 metric

Forward Inlet, entered between Kains and Montgomery points, is 6 miles long. Winter Harbour, located above the narrows at Greenwood Point, is the only secure all-weather anchorage along this part of the coast. The bitter end of the inlet shoals and becomes a saltwater lagoon that is encumbered with many pilings, booms and fish farms.

Forward Inlet offers nightly shelter to the bulk of the commercial fleet that fish the waters between Solander Island and Cape Scott. To be close to outside fishing grounds, the fleet uses Grant Bay, North Harbour, Winter Harbour and the area northeast of Kains Island for anchorages. Winter Harbour, the fish-buying and supply center, has a government dock with floats as well as private floats and wharves.

Kains Island Quatsino Light and Forward Inlet

Kains Island Quatsino Light

Chart 3686 metric; light: 50°26.48' N,
128°01.85' W

Quatsino Lighthouse is located on the southeast end of Kains Island. Its light flashes every 5 seconds with a range of 27 miles, and the fog signal consists of one blast every 30 seconds. The boat passage between Kains Island and the mainland is suitable only for small craft in fine weather. In settled weather many fishing boats anchor northeast of Kains Island.

North Harbour

Chart 3686 metric; anchor: 50°29.15' N,
128°02.70' W

North Harbour, the area northwest of Matthews Island, affords sheltered anchorage to much of the northwest fishing fleet. Three public mooring buoys lie close to the north shore of Matthews Island in 6 to 8 meters of water. A fish farm lies south of the buoys, and the area southwest of the buoys are full of fishing boats every night of the summer. Since they lie with their anchor lights on, you can pass carefully through them at night if necessary.

Anchor in 4 to 7 fathoms, midway between the island and Flint Rock, over a sand and gravel bottom with good holding.

North Dock—Winter Harbour

Browning Inlet

Chart 3686 metric

Browning Inlet is a narrow, scenic passage that leads northwest from North Harbour to a drying basin. Northwest winds that feed down the inlet are mild and of little concern. After the hectic fishing season is over, locals like to take a dinghy on the flood to the southern end of the basin. From there they hike three-quarters of a mile over a primitive trail to Grant Bay for an extended picnic. In the winter after a storm residents comb the shores of the beach looking for interesting driftwood. (If you take the hike, be sure to consult tide tables for your return trip, or you'll have a long messy haul over mud flats.)

The inlet is named after George Browning, second master of the *H.M.S. Hecate,* a survey vessel that charted the area in 1861 and 1862.

Small vessels can anchor along the inlet in 3 to 5 fathoms.

Winter Harbour

Chart 3686 metric; public dock: 50°30.77' N, 128°01.73' W

> *Winter Harbour...affords secure, well sheltered anchorage in a depth of about 15 meters (49 ft), mud bottom, 0.6 mile NNE of Greenwood Point.*(p. 288)

The village and wharves of Winter Harbour lie along the western shore. More than 600 feet of public float space is available close north of the fish packing plants. Since space on this float fills rapidly in the afternoon, you may have to raft. At night the floats tend to be noisy, so boaters who like quiet may want to do their business here during the day and anchor elsewhere. Free showers and laundry facilities on the floats are available for fishing boats. Yachtsmen wishing to use the facilities should inquire at the float office.

Winter Harbour is a beehive of activity during fishing season. The town is now connected by dirt road to Holberg, where a gravel road

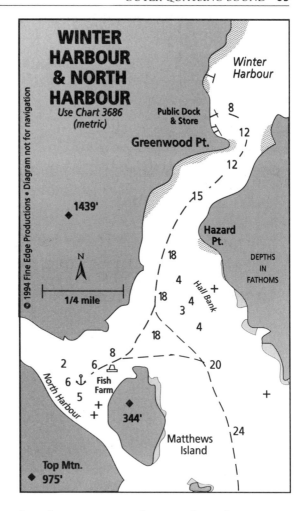

heads east to join the paved road into Port Hardy. (Allow 1 hour 45 minutes travel time. The roads are passable in a two-wheel-drive vehicle but four-wheel-drive is preferable.) The picturesque wooden boardwalk along the bay front is a major attraction of the town. Two pay telephones are located at the shore end of the public wharf. Demand is heavy and the phones are frequently out of order.

A store lies 100 yards south of the wharf. Open seven days a week during summer months, the store is well stocked with fresh produce, frozen and canned goods and bakery items; the government liquor area offers the only selection for miles along this coast in either direction. Limited hardware and fishing supplies are also available.

You can fill up on fuel and water at the Chevron dock below the store. In summer, the population of Winter Harbour swells to about 200 residents, but in winter the number dwindles to about 60. While a few fishing vessels berth here during winter, there are

Winter Harbour— South Dock

no winter live-aboards. The nearest school is located in Holberg.

Kwaksista Regional Park, near the village, has six campsites with toilets, fire pits, and a boat launching ramp. In 1993, sportfishing and sea kayaking businesses were in the infant stage of development here.

Anchorage can be taken north of the public floats, but during the night the bay is busy with activity and it is not too peaceful.

Nordstrom Cove

Chart 3686 metric; anchor west: 50°29.22' N, 127°55.61' W; anchor east: 50°29.15' N, 127°55.40' W

Nordstrom Cove...with drying and below-water rocks in it, is only suitable for small craft. (p. 288)

Nordstrom Cove, the first cove on the north shore of Quatsino Sound, is surrounded by ugly clear-cuts. If this doesn't bother you, the cove can be a good base from which to fish and explore the outer sound during stable weather. Prevailing northeast swells are faint, but since the cove is open to the south, it can be uncomfortable in any major blow from that direction.

In the eastern part of the cove a small, well-protected nook behind a reef and a rock makes a good anchorage that gives you a good view

out into the sound. Enter slowly and, before you turn east, make visual contact with the shoal marked 0.9 on the chart. Notice the rock in the center of the eastern part of the cove that bares—it's loaded with gigantic mussels.

Anchor in 2 fathoms, sand and gravel bottom, with fair holding.

The inner cove to the north is basically a flat 5-fathom hole with reasonable swinging room that affords good shelter from westerlies. It is somewhat protected from southwesterlies by a dangerous shoal on the southwest shore and a 1-meter shoal in the center of the bay. You can enter the inner bay from the east side of the 1-meter shoal.

This cove is surprisingly scenic and snug, and a thin layer of trees left standing along shore largely hides the ugly clear-cut slopes behind it. The northwest half of the cove shoals to mud flats.

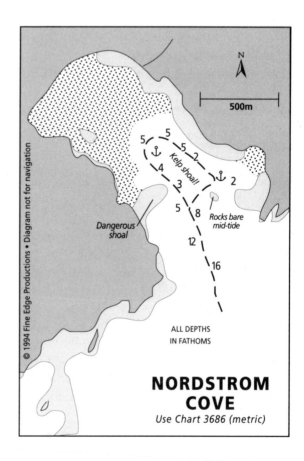

Anchor in the center of the cove in 5 fathoms over a sand and mud bottom with fair holding.

In good weather a small vessel can pass inside McAllister Islet, 3 miles to the west where crowded colonies of huge, brightly colored sun stars, sea stars and sea urchins live.

Nordstrom Cove

Koskimo Bay
Chart 3679 metric

> *Koskimo Bay, south of Bedwell Islands, affords anchorage on its east side, 0.4 mile NE of Chapman Islet, in 25 m (82 ft.), sand and mud bottom.* (p. 288)

Small boats will find good shelter behind Mabbott Island, off Mahatta Creek or in the Koskimo Islands.

Mabbott Island
Chart 3679 metric; anchor: 50°27.47' N, 127°23.67' W

Usually shunned by yachtsman as too deep, Koskimo Bay has several possible scenic anchorages. The first is located in the channel south of Mabbott Island. You can enter the narrow passage from either end.

Although a large operating fish farm nearly closes off the east entrance of this channel, it does create a buffer against down-canyon winds. Serviced by three employees who spend much of their time throwing scoops of feed to the growing salmon, the fish farm raises over 100,000 Atlantic salmon. The 35-foot square

pens are covered with nets to keep out the great blue herons circling greedily overhead. During prohibition Mabbott Island was known locally as Whiskey Island because of its clandestine trading operations.

Anchor in 4 fathoms over a flat gravel and rock bottom with fair holding just east of the narrows. Kelp, the size of banana leaves, may make anchoring a trifle difficult, but don't give up too easily—it's quiet and protected in here and well off the traffic lanes.

Above: Mabbott Island
Below: Mabbott Island looking east

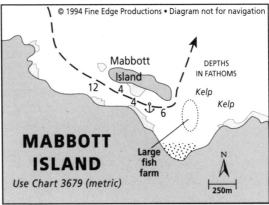

© 1994 Fine Edge Productions • Diagram not for navigation

Mabbott Island

DEPTHS IN FATHOMS

Kelp

Kelp

12 4

4 6

MABBOTT ISLAND

Large fish farm

N

Use Chart 3679 (metric)

250m

Mahatta Creek

Chart 3679 metric; anchor: 50°27.63' N, 127°51.70' W

The second anchorage in Koskimo Bay is just east of the outlet of Mahatta Creek. Because of its easy access at all hours, it is a popular anchorage among locals. Mahatta Creek is a great place to explore at high tide. It is navigable by dinghy most of the way to a beautiful pool and falls.

Anchor in about 4 fathoms behind the drying shoal.

Koskimo Islands

Chart 3679 metric; anchor: 50°28.17' N, 127°51.25' W

A rather well-protected, fair-weather anchorage can be found in the center of the Koskimo Islands just west of the passage between the mainland and the large island marked (77) on the chart. This intimate, scenic area is a good place for fishing or exploring by dinghy. You can land on a small shell beach on the mainland shore at the west end of the narrows. Fortunately these islets have been spared from woodcutters and are still covered with trees.

A small vessel can carefully navigate the passage to the east where the fairway has about 6 feet minimum at zero tide. It is important to locate the shoal awash at high tide in the center of the channel and stay north of it.

Anchor in 4 fathoms over a gravel bottom with fair holding.

Top: Koskimo Islands looking east
Middle: Looking west from Koskimo Islands
Bottom: Entrance to Koprino Harbour with Schloss Island on left

© 1994 Fine Edge Productions • Diagram not for navigation

N

300m

Kelp

Kelp

Koskimo

Islands

Kelp

Kelp

10

15

Kelp

4

Rocks awash at high tide; stay north

4

Kelp

DEPTHS IN FATHOMS

Kelp

Small beach with shells

5

10 15

5

1

5

2

Shoal dries

KOSKIMO ISLANDS

Mahatta Creek

Use Chart 3679 (metric)

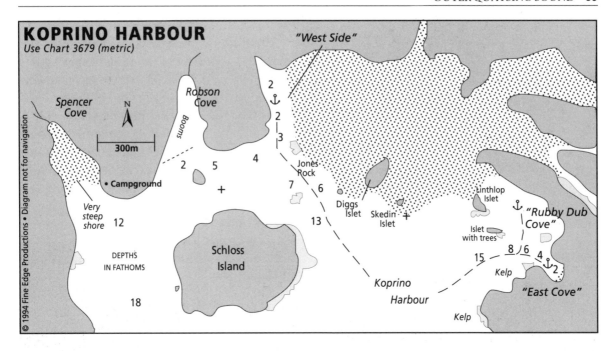

ruins on the eastern shore. The ruins were a pilchard cannery—a sister cannery to the one in Koskimo Bay. The bay shoals very rapidly without warning. We could not find a good place to anchor here.

Koprino Harbour
Chart 3679 metric

> *Koprino Harbour is only suitable for small vessels.... Anchorage for small vessels can be obtained in Koprino Harbour, west of Schloss Island, in 22 m (72 ft.), mud, or 0.1 mile NNW of Ives Islet in 15 m (49 ft.).* (p. 288)

This "harbour" was probably an inviting anchorage for old, deep-draft sailing ships that wanted to get out of the tidal streams but needed to be able to sail on and off anchor in any wind. However, it is a little too deep for small yachts. Although there are some conditional anchorages in the harbor, all have disadvantages.

Spencer Cove
Chart 3679 metric; entrance: 50°30.03' N, 127°52.53' W

Spencer Cove, the westernmost cove in Koprino Harbour, dries completely and seems to lack good holding ground. There is a narrow primitive camping area directly on shore, and a small boat launching ramp behind cement

Log booms, Robson Cove

Robson Cove
Chart 3679 metric; entrance: 50°30.20' N, 127°52.00' W

Robson Cove is a large, active, and noisy logging operation jammed with log booms; there is no anchoring room for yachts.

Entrance to East Cove, Koprino Harbour

"Koprino River (West Side)"

Chart 3679 metric; anchor: 50°30.31' N, 127°51.55' W

Koprino River (west side) has an anchorage site that we have not seen previously described. North of Jones Rock on the east side of a tree-covered peninsula that juts south just west of the river delta, a narrow channel runs almost the full length of the western shoreline.

From this anchorage your view doesn't suffer from the clear-cuts visible to the west, and you can watch interesting birds and wildlife on the mud flats to the east. The upper part of Koprino Harbour is shallow so navigate carefully. A word of warning: It is not easy to leave this anchorage by dark if conditions require it.

Anchor mid-channel in 2 fathoms—sand, mud and sea grass bottom, with good holding. There are shoals of 1 fathom or less on either side of the narrow channel. A stern and bow anchor in line with the channel, or a stern line ashore, provide secure anchorage.

East Cove

Chart 3679 metric; anchor: 50°29.83' N, 127°50.20' W

East Cove...affords no anchorage. (p. 288)

Once again, *Sailing Directions* tends to reflect the needs of larger commercial vessels, not smaller cruising vessels and sport-fishing runabouts. We found East Cove to be the best and easiest to access in Koprino Harbour.

Small, secluded and lined with trees the cove is well protected in almost any weather and has a good view. The depths are reasonable and we noted no problems in the fairway. The 1/2-fathom curve at the head of the bay is marked with sea grass and there is a small pebble-shell beach ashore. From here you can explore Koprino River and its delta. You often see large flocks of Canada geese feeding in the grasses nearby.

Anchor in 3 fathoms mid-channel near the head of the bay. Since swinging room is limited, both fore and aft anchors, or a stern line ashore, are advisable.

"Rubby Dub Cove"

Chart 3679 metric; anchor: 50°30.05' N, 128°50.49' W

Locals who like to gather mussels and clams find the spot just east of Linthlop Islet near the outlet to Koprino River an excellent anchorage. They call this Rubby Dub Cove.

Anchor is 5 fathoms; the bottom is undetermined.

South Entrance to Quatsino Sound and Restless Bight

Charts 3679 metric, 3686 metric

The area around the Gillam Islands and the rocks and reefs to the south off Restless Mountain—historically the summer work and play grounds of original natives—is seldom visited due to its fierce appearance. Behind the reefs, however, the coast offers fine beaches, great fishing, and tide pools and sea caves to explore.

According to Tom Cook, there are several attractive beaches along the shores of Restless Bight that small boats can visit by carefully maneuvering behind rocks and foam. We recommend checking out such places by sea kayak or motorized inflatable before committing your cruising vessel. Gooding Cove makes a good base from which to explore this region.

Harvey Cove

Charts 3686 metric, 3679 metric; entrance:
50°25.76' N, 127°55.38' W

*Harvey Cove is exposed to the west and not
recommended as an anchorage.* (p. 288)

Extensive and recent clear-cutting to the water
line has left ugly scars that make visiting
yachtsmen cringe. As *Sailing Directions* says,
there is little to recommend this place. If
Gooding Cove is crowded or you want to fish or
explore Gillam Islands, this is a reasonable
temporary anchorage.

Anchor in 5 fathoms off the north side of the
cove. Bottom and holding are undetermined.

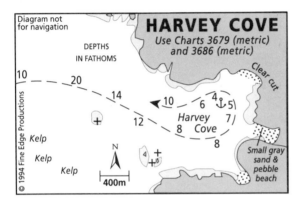

Gooding Cove

Charts 3686 metric, 3679 metric and 3624;
anchor: 50°23.95' N, 127°57.18' W

*Gooding Cove affords anchorage in fine
weather for small craft in a depth of about
10 meters (33 ft) sand bottom.* (p. 288)

Rowley Reefs and the rocks off the western
edge of Gooding Cove offer a fair amount of
protection from prevailing northwest swells.
You can find comfortable anchorage in stable
weather by tucking into the cove's southwest
corner.

You can land easily on the gray pebble/
sand beach and hike to the east side of the
creek on a newly made trail. The thick spruce
forest here is covered with moss and ferns.

Gooding Cove entrance

Kayakers or canoeists can find primitive campsites on the beach near the entrance to the trail.
Forest buses bring tourists to this area in the
summer via a dirt road that climbs the rocky
bluff to the east.

Anchor in 3 fathoms over a mixed bottom of
pebbles, hard sand and grass. Although you
may have difficulty setting your anchor, once
set it should hold well.

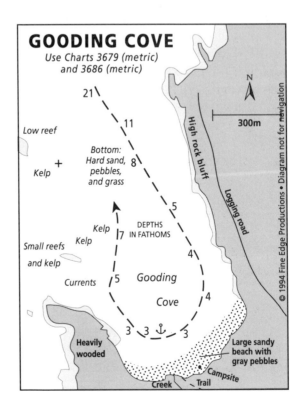

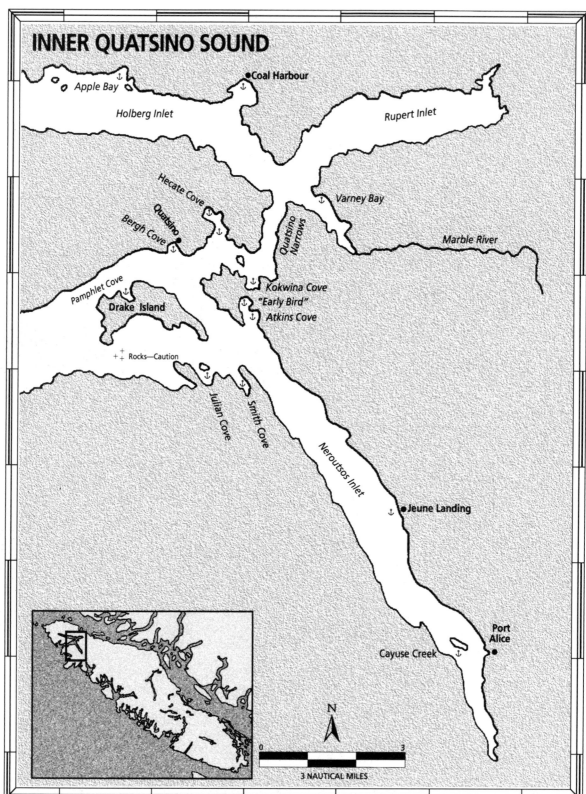

INNER QUATSINO SOUND

Apple Bay

Coal Harbour

Holberg Inlet

Rupert Inlet

Hecate Cove

Varney Bay

Quatsino

Bergh Cove

Quatsino Narrows

Marble River

Pamphlet Cove

Kokwina Cove

"Early Bird"

Drake Island

Atkins Cove

Rocks—Caution

Julian Cove

Smith Cove

Neroutsos Inlet

Jeune Landing

N

Port Alice

Cayuse Creek

0   3

3 NAUTICAL MILES

9

Inner Quatsino Sound

Inner Quatsino Sound is a large area with some interesting cruising. Here, no signs of Pacific swell remain, and the microclimate is favorable.

Boats entering Coal Harbour can visit the site of the last whaling operation on the Pacific coast. Except for the two industrial plants and a few logging operations, the inner sound is quiet, and time moves at its own slow pace.

Pamphlet Cove ("Quiet Cove")

Chart 3679 metric; anchor: 50°31.11' N, 127°39.30' W

Pamphlet Cove, on the north side of Drake Island, affords sheltered anchorage for small craft. Keep in the middle when entering to avoid drying rocks on either side. (p. 289)

Heading east in Quatsino Sound toward Drake Island you pass several active log booming operations along the south shore. These are of little interest to yachtsmen. Pamphlet Cove on Drake Island is a favorite of locals who call it Quiet Cove. The cozy anchorage is located inside a provincial recreation reserve.

Well protected from all winds and seas, the cove has easy access, but use caution to avoid the rocks close to shore. The shoreline is heavily wooded, with many varieties of trees and bushes coexisting in profusion. It's fun to row along the shore and count the different species. You might be interested in inspecting an old boat grid located on the east shore as well as the

Boat cradle, Pamphlet Cove

saltwater lagoon to the south. Locals mention a trail that goes from the lagoon to the south shore of Drake Island, but we have not taken it.

Anchor in 4 fathoms over a relatively flat bottom that varies from mud to sand and gravel with some kelp and sea grass. Holding is good.

Ildstad Island

Chart 3679 metric; anchor: 50°31.10' N, 127°42.00' W

In fair weather only, temporary anchorage can be taken off the northwest corner of Ildstad Island.

Anchor in 10 fathoms or less for a fishing or lunch stop only.

PAMPHLET COVE ("QUIET COVE")

Use Chart 3679 (metric)

DEPTHS IN FATHOMS

Kelp

15

+ Dry rock

8 Kelp

6 • Boat grid

⚓ 4

N

1/4 mi.

+

Tidal lagoon

© 1994 Fine Edge Productions • Diagram not for navigation

Entrance to Pamphlet Cove

Buchholz Channel

Chart 3649 metric

> *Buchholz Channel, on the south side of Drake Island, is not recommended to be used at night or without the aid of local knowledge. The best time to enter is stemming the ebb stream. It should be noted that the flood stream sets strongly toward Farmer Islets and the dangers in their vicinity.* (p. 289)

As Tom Cook puts it, "The approach to Buchholz Channel is an extremely foul bit of ground. My livelihood as shipwright has been repeatedly augmented by people not paying close attention to areas north and east of Bland Island and south and west of Norgar Islet. Extra caution is advised."

Kultus Cove

Chart 3679 metric; anchor: 50°29.00' N, 127°37.00' W

> *Kultus Cove has irregular depths and affords no anchorage except to small craft.* (p. 289)

Kultus Cove on the south side of Drake Island is deep, full of log booms and is of little interest to cruising boats. Tugs with log barges moor to the log rafts to load. A yellow and black buoy marks a shoal area. Some protection can be found close to shore at the head of the cove, but beware of floating and attached logs. A better choice lies one mile east in Julian Cove.

Neroutsos Inlet

Chart 3679 metric and 3681 metric

East and south of Drake Island, Neroutsos Inlet, one of the major arms of Quatsino Sound, turns south. Thirteen miles long, this inlet terminates in a drying mud flat. For cruising boats, there are three excellent anchorages within less than 2 miles of Drake Island at the top of Neroutsos Inlet. The southern part of the inlet is the home of Western Pulp, a large industrial complex located at Port Alice.

Julian Cove

Chart 3679 metric; anchor: 50°29.08' N, 127°36.48' W

> *Julian Cove...has depths of 10 to 15 m (33 to 49 ft.), mud, and limited swinging room but is a useful anchorage for small craft.* (p. 289)

A bombproof cove, Julian is scenic and picturesque. A few deadheads attached to the bottom and remnants of an old log boom are the only reminders of man-made intrusions here. This is a great cove for cruising boats and is worth the trip to get here.

A mixed forest of yew, cedar, blue spruce and birch packs the shore, with their branches spreading out over the water just above the high tide line. Small Julian Creek enters the cove through the meadow. High peaks to the

Entrance to Julian Cove

south form a magnificent backdrop to the lush green meadow where Julian Creek wends its way to the saltwater. There is room for two or three cruising boats in Julian Cove.

Anchor in 2 fathoms over mud bottom with good holding.

Smith Cove

Chart 3679 metric; anchor: 50°29.09' N, 127°35.13' W

Smith Cove, 0.5 mile east of Julian Cove, is foul and only available to small craft. (p. 289)

Immediately east of Julian Cove, nature does her best

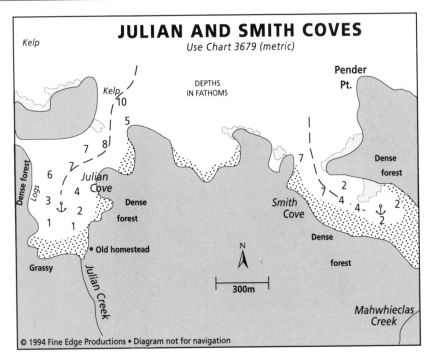

south form a magnificent backdrop to the lush green tricks again. Smith Cove is another beautiful, well-protected cove that, from the inside, ap-

Entrance to Smith Cove; inside looking north

pears to be nearly landlocked, and it is unlikely that any chop could ever build up here. Mahwhieclas Creek flows down from Comstock Mountain, 1,000 feet above, entering the cove at the large drying flats. Dense trees grow on shore and there is nothing manmade in sight. There is wonderful view of the ridge to the south from the top of limestone bluffs on the north shore.

Small craft can anchor anywhere southeast of a rocky, grass-covered shoal that extends 100 yards or so from the eastern shore. The head of the bay is a drying shoal.

Anchor in 2 fathoms over mud bottom with good holding.

Atkins Cove and "Early Bird Cove"

Chart 3679 metric; anchor Atkins: 50°30.57' N, 127°34.70' W; anchor Early Bird: 50°30.85' N, 127°34.83' W

Atkins Cove has drying flats with boulders extending from its east shore and is exposed to the south. A narrow passage, with depth of 1.1 m (4 ft.), leads into a small lagoon at its head. (p. 289)

If you cross to the eastern shore of Neroutsos Inlet, you find another interesting anchorage—Atkins Cove. Surrounded by second growth, the shore has a less intimate feeling than Julian and Smith coves to the west, but there is a certain wildness to it. The cove offers good protection from all but southerly blows.

The outer cove of Atkins has large shoaling areas on its eastern side. In late summer, this is a favorite scavenging place for black bear.

Anchor in 5 fathoms near the head of the cove in mud with good holding.

If you would like to venture into one of the most landlocked coves on the West Coast, check out the sizeable inner lagoon known locally as Early Bird Cove, which offers total protection from any seas. It's a good idea to investigate the entrance first by dinghy before committing your vessel.

This is a bigger challenge than the north end of Julia Passage in Barkley Sound, and you should try it only if the weather is good and you feel comfortable doing it. The entrance is extremely narrow and shallow; a moderate current runs and there is no turning room. Tom Cook remembers a rock in the narrows that

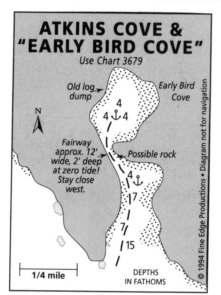

ATKINS COVE & "EARLY BIRD COVE"
Use Chart 3679

Old log dump

Early Bird Cove

N

4
4 ⚓ 4
|

Fairway approx. 12' wide, 2' deep at zero tide! Stay close west.

Possible rock

4 ⚓
|
.17
|
7/
|
/ 15
|

1/4 mile

DEPTHS IN FATHOMS

© 1994 Fine Edge Productions • Diagram not for navigation

caused him concern 10 years ago when he was towing bundles of logs out of here.

Although *Sailing Directions* states there is 4 feet at zero tide, we think it is more like 2 feet. The fairway is hardly more than 12 feet wide! This means you have to enter at or near high water slack. Kelp beds may hide uncharted rocks, but the bottom is clearly seen the entire way, so dangers are easy to spot. We found the fairway by favoring the west bank all the way through the narrows and by staying west of the kelp bed that lines the middle of the channel. As you pass through the narrows, tree branches almost sweep your deck!

Inside the lagoon stay clear of the visible deadhead on the east shore. A short distance to the north a trail leads to Kokwina Cove.

Anchor in 4 fathoms in a bottom of mud and light debris with good holding.

Jeune Landing

Charts 3681 metric, 3679 metric; entrance: 50°26.45' N, 127°29.90' W

Halfway down Neroutsos Inlet on the east side, Jeune Landing has a public wharf and a small float. This is the beginning of the residential district for the Port Alice pulp operation, centered a mile south at Rumble Beach.

From here you can walk south to Rumble Beach, where you'll find a modern shopping center with a liquor store, restaurants, hotel and laundromat. A hospital with heliport is located here, and the community is served by radio station CBUX, on 1170 kHz. A paved road connects this area to Vancouver Island's main highway between Port Hardy and Port McNeill.

Entrance to "Early Bird Cove"

Leaving "Early Bird Cove"

Rumble Beach

Charts 3681 metric, 3679 metric; wharf:
50°25.42' N, 127°29.13' W

Rumble Beach, the residential town that serves Port Alice, has full services as mentioned above. Port Alice Yacht Club has a private float where you can tie up, but you may need to make prior arrangements for a gate key. Shopping facilities are within easier walking distance from the yacht club than from the wharf at Jeune Landing. A log breakwater gives some protection from the chop, and there is a boat launching ramp here.

Port Alice

Chart 3681 metric; 50°23' N, 127°27' W

> *Port Alice is the site of a large pulp mill owned by Western Pulp Limited. The port is used mainly for shipping pulp.* (p. 290)

Port Alice, 3 miles south of Rumble Beach, is the site of the large pulp mill complex. Long loading wharves accommodate seagoing vessels, and the sights, sounds and smells offer little for a cruising boat.

This was once the northerly terminus for the coastal steamers *Princess Maquinna* and *Princess Norah*, which made the round trip from Victoria every seven days. Paved roads to the east now offer the main link for supplies and travelers, and the port is active only as a transfer point for the huge freighters that carry

pulp to worldwide destinations.

Just south of Cayuse Creek and inside Ketchen Island, on the west side of the inlet, a small boat can take anchorage in about 6 fathoms and sometimes escape the sights and sounds of the mill.

Quatsino Narrows

Chart 3681 metric

> *...Tidal streams attain 9 kn on the flood and 8 kn on the ebb in the vicinity of Makwazniht Island. North of Quattische Island and east of Ohlsen Point maximum rates are approximately 5 kn and run past the entrance to Hecate Cove at 1 to 3 kn. Strong turbulence is encountered throughout the main channel. Predictions of the times and rate of the maximum current, and the time of slack water, are given in current station Quatsino Narrows in the Tide Tables, Volume 6.* (p. 290)

Entrance to Quatsino Narrows

Quatsino Narrows separates Holberg Inlet and Rupert Inlet from Quatsino Sound proper and is one of the more scenic places within the sound. East of Bergh and Hecate coves the channel narrows and shoals somewhat; the current becomes a major factor in navigating.

The narrows form a straight channel nearly a mile and a half long and 250 meters wide. The bottom is relatively deep and steep, and it is fair the entire length except for a couple of 8-meter shoals at the north end. The minimum

Typical Quatsino anchorage; note Spanish moss on trees.

fairway depth at the north end is 54 feet. If you're heading south, a range bearing 193° true helps keep you in the fairway.

The speed of the current—which varies according to the differences in the level of tides—can reach 9 knots maximum on flood and 8 knots on ebb at the north end. Normally, however, the speed is 5 knots or less on both flood and ebb throughout the narrows.

Dangerous tide rips and overfalls occur off the north entrance west of Makwazniht Island. During both flood and ebb currents, a rip forms off Ohlsen Point, and a large back-eddy occurs east of Quattische Island. There is only a brief time of slack water, and the time of the turn may not be the same on the surface as below it. According to locals, the turn to ebb at the south end of the narrows occurs approximately 30 minutes later than the ebb at the north end! *Sailing Directions* states that strong turbulence is encountered throughout the main channel.

Skippers accustomed to the tortuous rapids and ever-changing whirlpools north of Desolation Sound may find these narrows less threatening. Locals generally transit the narrows with the current. Be on the lookout for large ships transiting to and from the copper mine on Rupert Inlet. Tofino Vessel Traffic Management Zone on Channel 11 VHF controls these vessels.

Passing through Quatsino Narrows can be a particularly pleasant visual experience because the narrows remain untouched by development on either shore. As the current rushes through at ebb or flood, you can hear the sound of the "river."

Bergh Cove

Chart 3681 metric; entrance: 50°32.23' N, 127°37.55' W

Bergh Cove, 2 miles west of Quatsino Narrows, is a good place to bide your time while waiting

Entrance to Bergh Cove

for favorable current conditions through the narrows. The village of Quatsino consist of a series of attractive homes spread along the shore between Bergh Cove and Hecate Cove, a mile and a half to the east. A number of float houses are located on the western shore of Bergh Bay.

Enter the cove by passing east of Leeson Rock. The rock is marked by a red buoy, "M10," shown on the Quatsino Narrows new metric chart 3681.

There is a public dock with the traditional red railings of government wharves. The cove is small and busy; anchorage is not recommended here.

Hecate Cove

Chart 3681 metric; Kitten Islet anchor:
50°32.54' N, 127°35.52' W

Hecate Cove is a moderate-sized cove, well protected from all winds.

Buildings and homes dot the shoreline, and there are a number of private piers. This is a good place to wait for a fair tide in the narrows.

Quatsino Boat Yard on the west shore, in operation for some 50 years, offers complete services, a machine shop and marine ways capable of hauling up to 27 tonnes. Tom Cook is their shipwright. You can reach the boatyard by telephone at (604) 949-6651. The 39-foot double-ender, *Zoe,* Tom is building for himself is docked in front of his tidy red float house at Kitten Islet.

Hecate Cove was named after H.M.S. Hecate, a brigantine-rigged, paddle-wheel sloop that surveyed the coast from 1860 to 1862 under the command of Captain George Henry Richards.

Although strong tidal streams exist outside Hecate Cove, little effect is noticed inside the cove itself.

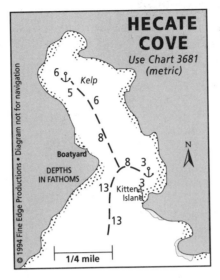

Anchor near the head of the bay in 6 fathoms with sand, gravel or mud bottom and good holding.

In southeast winds, this end of the bay could be a little shaky. Kitten Island which is a more scenic and isolated anchorage would be a better choice in that case. The area northeast of Kitten Islet gives good protection from southerly winds.

Anchor in 3 fathoms, mud, sand and gravel bottom. Holding is fair.

Kokwina Cove

Chart 3681 metric; anchor:
50°31.45' N, 127°34.40' W

Kokwina Cove ...is only suitable as a small craft anchorage. (p. 293)

Kokwina is a strategic place to wait and watch for proper conditions before transiting Quatsino Narrows. Inside the northeast point of Kokwina you do not feel the strong effects of the current. This cove, surrounded by uniform second growth, abandoned heavy equipment, log floats and several deadheads, is not a particularly attractive place. The view north into the pristine Quatsino Narrows makes it appear even less attractive.

Float house, Hecate Cove

Entrance to Kokwina Cove

Anchor in 6 fathoms just inside the north point, favoring the east side. The bottom is mud, the holding is undetermined.

Rupert Inlet

Chart 3679

Rupert Inlet extends 5 miles ENE from Quatsino Narrows and terminates in an extensive drying reef. (p. 293)

The north shore of the inlet is dominated by the large industrial complex owned by Inland Copper Mine (Utah Mines Limited). Tailings from the mine now cover a channel that formerly separated Narrow Island and Red Island from shore. The operation has extensive ship and barge loading areas. Except for Varney Bay at its entrance, the inlet holds little of interest to yachtsmen.

Varney Bay

Chart 3679; anchor: 50°3.37' N, 127°31.73' W

Varney Bay is only useful as an anchorage for small vessels. (p. 293)

Varney Bay is the outlet for the Marble River, which drains 5-mile-long Alice Lake to the southeast. There are no manmade blights to spoil your view here, and you can explore Marble River by dinghy or sportfishing boat for 2 to 3 miles at high tide. A high bluff 2 miles up-river at "Hole in the Wall" has a cavern big enough to enter by dinghy. There is a good picnic spot next to the cave. During heavy rains,

Sundown—Varney Bay

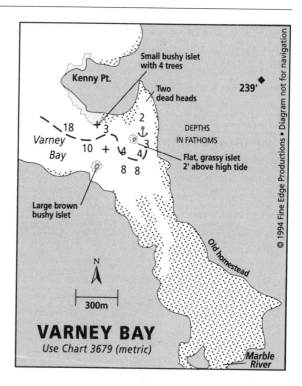

primarily during winter storms, the river becomes a white water nightmare! Where the river narrows, you can sometimes catch sight of weasels, deer and river otters.

A small V-shaped nook in the northeast corner of the bay behind Kenny Point offers good, quiet protection. Varney Bay makes a good base from which to visit Coal Harbour and Holberg Inlet; it is also useful as a short layover while you wait for favorable current in Quatsino Narrows. The head of the bay has extensive drying mud flats. An old homestead located on shore was settled in the early 20th Century; a number of exotic plants, shrubs and trees were imported for the property.

As you enter Varney Bay, be careful in navigating this S-shaped route; avoid below-water and drying rocks, and keep a sharp lookout for deadheads.

Anchor in 2 fathoms, tucked behind a small grassy islet. The bottom is hard mud with good holding. Swinging room is limited, and larger vessels may feel safer anchoring in 4 fathoms in a "hole" in the center of the bay.

Holberg Inlet

Chart 3679 metric

> *Holberg Inlet...extends 18 miles west from Quatsino Narrows and terminates in an extensive drying flat.* (p. 293)

Holberg Inlet is a long, narrow, quiet inlet that resembles a fjord. Coal Harbour, an active commercial port, is located inside the narrows on the north shore. The settlement of Holberg is located at the extreme west end. The Straggling Islands, 4 miles west of Coal Harbour and Apple Bay, offer the only anchoring opportunities in Holberg Inlet.

Coal Harbour

Chart 3679 metric; wharf: 50°35.88' N, 127°34.80' W

> *Anchorage in Coal Harbour can be obtained 0.3 mile NNE of Stewart Point in 22 m (72 ft.), mud bottom; do not anchor west of a line drawn south from the public wharf.* (p. 293)

Coal Harbour is the only all-weather protection north of Quatsino Narrows. The village of Coal Harbour has a cafe, store, post office and several public telephones. One pay telephone is located outside the cafe; the other is on the opposite side of the street. A paved road leads 12 miles to Port Hardy, where full supplies are available.

The Moby Dick store is located on the first

Coal Harbour fuel and fishing dock

street left, at the site of a whale jaw bone arch. Summer hours posted are 11 a.m. to 9 p.m. The town has a marine way that can haul craft up to 50 feet in length.

This quiet village of a few hundred friendly inhabitants has witnessed a number of changes over the years. It was first settled in the late 1800s by coal miners who gave it its name.

Coal Harbour whaling harpoon gun

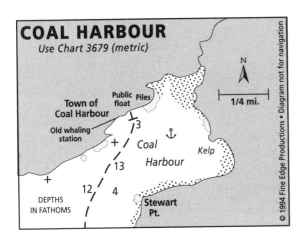

COAL HARBOUR
Use Chart 3679 (metric)

N

Town of
Coal Harbour

Public
float

Piles

1/4 mi.

Old whaling
station

3

Coal

Harbour

Kelp

13

12 / 4

DEPTHS
IN FATHOMS

Stewart
Pt.

© 1994 Fine Edge Productions • Diagram not for navigation

Baidarka *at Coal Harbour*

Later it served as a supply center for the Quatsino Sound settlements. During World War II it became a base for amphibious seaplanes, and after the war it became one of the last whaling stations on the West Coast of North America. It now serves a small commercial fishing fleet and is becoming a bedroom community for Port Hardy and the copper mine in Rupert Inlet.

Signs of Coal Harbour's past can be seen near the wharf. Only one seaplane hangar remains now; the second, used for the whaling operation, had to be removed because the residual smell was too unpleasant for the residents. Photos on the wall of the cafe show sperm and fin whales being slaughtered. The whaling station, which ceased operation in 1967, at one time had seven pack boats (killer vessels) based here.

The bottom of the mile-deep pit at the copper mine in Rupert Inlet is 1,084 feet below sea level. Locals claim that below-sea-level records were set here by helicopters and scuba divers in the pond at the bottom of the pit.

Free bus tours of forest logging operations

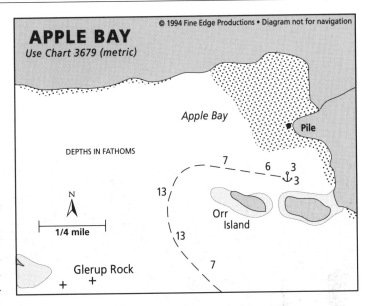

Whale's jawbone, Coal Harbour

and the copper mine leave Coal Harbour during summer months. Call ahead to make arrangements—the telephone numbers are posted near the cafe.

Coal Harbour has a public wharf with two sizeable floats. Fuel and water are available on the eastern float, which supports the local fishing fleet and commercial operations. The westernmost float is used for temporary tie-ups. A marina and boat launching ramp are close west of the public wharf.

Anchor in 4 fathoms, mud bottom, east of the public wharf, keeping clear of commercial traffic. A no-anchor zone is in effect west of a line drawn south from the public wharf.

Apple Bay

Chart 3679 metric; anchor: 50°36.11' N, 127°39.30' W

Apple Bay has extensive drying flats of gravel and boulders. (p. 294)

Local small boats take shelter behind the lee afforded by Orr Islet and Off Reef, 3 miles west of Coal Harbour. This area and the Straggling Island complex just to the west are used for sportfishing and recreational purposes.

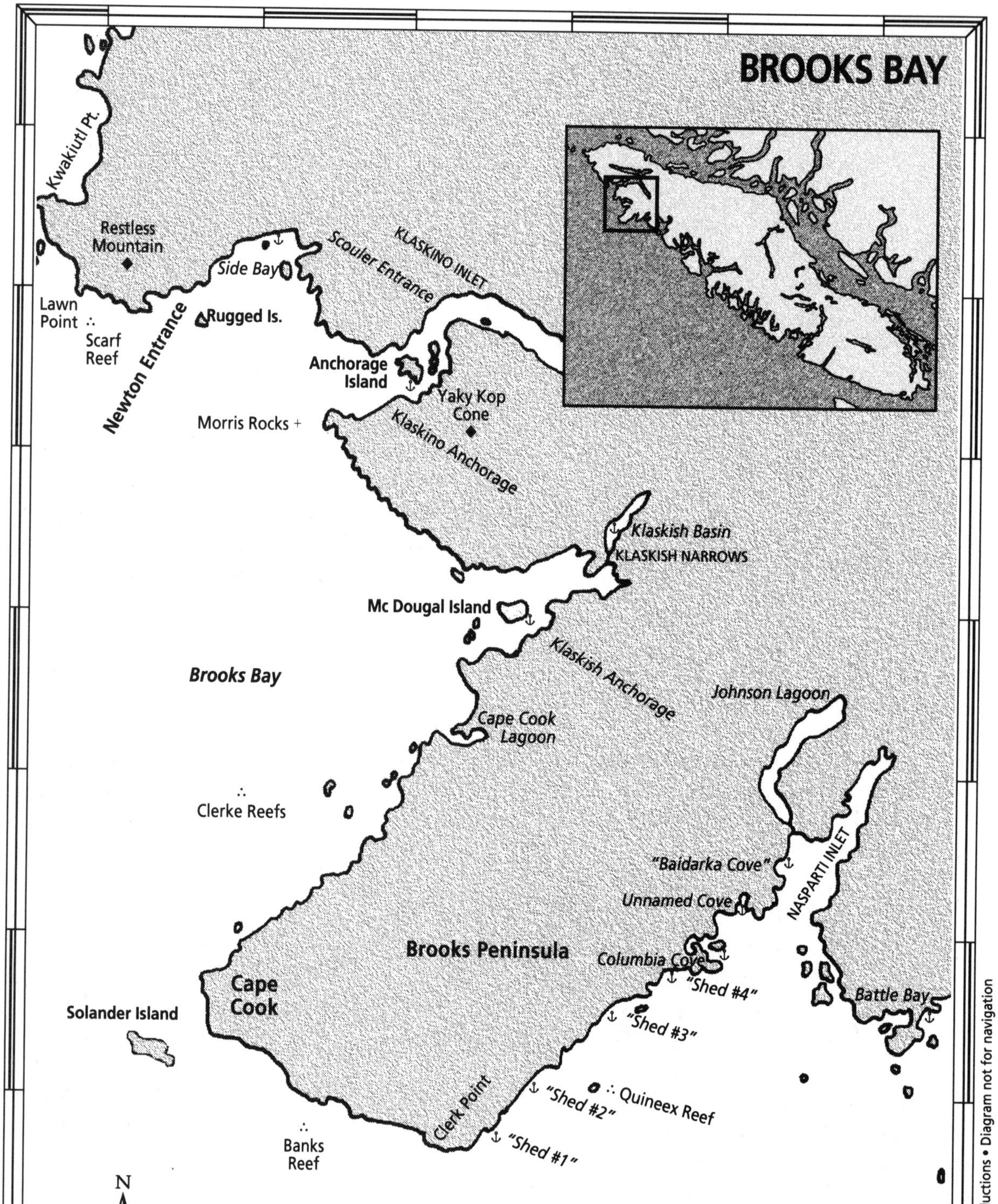

Kwakiutl Pt.

Restless
Mountain

Side Bay

Scouler Entrance

KLASKINO INLET

Lawn
Point

Scarf
Reef

Newton Entrance

Rugged Is.

Anchorage
Island

Yaky Kop
Cone

Morris Rocks +

Klaskino Anchorage

Klaskish Basin

KLASKISH NARROWS

Mc Dougal Island

Klaskish Anchorage

Johnson Lagoon

Brooks Bay

Cape Cook
Lagoon

Clerke Reefs

"Baidarka Cove"

NASPARTI INLET

Unnamed Cove

Brooks Peninsula

Columbia Cove

"Shed #4"

Battle Bay

Cape
Cook

Solander Island

"Shed #3"

Clerk Point

"Shed #2"

.:. Quineex Reef

"Shed #1"

Banks
Reef

N

0 _____ 3

3 NAUTICAL MILES

10

Brooks Bay

Brooks Bay is a region of high, rugged and unspoiled mountains frequently shrouded in clouds that give it a Poe-like aspect. It is a widely beautiful place, complete with "brooding peaks."

Brooks Bay is perhaps the most pristine area of all the West Coast. It seems a long way from Seattle and Vancouver, and it's understandable why many skippers pass it by. Your feeling about Brooks Bay may depend on how much you like crashing swells that burst into white fountains in all directions. Later on, when civilization starts creeping in around you, this is one of the places you yearn for!

Kwakiutl Point to Cape Cook
Chart 3680

The area between Kwakiutl Point and Cape Cook has ill-defined reefs up to 2 miles or more offshore. Lending an additional touch of apprehension are breakers that explode into white spray and foam as they hit numerous rocks and shoals and shoot into the air. Brooks Bay is between Lawn Point (aptly named because of its golf course appearance) southwest of Restless Mountain and Cape Cook on the western extremity of Brooks Peninsula. Lawn Point, a good place to explore, can be reached on foot from sandy beaches to the north or east.

Frequent summer weather forecasts for this area say, "Brooks Peninsula—locally small craft warnings/rising to gale force afternoon winds." This condition, caused by a "lee trough," is a Brooks Peninsula phenomenon that occurs during the summer. It should not be confused with a widely felt low pressure gale.

To make sure this is a local condition only, compare wind reports and forecasts from Cape Scott and Quatsino with those of Solander Island. Passage around Brooks Peninsula under these conditions is best made very early in the morning before the wind picks up.

Brooks Bay
Chart 3680

Although Brooks Bay is a large open roadstead with no protection, two deep, narrow inlets—Klaskino and Klaskish—have public mooring buoys and are secure, well-sheltered anchorages offering a classic cruising experience.

As you enter Brooks Bay you must navigate carefully to avoid the numerous unmarked rocks and reefs. Only the Rugged Islands show up well on radar—other low-lying obstacles do not. For a safe passage, be vigilant, take frequent position fixes and keep a sharp lookout in all directions. Your reward will be a secure, solitary anchorage with exceptional views.

Klaskino Inlet
Charts 3680, 3651 metric; Scouler Entrance way-point: 50°18.10' N, 127°50.00' W

Klaskino Inlet, entered north of Heather Point, offers two sheltered anchorages. Its shores are steep and mountainous. A logging road follows the north shore from Red Stripe Mountain to its head. A small float is near the head of the inlet (1988), NE of the small island.(p. 273)

Fishing boats will often be seen crossing Steele Reefs directly from the west, but this is a risky proposition for cruising yachts and is not recommended.

The recommended entrance to Klaskino Inlet—Newton Entrance—is shown on Chart 3680. From a good offing 2.5 miles south of Lawn Point, head northeast, keeping Rugged Islands to starboard, then turn southeast and pass between buoys "M17" and "M18" before you turn east toward the Scouler Entrance way-point listed above.

Klaskino Inlet is a beautiful classic fjord, but the water is deep and there is no local knowledge on anchoring opportunities. Fishing vessels and cruising boats stay west of Anchorage Island in one of two protected spots.

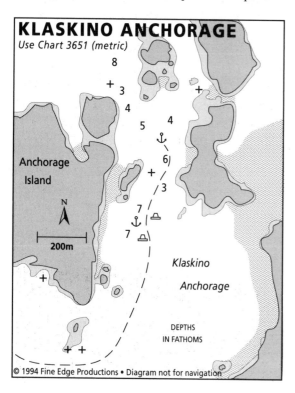

Entering Klaskish Inlet to the south is a bit more straightforward and equally as beautiful. Fishing boats take refuge in both inlets.

Klaskino Anchorage
Chart 3651 metric; anchor west of buoys: 50°18.18' N, 127°49.00' W, anchor north nook: 50°18.36' N, 127°48.95' W

Klaskino Anchorage...is well sheltered with depths of 8 to 10 fathoms (15 to 18 m). Its entrance is slightly less than 0.1 mile wide between the islets and rocks off the south extremity of Anchorage Island and the drying flat extending from the south shore of the inlet. A rock, 3 feet (0.9 m) high, and several drying rocks lie 0.3 mile west of the entrance and slightly more than 0.1 mile off the south shore. Four public mooring buoys are in Klaskino Anchorage.(p. 273)

Klaskino Anchorage, on the southeast side of Anchorage Island, is well sheltered in all directions with depths of 7 to 8 fathoms near the large public mooring buoys. Going ashore here is a treat. If you follow the small creek east of your anchorage and head upstream through thick rain forest, you come to a series of pools and a beautiful waterfall.

If the buoys are crowded, anchor between the buoys and Anchorage Island in 7 fathoms.

The north nook, a few hundred yards north, is a more intimate anchorage for small boats and offers more shelter. Avoid the rock that dries at 4 feet just north of the line of buoys by favoring the east side of the channel. Minimum fairway depth into the nook is about 3 fathoms.

Anchor in 5 fathoms as indicated. The bottom is a combination of mud, rock, shingle and stones, depending on where you anchor.

Scouler Entrance and Pass
Chart 3651 metric

Scouler Pass leads through the chain of islands and reefs obstructing Klaskino Inlet NE of Anchorage Island. The north passage is about 250 feet (76 m) wide with a least depth of 14 feet (4.3 m). The South passage is about 400 feet (122 m) wide with a least depth of 7 feet (2.1 m).... Anchorage can be obtained in about 20 fathoms (37 m), mud, east of the chain of islands just described. (p. 273)

Scouler Entrance leads into Klaskino Inlet. The shoaling bar shown on Chart 3651 can be crossed in two different spots at Scouler Pass. The north passage is deeper. Inside the fjord proper, anchorage can be taken to the immediate southeast behind the large island. However, the depth—25 to 35 meters (80 to 110 feet!)—makes it inconvenient for small vessels to anchor. The inlet continues for another 3 miles to a small basin. The shore, steep and majestic, teems with cascading streams during rainstorms.

No local knowledge is available about anchoring opportunities behind the south shore islets or in the cove at the head of the inlet.

Klaskish Inlet

Chart 3680; McDougal Island way-point:
50°14.26' N, 127°47.52' W

> *Klaskish Inlet, entered between Orchard Point and Sapir Point, offers sheltered anchorage SE of McDougal Island and in the basin at its head.* (p. 273)

Klaskish Inlet is deep in the apex of Brooks Bay, but it is a less difficult route than the circuitous one into Klaskino Inlet. It is important to identify and avoid Hughes Rock. Since swell breaks on it, it is usually visible for quite a distance.

Once you have safely passed the shoals off Gould Rock, you can steer directly for the low saddle on McDougal Island. The navigation light and day mark on Donald Islets, below tree line, are difficult to see in some light conditions.

The trees on McDougal Island have a windswept appearance, testimony to severe winter storms in the past. Just behind the island the

Entrance to Klaskish Inlet, seen from 3 miles out.

impressive twin summits of Harris Peak rise nearly 3,000 feet.

The prevailing northwest swell smoothes out quickly just east of McDougal Island.

Klaskish Anchorage

Chart 3680; anchor: 50°13.90' N, 127°45.82' W

> *Klaskish Anchorage, SE of McDougal Island, offers small craft well sheltered anchorage in 10 to 13 fathoms (18 to 24 m) but the bottom is irregular. Two public mooring buoys are in the anchorage.* (p. 273)

Klaskish Anchorage is located on the southeast side of McDougal Island. There are two public mooring buoys here. From this anchorage you can get a good feel for conditions off Cape Scott. Most yachtsmen, however, prefer to continue

South entrance to Klaskish Anchorage

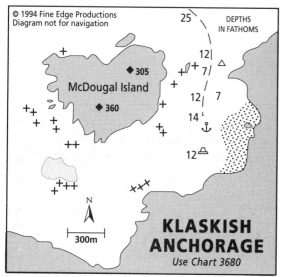

© 1994 Fine Edge Productions
Diagram not for navigation

DEPTHS IN FATHOMS

McDougal Island

KLASKISH ANCHORAGE
Use Chart 3680

300m

east another mile and a half into Klaskish Basin for an unforgettably scenic experience and a secure anchorage.

Anchor in 8 fathoms just north of the buoys over an irregular bottom.

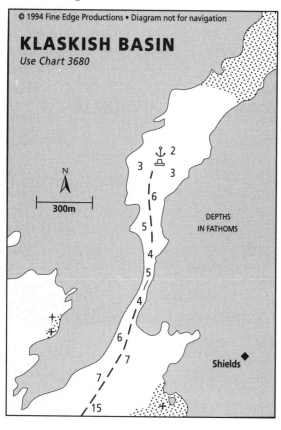

© 1994 Fine Edge Productions • Diagram not for navigation

KLASKISH BASIN
Use Chart 3680

DEPTHS IN FATHOMS

300m

Shields

Klaskish Basin

Chart 3680; anchor: 50°15.37' N, 127°43.85' W

Klaskish Basin, at the head of Klaskish Inlet, has a very narrow entrance, less than 300 feet (91 m) wide, but the least depth is 7 fathoms (13 m). The basin provides protection from all seas but strong winds blow down the mountains and through the Klaskish River valley. Eight public mooring buoys are in the basin. (p. 273)

The entrance to Klaskish Basin is famous for its narrow gorge, where trollers are obliged to raise their side poles in order to clear the trees. The gorge is straight, and the bottom has a least depth of 7 fathoms. The steep, rocky cliffs on either side make good echo targets in foggy weather.

Boaters fortunate enough to visit this basin

Klaskish Basin

are struck with its wild yet quiet beauty. The terrain is magnificent—the U-shaped valley clearly indicates its glacial origins. Klaskish Basin marks the southern limit of the once powerful Kwakiutl people, and it must have been one of their favorite places.

Inside the basin, the water is flat calm, and you are completely cut off from the outside world, including most radio reception!

Williwaws—gusty katabatic winds—occasionally offer a command performance of primeval power, thundering down high slopes and funneling through the river valley on their way to sea. At rising tide, you can take a dinghy up the Klaskish River until your progress is blocked by blowdowns that attest to the

Klaskish Basin—entrance, Narrows and anchorage, top to bottom

strength of these williwaws; you can explore the river on foot as well. A large pool 3 miles inland that marks the limit to which salmon can migrate and is a good serious hike.

Wildlife abounds here; tents seen in the summer at the pristine meadow near the Klaskish River outlet belong to volunteer researchers who keep track of animals combing the shores of the Klaskish. A single observation on the beach one September morning yielded a bear with cubs, several deer and a very large wolf estimated at over 100 pounds. Numerous bald eagles circle overhead hour after hour.

Eight large public mooring buoys are available and well spaced in 4 fathoms.

Anchor in 3 fathoms between the buoys and the large drying flats to the northeast.

Klaskish Basin bouys

"Cape Cook Lagoon" from inside, looking west.

Brooks Peninsula

Chart 8360; position: 50°09' N, 127°50' W

> *Brooks Peninsula...separates Brooks Bay from Checleset Bay. Its shores are rocky and the mountains rise abruptly to elevations in excess of 2,000 feet (600 m). The shelf edge lies only 4 miles SW of Brooks Peninsula where depths increase steeply into Ououkinsh Canyon.* (p. 273)

Brooks Peninsula is the odd, square-shaped peninsula that juts out into the Pacific just north of the 50th parallel. Six miles in length, this natural mountainous barrier divides the colder, more forbidding north island from the milder, more protected coastline of the south. (The first ocean water that exceeds 60°F is usually found south of Brooks Peninsula.) Dozens of peaks over 2,000 feet high rise steeply over the peninsula. Weather-beaten grasses, brush and salal cover the northern shore, and rocks, reefs and jumbled masses of logs and flotsam lie offshore.

The forest has not been logged here, giving the knobby high peaks an austere alpine appearance. Preservation as a natural area, which is currently under consideration, would save this pristine environment for generations to come. Because the peninsula escaped the last ice age, its flora and fauna are of special interest to biologists.

"Cape Cook Lagoon"

Chart 3680; entrance: 50°11.95' N, 127°48.13' W

A fine, wide, sandy beach extends for nearly a mile south of rugged Orchard Point. Near the southwest end of the beach, a large rock outcropping covered with trees extends into Brooks Bay. Immediately southwest of the outcropping is the narrow scenic entrance to an unnamed and beautiful saltwater lagoon, brought to our attention by Tom Cook of Quatsino. Fine camping spots are located on the inside of the south sand spit. This is truly a kayaker's haven; this large protected tidal lagoon is surrounded by lush undisturbed rain forest. At the east end of the lagoon fresh creek water mixes with saltwater.

Nature restricts entering Cape Cook Lagoon to kayaks and runabouts, and then only when prevailing northwest swells are calm enough to allow it. While you can get some lee effect from Clerke Islets and the rocks and shoals just offshore, this is a dangerous lee shore and caution is advised.

"Clerke Reef Passage"
Chart 3680; north entrance way-point:
50°13.40' N, 127°49.96' W

> *No attempt should be made to pass between Clerke Reefs, Hackett Island, Guilliams Island or Clerke Islet and Brooks Peninsula, except with local knowledge.*
> (p. 273)

The author found that in *stable* weather you can save a few miles and get some protection from swells by passing inside Clerke Reef, outside (west) of Clerke and Hackett islets. This channel which we call Clerke Reef Passage has a flat bottom with a minimum depth of 20 fathoms and keeps a straight course for its entire length to Solander Island. Since this route is risky in poor visibility, you should stay well offshore in foul weather.

To enter Clerke Reef Passage, start at way-point 50°13.40' N, 127°49.96' W, 1.25 miles west of Orchard Point. From Klaskish Basin proceed to the way-point by passing north of McDougal Island and Donald Islets. From the way-point the course is 195° magnetic for 8 miles until you

are abeam Solander Island. (See paragraph on Solander Island for both north and south way-points. See way-point, given for Clerke Point at the south end of Brooks Peninsula, at the end of this chapter.)

You can also enter Clerke Reef Passage from the south entrance of Klaskish Anchorage (4 fathom minimum, rather than 8 fathoms marked on the chart!); head 247° magnetic until you reach Clerke Reef way-point (50°13.40' N, 127°49.96' W). Avoid the underwater rock 0.85 mile west of Orchard Point. Once again, note that this shortcut is for fair weather only.

Cape Cook
Chart 3680; position: 50°08' N, 127°55' W

> *Cape Cook...is a conspicuous wooded bluff.*
> (p. 274)

Cape Cook, on the northwest corner of the Brooks Peninsula, has a reputation for bad weather and high seas from both the north and south. With a microclimate of its own, Cape Cook catches the first winds of the day and those of highest velocity along this part of the coast. Afternoon small craft or gale warnings are frequent in this area when the rest of the coast is reporting moderate prevailing northwesterlies. Locals say the West Coast supply ship, *Princess Maquinna*, that ran from Victoria to Quatsino, was sometimes forced to

Approaching Cape Cook
and Solander Island from the north.

turn back on its southbound route because of severe weather, something she never had to do along the rest of the West Coast.

Cape Cook, named Woody Point by Captain James Cook when he first sighted it in 1778, was later renamed after the admired navigator.

Atmospheric conditions along the Cape create a cloud known as Cap on the Cape, which local fishermen say portends a strong west-northwest wind.

Shoals off the cape, as well as the mixing of currents and swells from all directions, cause the summer northwest prevailing swells to reach impressive heights. Passage early on a calm morning is advised, as well as a willingness to turn around and wait for more favorable conditions.

On summer days you often count more than 50 commercial fishing boats trolling off Solander Island; watch them for an indication of offshore conditions.

Solander Island

Chart 3680; north way-point: 50°07.07' N, 127°57.27' W; south way-point: 50°06.37' N, 127°57.16' W

Solander Island, 1.3 miles SW of Cape Cook, is conical shaped. (p. 274)

There is foul ground between Solander Island and Cape Scott. The rocky ramparts of the island are swept clean by crashing swells, and a ring of white foam surrounds it and the islets to the north.

The navigation light atop the island flashes every 10 seconds; the automated weather reporting station here does an important service keeping vessels up-to-date on conditions. By monitoring current weather reports for Solander Island you can get an idea of what to

Solander Island with Brooks Peninsula in background

expect at this strategic site.

This barren and austere rock has been likened in appearance and function to Cape Horn off South America. It marked the division between the Kwakiutl peoples of the north and the Nuu-chah-nulth peoples of the south. For yachtsmen, it announces the beginnings of the more protected and warmer inner waterways. This is also the half-way point if you're making a circumnavigation of the island from Vancouver.

Clerke Point, on the southwest corner of Brooks Peninsula, has a way-point of 50°03.46' N, 127°48.30' W.

Solander Island from the south

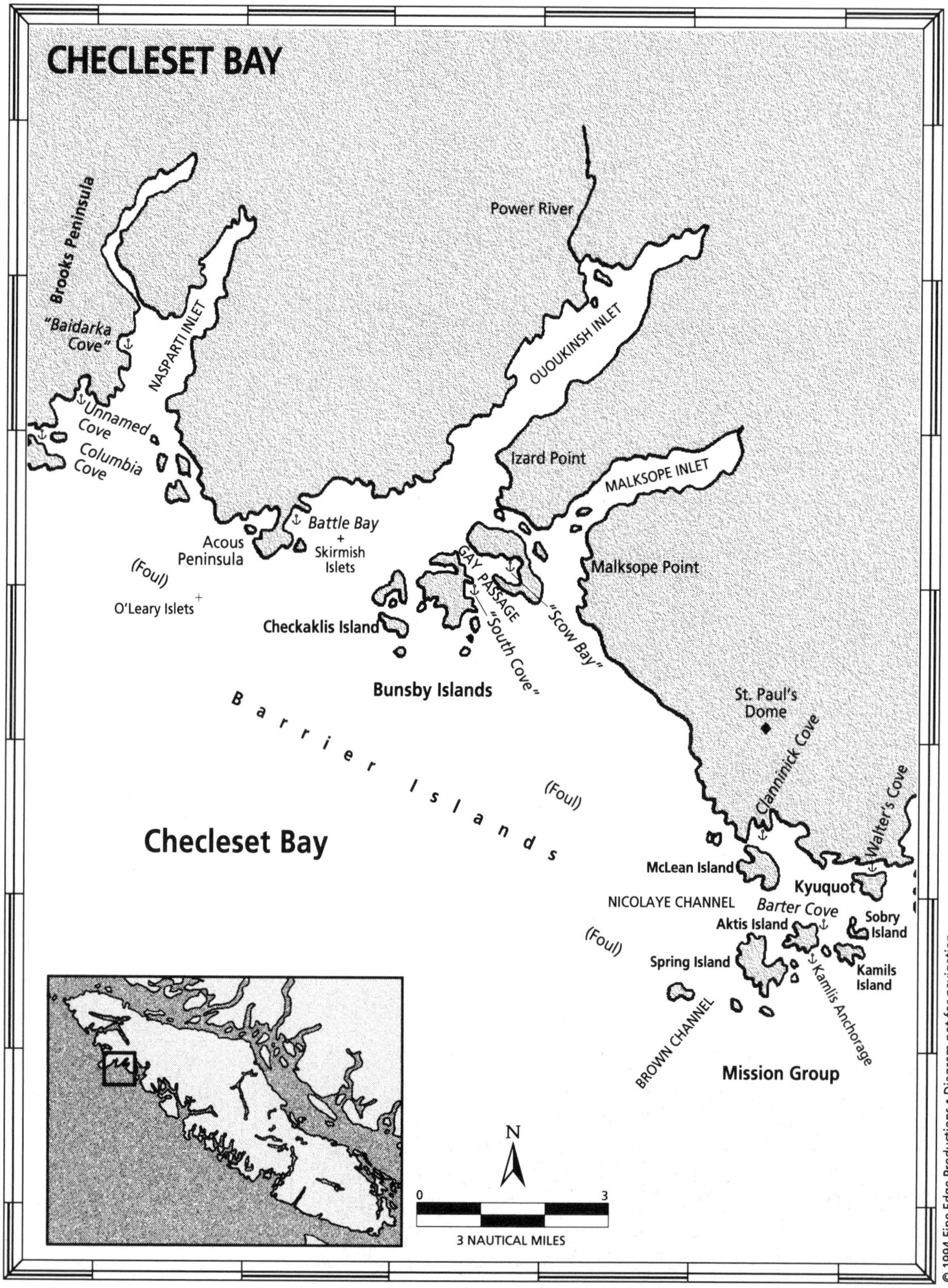

CHECLESET BAY

Brooks Peninsula

"Baidarka Cove"

NASPARTI INLET

Power River

OUOUKINSH INLET

"Unnamed Cove"

Columbia Cove

Izard Point

MALKSOPE INLET

Battle Bay

+ Skirmish Islets

Acous Peninsula

Malksope Point

(Foul)

O'Leary Islets +

GAY PASSAGE

"Scow Bay"

Checkaklis Island

"South Cove"

St. Paul's Dome

Bunsby Islands

Clanninick Cove

B a r r i e r   I s l a n d s

(Foul)

Walter's Cove

Checleset Bay

McLean Island

Kyuquot

NICOLAYE CHANNEL

Barter Cove

Sobry Island

Aktis Island

Kamils Island

Spring Island

Kamils Anchorage

BROWN CHANNEL

Mission Group

N

0 ——— 3

3 NAUTICAL MILES

11
Checleset Bay

It is easy for a skipper to tell when he rounds Clerke Point and heads into Checleset Bay. With Brook Peninsula astern, the water calms, the air becomes balmy and food and drink reappear on the galley table. The crew comes alive, starts comparing notes on the differences between Cape Scott and Cape Cook and focuses on swimming and beachcombing. You are below the 50th parallel now, in the banana belt and things are warming up.

Cape Cook to Nasparti Inlet
Charts 3680, 3683

Since numerous rocks, reefs and shoals fringe Brooks Peninsula, it's essential to maintain a good offing. East of Clerke Point, the prevailing northwest swell decreases rapidly, and Checleset Bay takes on a more welcoming appear-ance. The bay, however, is full of a variety of rocks and islets, known collectively as the Barrier Islands, and navigation can be a challenge.

If you are in a hurry, take the outside option and skirt the hazards by staying well offshore. If you have time, though, the route inside the Barrier Islands is almost completely protected from swell, and you can poke your bow into a number of intimate and seldom-visited coves.

Clerke Point
Chart 3683; way-point: 50°03.46' N, 127°48.30' W

Clerke Point, the south extremity of Brooks Peninsula, lies 5 miles SE of Cape Cook. The coast between is foul and should be given a wide berth. Banks Reef dries 13 feet (4m). Eldridge Rock has 13 feet (4m) over it and breakers are nearly always present. (p. 274)

Clerke Point is named after Commander Charles Clerke, who was second in command on Cook's third and fateful expedition to the Northwest in the *Discovery*. When Cook was murdered in Hawaii, Clerke took over command, but died later on the expedition of tuberculosis.

The way-point for Columbia Cove is Jackobson Point (50°07.87' N, 127°40.34' W).

Barrier Islands

Shelter Shed

Charts 3680, 3683

> *Anchorage.—The coast along the SE side of Brooks Peninsula, NE of Clerke Point, is used as an anchorage by fishing vessels during NW winds. It is known locally as Shelter Shed.* (p. 274)

Once you round Clerke Point, you are out of the big northwest swells, and although winds gust down gullies along the southeast side of the peninsula, there is little fetch for the seas to build on. From Clerke Point to Jackobson Point, outside the 5-fathom curve, the shore (except for Quineex Reef) is relatively free of rocks and obstructions.

In stable summer weather, fishing boats run in against shore to what is called Shelter Shed (or just Shed) along the southeast side of the peninsula and find shelter from northwest winds and swells. This region is an open roadstead and offers no protection from southerly winds or seas. If you anchor here you should have an alternate plan if conditions start to deteriorate.

There are several beaches nearby that make good landing spots for sea kayaks, dinghies or sportfishing boats. Temporary anchorage can be taken off several beaches in 3 to 4 fathoms. For convenience, we have named them Shed 1 through Shed 4.

Shed 1 (anchor: 50°05.20' N, 127°46.47' W) is the closest anchorage to the fishing grounds. Boats simply stay close to shore southeast off the first mountain peak (1,415 ft.) where there is a small landslide scar, and they anchor outside the reef line in about 8 fathoms.

Shed 2 (anchor: 50°06.32' N, 127°45.12' W) is located 2.75 miles from Clerke Point inshore from Quineex Reef. This small beach is at the outlet of a U-shaped valley drained by a major creek. Anchor in 4 fathoms.

Shed 3 (anchor: 50°07.32' N, 127°43.32' W) is located 1.75 miles northeast of Quineex Reef. This spot has a beautiful white sand beach, in-

Shelter Shed 4 on left

teresting islets, and rocks and a reef close offshore that give additional protection and a nice view. Enter carefully and anchor in 3 fathoms. Used by local sportfishing boats in northwest weather, it is also a good kayak campsite.

Shed 4 (anchor: 50°07.68' N, 127°42.20' W), the long grey beach covered with driftwood, is less than a mile from Jackobson Point. The shore is shallow. Anchor in 2.5 fathoms about 600 yards offshore.

The Brooks Peninsula is a wildly beautiful, unspoiled natural playground. It has special charms for visiting yachtsmen and we hope it will remain like this for future generations.

Nasparti Inlet

Chart 3683

> *Jackobson Point, the west entrance point of Nasparti Inlet, is low and a drying rock spit extends south from it. Boit Rock, 0.3 mile NE of Jackobson Point, has less than 6 feet (1.8 m) over it.... Nasparti Inlet has high shores and a drying flat at its head. Booming grounds line the west shore, 1 mile north of Lorenz Point.* (p. 274)

Nasparti Inlet advances several miles into Vancouver Island at the south edge of Brooks Peninsula. Like Klaskish Inlet to the north, Nasparti Inlet sets off the landscape, accentuating the uniqueness of Brooks Peninsula.

Nasparti is a quiet, primitive place and a

good spot to relax before you head south into the hustle and bustle of people and machines. Out of sight of man's noise, the rain forest and wildlife are still at their finest here.

Nasparti is a European adaptation of the name of a tribe that lived here in fur trading days. There are several places where you can drop your hook and explore an overwhelmingly peaceful region. Columbia Cove is the most accessible.

Columbia Cove ("Peddlers Cove")

Chart 3683; anchor: 50°08.33' N, 127°41.48' W

Columbia Cove, on the north side of Jackobson Point, affords sheltered anchorage to small craft and has two public mooring bouys. (p. 274)

Columbia Cove, known locally as Peddlers, is not identified on the chart. It is a small, well-sheltered channel north of an unnamed island and is entered northwest of Jackobson Point. This is a scenic, calm spot that feels cozy after the wide open horizons off Cape Cook. The eastern entrance is foul with rocks.

Bear, cougar and smaller animals regularly ply the large drying mud flats of Columbia Cove. An old coast guard cutter, beached and tied to the shore at the west entrance, is slowly breaking up—evidence of some business venture gone sour. There is a deserted cabin on shore. A primitive quarter-mile-long trail leads

from the southern end of the beach to the outside beach, listed as Shed 4 above.

In 1791 Captain Robert Gray, master of the fur-trading *Columbia Rediviva*, visited the cove and named it in honor of his vessel. His first mate described the cove as "...entirely landlocked in an excellent harbour." The *Columbia* revisited the cove a year later and, fear-

Entrance to Columbia Cove

ing an attack, fired cannon and muskets at the natives, tragically killing twenty of them. Gray, who played an important part in early European exploration of this coast, established Fort Defiance in Clayoquot Sound (see Meares Island).

There are now three public buoys in the cove, but they are quite close together; the swinging room is somewhat small and the water is shallow. Additional anchorage can be found in the entrance to the west of the buoys.

Anchor in 2 fathoms over mud and gravel bottom with fair holding.

"Cove Northeast of Columbia Cove"

Chart 3683; anchor: 50°08.93' N, 127°40.38' W

There are two unnamed coves close northeast of Columbia Cove. The first, shallow and rocky, is of marginal use to yachtsmen. The second has two potential anchorages in stable summer weather, as shown on the accompanying

COLUMBIA COVE

Sandy beach

Use Chart 3683

Foul: no exit

Shipwreck

Kelp

DEPTHS IN FATHOMS

N

200m

Jackobson Pt.

© 1994 Fine Edge Productions • Diagram not for navigation

Combing the shore

diagram.

When we visited it, this scenic cove was calm while west-northwest gales were blowing off Brooks Peninsula. However, sharp gusts can whip down the deep gully off high peaks to the northwest. Several small pebble beaches are good for landing and exploring. There is a good view to the south, and rocks and reefs off the eastern side of the cove give small craft some protection from light southerlies. A slight swell from the southwest can be felt here at all times, however.

Anchor in 5 fathoms over a flat bottom of rock, mud, gravel and kelp. The anchor is somewhat difficult to set because of kelp, but holding can be good.

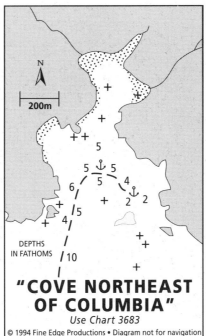

"COVE NORTHEAST OF COLUMBIA"
Use Chart 3683
© 1994 Fine Edge Productions • Diagram not for navigation

"Baidarka Cove"
Chart 3683; anchor 50°09.60' N, 127°39.35' W

Another mile and a half inside Nasparti Inlet, due west of Lorenz Point and three quarters of a mile south of the Johnson Lagoon tidal rapids, lies a second unnamed cove, beautiful and peaceful, that offers sheltered anchorage in most summer weather. We call it Baidarka Cove.

The cove has room for several boats as well as outstanding views in all directions. The rocky, tree-lined shore has small pebble beaches and a drying flat, and several islets you can explore by dinghy. This is also a good place to explore the Johnson Lagoon tidal rapids to the immediate north in case you wish to make a transit. You can also use it as a base to explore Nasparti Inlet.

The high alpine peaks on the peninsula to the west are rugged and bare, while the peaks to the northeast have a long, serrated ridge with trees growing to their summits. Some logging scars on the eastern shore of the inlet tell of man's past here.

Baidarka Cove has a number of small rocks above and below water that necessitate careful navigation, but kelp marks many of the dangers. The head of the cove shoals abruptly. This is an excellent place to enjoy the quiet solitude and warmer water, and to plan the remainder

Entrance to "Baidarka Cove"

of your route south.

I took the liberty of naming this cove after my faithful vessel, *Baidarka,* which we use for exploring the Northwest coast on annual trips from Puget Sound to Glacier Bay and back. (*Baidarka* is the Russian word for skin-covered kayaks, particularly the three-holed kayaks used by the Aleuts.)

Anchor in 10 fathoms in the center of the cove. If you anchor close in on the south side, you can tie a stern line to shore. The bottom is mud, gravel and kelp with good holding.

Johnson Lagoon

Chart 3683; entrance: 50°10' N, 127°39' W

Johnson Lagoon, on the west side of Nasparti Inlet, has a very narrow rock encumbered entrance. There are tidal rapids in the narrows and entry by small craft can be made only at HW slack. At spring tides slack water is 2 hours after HW and 2h. 30 min. after LW. (p. 274)

Johnson Lagoon is a narrow 3-mile-long fjord. The sides are steep, and inspiring peaks tower overhead in all directions. The lagoon is reputed to offer good shelter from the notorious southeast storms that hit Brooks Peninsula.

This area has been used as a booming ground, but little is known about its attractions for yachtsmen. The lagoon is wonderfully placed for those seeking the grandeur of this part of the coast. The entrance is extremely narrow with fast-flowing tidal rapids, and its successful navigation requires careful personal observation and good judgment.

It is said you can anchor in Johnson Lagoon in moderate depths off several gravel and mud bars, but we were unable to confirm this.

Southwest cove of Battle Bay

Nasparti Inlet to Ououkinsh Inlet
Chart 3683

These two inlets are separated by the O'Leary, Cuttle and Skirmish islets and the Acous Peninsula. These islets, part of the Barrier Islands that moderate the swells along this part of the coast, create navigational challenges for visiting yachtsmen. According to your experience, you will find this maze either exhilarating or frightening!

Since so many of these rocks, reefs and islets looks similar, you need to keep an accurate dead-reckoning position on the chart and a sharp lookout for a safe passage. It's helpful if you draw your route ahead of time and list the headings and distances so you can keep track of them easily.

O'Leary Islets
Chart 3683; "Bowler Islet": 50°06.13' N, 127°39.87' W

O'Leary Islets (50° 06' N., 127° 39' W.) are sharp topped and steep sided. Yule Rock, 0.6 mile north of O'Leary Islets, is 19 feet (5.8 m) high. Ferey Rock, 0.7 mile NNW of Yule Rock, dries 10 feet (3 m). (p. 274)

Heading south from Nasparti Inlet you need to take the O'Leary Islets to port. These and many islets to the east are the hunting areas and playgrounds for cavorting sea lions and sea otters. The most prominent and westerly of these islets is treeless and has the shape of a bowler hat, clearly seen from some distance.

Battle Bay
Chart 3683, 3680; anchor: 50°06.92' N, 127°35.50' W

Battle Bay, with Skirmish Islets in its centre, is not recommended as an anchorage. Longback Rocks lie east of the north entrance point of the bay. (p. 274)

Sailing Directions does not recommend Battle Bay as an anchorage. It certainly is a challenge to enter and there is a lot of foul ground, but it is

Above: Approaching Battle Bay, with Skirmish Island to right. Below: Anchored in Battle Bay.

a beautiful place with an interesting shoreline. In Battle Bay you can appreciate the undisturbed natural environment as in few other places.

The best way to visit is to cruise the shore by dinghy or kayak and walk the beaches. Keep in mind that this is an Indian Reserve and no artifacts may be removed or defaced in any way. From here to Rugged Point there are a number of ancient buriel grounds; the Checleset and Kyuquot First Nation's Peoples ask that all tourists contact the band office for permission to visit their area.

This is the ancestral home of a powerful Checleset tribe; you can still see an erect totem

pole on the neck of the peninsula and evidence of their reign here. (The Checleset were probably the ones involved in a skirmish with Captain Gray in Columbia Cove.) The old growth rain forest is magnificent: spruce, cedar, hemlock, yew, fungus pods, moss, tall ferns, madrone, salmon berry, blackberry, cowsnip, and saltweed all mingle here; and occasionally you see evidence of bears.

A small trail leads between the eastern shore of the peninsula and island (195) to the east. This lagoon is interesting to view, and the coast off the south side is literally breathtaking! The native peoples were superb navigators of this maze with their canoes and obviously they found plenty to eat—there is an abundance of oysters, mussels and clams among the rocks and tide pools.

The main part of Battle Bay northeast of Battle River and its lagoon has larger beaches and is a favorite destination for sea kayakers. This wonderful cruising area should be maintained in its primitive state for everyone to enjoy.

Battle Bay is encumbered with rocks of all sizes, and you need to enter it at dead-slow. Find a clear channel to the south side of Skirmish Islands and the small reef to the south. Stay mid-channel with a heading of about 260° magnetic. When a northwest gale blows off Cape Cook, this part of the bay frequently receives a light to moderate easterly back-eddy breeze that blows out of Ououkinsh

---

Facing page: A watch at the bow

Inlet! Small vessels can take anchorage on the western side of the bay near Acous Peninsula, where the water is calm.

Anchor in 5 fathoms off the southwest corner of the beautiful sandy beach. Bottom is sand and mud with good holding.

Ououkinsh Inlet
Chart 3683

Anchorage in 16 fathoms (29 m), mud, can be obtained about 0.3 mile off the drying flats at the head of Ououkinsh Inlet. (p. 274)

This inlet is seldom visited by yachtsmen and is truly off the beaten path. It has the rugged ap-

© 1994 Fine Edge Productions • Diagram not for navigation

BATTLE BAY
Use Charts 3683 and 3680

Battle Bay—southwest corner

pearance of a northwest fjord, with tree limbs that extend gracefully out over the water. Six miles long, it is deep for the most part, with precipitous sides.

Anchorage is reported to be available behind small islands off the south side of Powell River which comes in from the northwest.

Ououkinsh Inlet to Malksope Inlet and Walters Cove

Between Ououkinsh Inlet and Malksope Inlet to the south is a peninsula fronted by the Bunsby Islands.

To continue south from here, you can go "outside," back into the Pacific and around the rocks and reefs scattered up to 5 miles offshore. Or you also can stay "inside" by carefully navigating the Bunsby Islands via Gay Passage.

Bunsby Islands
Chart 3683; 50°06' N, 127°32' W

The Bunsby Islands are a group of low, windswept, densely treed islands with fascinating geometry that includes innumerable rocks and reefs. The beauty of this corner of Checleset Bay rivals the outer islands of the Broken Group in Barkley Sound and it has better all-weather anchorages. It is well worth a stop on your West Coast itinerary.

In 1983 an experiment to reintroduce the sea otter was begun on this part of the coast. Now, from here to Clanninick Cove, several hundred pairs of sea otters look happy and healthy, and their comeback has been a huge success. Watching these animals watch *you* is a most enjoyable experience.

Close to the Vancouver Island mainland there are a number of inviting small gunkholes, private "fiefdoms" of those lucky to know the secrets of their entrances. The first is immediately south of Izard Point. Its boat passage and shallow landlocked cove look bombproof, but we have no local knowledge about it.

The channel between the largest Bunsby Island and the peninsula has several snug anchorages. The area is known as Upsouis by locals; we have had difficulty entering.

"False Gay Passage"
Chart 3683

The inner passage along the coast to Walters Cove follows Gay Passage between the two biggest Bunsby Islands. When approaching from the northwest, *do not mistake False Gay Passage* (50°06.3' N, 127°33.0' W) for Gay Passage and turn south too soon. If you do, you will enter the foul channel west of Bunsby Island (260). Gay Passage is one mile northeast, and although it is similar in appearance, it is much safer to transit.

Local fishermen use the small, shallow cove

False Gay Passage from the north

north of Checkaklis Island for anchorage as well as the small bight in Bunsby Island northeast of Checkaklis Island; however, entrance is not recommended unless you have investigated the area first by dinghy.

Gay Passage

Chart 3683; north entrance: 50°06.63' N, 127°31.70' W

> *Gay Passage, between the two largest Bunsby Islands, has a number of rocks in it but can be used by small craft; local knowledge is required.* (p. 274)

Gay Passage is the secret to a pleasant, smooth ride down this part of the coast. See the diagram of its entrance from the north, and do not confuse it with False Gay Passage a mile to the west. From the south, the correct Gay Passage

"Scow Bay"

is easier to recognize as the route one mile due west of Malksope Point.

It is not difficult to navigate Gay Passage in good visibility from either north or south if you proceed slowly and pay strict attention to identifying and avoiding the charted rocks on either side of the fairway. The minimum depth is about 6 fathoms, but you must be careful; the fairway curves and narrows to about 100 yards, and it contains enough obstacles to keep you on your toes.

If you avoid patches of kelp, you will generally steer clear of underwater rocks. If someone in your party wants to take a picture of the sea otters, it is best to stop the boat dead in the water and shoot photos *before* you proceed.

Above: North entrance, Gay Passage
Below: Inside Gay Passage

"Scow Bay"

Chart 3683; anchor: 50°06.27' N, 127°30.83' W

Scow Bay, the local name for the north cove in Gay Passage, is a scenic, well sheltered and comfortable anchorage.

Since the southern side of the entrance to Scow Bay has a sizeable shoal extending well northwest of the islet, you should favor the north shore while transiting the bar. Small boats can enter the inner cove, avoiding the large, dangerous underwater rock and anchor in about 2 fathoms.

This is a quiet, secure anchorage where you

"South Cove"—Bunsby Islands

can relax in just about any weather. It's also a good place to launch a dinghy for exploring the Bunsby Islands.

Anchor in the outer cove in about 7 fathoms. The bottom is mixed mud, gravel and kelp and appears to hold well if your anchor is well set.

"South Cove"
Chart 3683; anchor west nook: 50°05.94' N, 127°31.47' W

On the south side of Gay Passage is a second Bunsby Island anchorage with two pictur-esque spots to drop the hook. Sea otters live here and will constantly entertain you. The southern end has an excellent, rather wild view across the reef with its waves and spray, and it is protected in most sum-mer weather.

Anchor in 4 fathoms in the center of the cove over a mixed bottom of undetermined hold-ing power.

The western nook in the large Bunsby Island is well pro-tected. Anchor in 7 fathoms over a mixed bottom with fair to good holding.

Malksope Inlet
Chart 3683

Malksope Inlet, entered be-tween Upsowis Point and Malksope Point, affords an-chorage in 11 to 18 fathoms (20 to 33 m), mud. Several is-lets and rocks, 1.5 miles north of Malksope Point, obstruct the fairway. Pass NW of these islets to enter the inner part of the inlet (p. 274)

Malksope Inlet is a 4-mile long

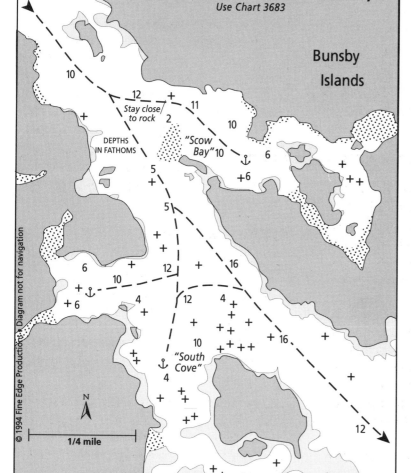

GAY PASSAGE
("SCOW BAY" & "SOUTH COVE")
Use Chart 3683
♦ 430'

Bunsby Islands

Stay close to rock

DEPTHS IN FATHOMS

"Scow Bay"

"South Cove"

N

1/4 mile

© 1994 Fine Edge Productions • Diagram not for navigation

fjord with precipitous sides, mountains that tower overhead, and deep water that affords little protection for cruising yachtsmen. The log booming area shown on the chart is no longer located off the north shore near the large drying flat of the Malksope River.

Malksope Inlet to Walters Cove
Charts 3651 metric, 3683

From the southern entrance of Gay Passage you can head south using buoys "M28" and "M27" and then lay a course towards McLean Island, staying north of Cole Rock.

A more scenic, intimate and less-rolling route—if you discount giant ugly clear-cut areas—is to hug the Vancouver Island coast south of Malksope Inlet for nearly 3 miles. St. Paul's Dome, the conspicuous 1,880-foot peak on the southern end of this coastal chain, is a good leading mark.

As you close the coast near several sea caves, pick up the small island marked (180) on the chart (with trees), turn south and pass island (180) on the port hand, staying well inside the reefs to the west and heading straight for Cole Rock. Minimum depth in this passage is about 7 fathoms

Turn 0.6 mile north of Cole Rock toward the north end of Spring Island and follow around McLean Island to your port. After you pass the buoy on Chief Rock (portside), you can turn north into Clanninick Cove (a good idea in poor visibility) or continue east for the somewhat tricky entrance to Walters Cove or Barter Cove to the south.

From here south to Tofino, you start a slow transition to civilization.

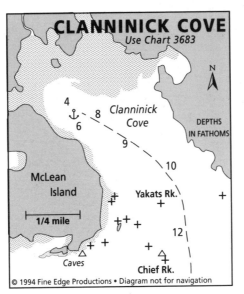

Kyuquot Sound Approaches

Barrier Islands are a chain of islets and reefs extending 20 miles NW from Jurassic Point...to the entrance of Ououkinsh Inlet.... Brown Channel is the most direct and safest approach for Clanninick Cove anchorage and Kyuquot. Kyuquot Channel is the safest and most direct approach for Kyuquot Sound.(p. 275)

If you bypassed Nasparti Inlet, and are approaching Kyuquot Sound from outside the Barrier Islands, Brown Channel, on the east side of Lookout Island, is the most direct and safest approach for Clanninick Cove and Kyuquot. (The way-point for Lookout Island light is 49°59.88' N, 127°26.87' W; the way-point for Brown Channel light and whistle buoy "MC" is 49°59.46' N, 127°26.81' W.)

To enter the sound directly, Kyuquot Channel south of Union Island, is the safest and most direct route.

Note: Kyuquot is pronounced Ky-oo-Kit.

Clanninick Cove
Chart 3683: anchor: 50°52.09' N, 127°24.65' W

Clanninick Cove, east of McLean Island, affords anchorage for small vessels in 9 fathoms (16 m). Yakats Rock, 0.3 mile north of Chief Rock, lies in the entrance of the cove and has less than 6 feet (1.8 m) over it. A rock, 2 feet (0.6 m) high, lies 0.2 mile east of Yakats Rock.(p. 275)

This is a good place to stay if visibility does not allow your safe entrance into the intricate Walters Cove, and you'll have a good time watching the many sea otters that live in the rocks northwest of Chief Rock.

Clanninick Cove with Chief Rock in foreground

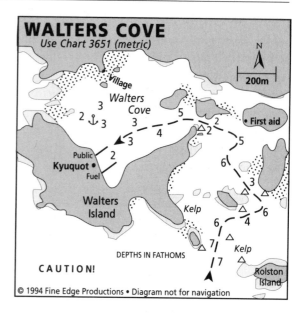

Clanninick Cove is fairly large, with Yakats Rock (less than 6 feet of water over it) and two shoals that encumber an otherwise easy entrance east of Chief Rock buoy.

Anchor in 7 fathoms on a broad flat near the head of the cove; you will find plenty of swinging room.

Dinner at Walters Cove

Walters Cove

Chart 3651 metric (it is large scale and must be consulted)

> *Kyuquot* [Walters Cove]*...has a store and a Red Cross Outpost Hospital under the charge of a resident nurse. A doctor makes scheduled visits. Diesel fuel, gasoline, lubricants and fresh water are obtainable. A marine ways in the cove is capable of hauling vessels up to 40 feet (12 m). Air service is available.... Two floats, one attached to the north and the other to the south side of the public wharf, are each 170 feet (52 m) long and for the use of small craft.... A fuel float, south of the public wharf, is the site of the marine service station.* (p. 276)

Walters Cove, situated on the east side of Walters Island, has an intricate entrance, and you must use Chart 3651 metric for a safe transit, or stand off in Nicolaye Channel west of Rolston Island until a local boat passes inbound that you can follow. The red flashing light at the west end of Rolston is the first of several critical aids to navigation for a safe passage into the cove.

Walters Cove is a secure, interesting and friendly little port. A favorite for many yachtsmen, it has fuel, water, telephone, store, and a restaurant; it is also alcohol-free. A telephone is located at the head of the wharf; the store is at its foot. The restaurant, open during the summer season, is just a short walk along the path to the south; the fuel dock (with water) is the main float south near the cannery.

The public wharf has floats on either side for small boats. If the floats are congested, you can anchor close west of the wharf in 3 fathoms, mud bottom, or in the north side of the cove off the village in 3 fathoms, mud bottom.

The Kyuquot Coast Guard Auxiliary requests that all persons and boats travelling through the sound do so with caution, remembering that the weather can change very quickly. (This is particularly important for kayakers who frequent the area in large numbers in summer.) Kyuquot Coast Guard Auxiliary monitors VHF Channel 06 and Channel 16. Martha Tyerman, their leader, can be reached at 604-332-5222.

Note: *Canadian Chart 2, Pacific Coast Catalogue,* does not list Chart 3651 as metric; however the chart itself *is* metric.

Above: Inner entrance to Walters Cove
Below: Walters Cove public wharf

First aid station (hospital)—Walters Cove

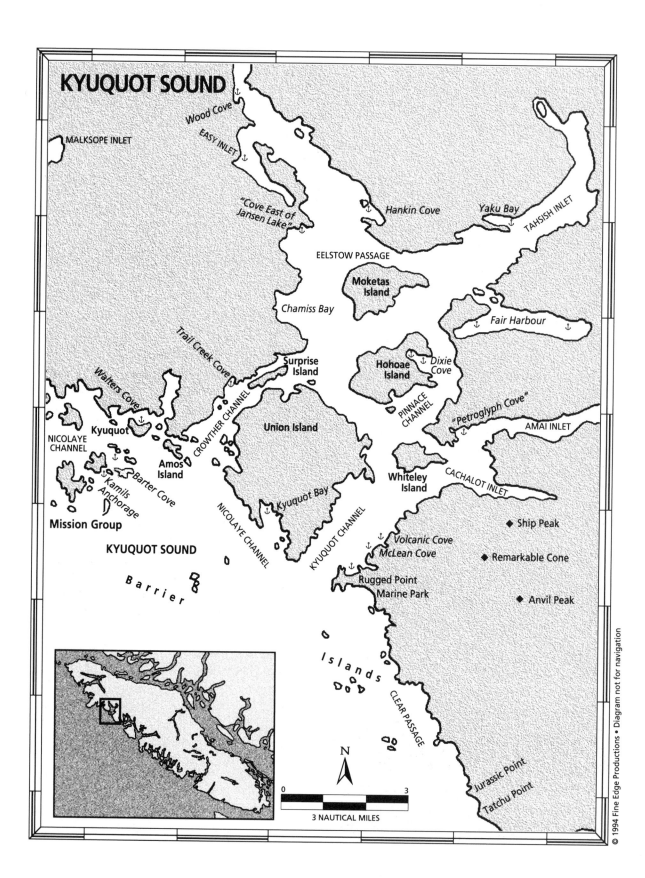

KYUQUOT SOUND

MALKSOPE INLET

Wood Cove

EASY INLET

"Cove East of Jansen Lake"

Hankin Cove

Yaku Bay

TAHSISH INLET

EELSTOW PASSAGE

Moketas Island

Chamiss Bay

Fair Harbour

Trail Creek Cove

Surprise Island

Hohoae Island

Dixie Cove

Watters Cove

Kyuquot

NICOLAYE CHANNEL

Amos Island

Barter Cove

Kamils Anchorage

Mission Group

CROWTHER CHANNEL

Union Island

PINNACE CHANNEL

"Petroglyph Cove"

AMAI INLET

Whiteley Island

CACHALOT INLET

KYUQUOT SOUND

NICOLAYE CHANNEL

Kyuquot Bay

KYUQUOT CHANNEL

Ship Peak

◆ Remarkable Cone

Volcanic Cove

McLean Cove

Rugged Point Marine Park

◆ Anvil Peak

B a r r i e r

I s l a n d s

CLEAR PASSAGE

N

Jurassic Point

Tatchu Point

0   3

3 NAUTICAL MILES

12
Kyoquot Sound

As you head south, Kyuquot Sound is the second of the five big sounds that cut deep into Vancouver Island's West Coast. It is bounded by Walters Cove (Kyuquot) on the north and Rugged Point to the south. There are two main inlets and several smaller ones.

The friendly, unhurried pace in Walters Cove sets the tone for exploring Kyuquot Sound. With no road access, and protected by a maze of islets and islands, the tempo is slow and inviting.

Inside Kyuquot Sound, the possibilities for anchorage are many, your choice frequently limited only by your imagination and prudence. Of the five sounds on the West Coast, this is probably the most protected, and the one where outside swell diminishes the fastest. Outflow winds (williwaws) sometimes blow at night, however.

Numerous islands and small peninsulas on the sound provide excellent anchorages for cruising boats, including two attractive and bombproof coves for small boats—the well-known Dixie Cove and a newly described cove we call "Petroglyph Cove."

Because the Barrier Islands, with their offlying reefs and rocks, discouraged early sailing ships from exploring Kyuquot Sound, it was one of the last areas of Vancouver Island to be charted and named. With modern boats, however, the protection afforded by the Barrier Islands provides opportunities for good sportfishing and kayaking.

Kyuquot Sound

Charts 3682, 3683, 3623, 3651 metric;
position: 50°00' N, 127°13' W

> Brown Channel is the most direct and safest approach for Clanninick Cove anchorage and Kyuquot. Kyuquot Channel is the safest and most direct approach for Kyuquot Sound. (p. 275)

The easiest and safest entry into the sound, which is also the only all-weather route, leads through Kyuquot Channel to the south of Union Island. *Sailing Directions* does not recommend Crowther Channel because the south entrance is encumbered with islets and rocks and the northeast end is narrow (300 feet).

In fair weather, however, small vessels heading south from Walters Cove can turn east using Crowther Channel. (Most of the charted hazards appear to be awash and can be

Rugged Point Marine Park beach

spotted easily in good visibility.) Pass close to the islet due west of Union Island, paying careful attention to the currents, which can be significant at spring tides. Some locals prefer to pass just east of Amos Island through a narrow, shallow channel; the south point of the island is prominent for its sculpture of a native mounted on a horse.

Proceeding in a clockwise direction within the sound, a few of the possibilities for anchoring are described below.

Barter Cove

Charts 3651 metric, 3682, 3683; anchor: 50°00.8' N, 127°23.2' W

This austere little anchorage has an interesting history. Kamils Island on the south side of Barter Cove is known locally as Cemetery Island. A white picket fence marks the remains of a fierce battle that took place here between the Kyuquots and the Clayoquots, their rivals to the south. In 1855—with the help of Mowachahts, Ehatisahts and Checlesets—the Clayoquots launched a vicious surprise attack against the Kyuquots, massacring most of them and leaving the survivors of the once most powerful tribe in disarray.

Nowadays, a few descendants of the Kyuquots live in a settlement on the east shore of Aktis Island, but the majority live on a reserve across from Kyuquot settlement in Walters Cove. Most of these islands are Indian Reserves; if you wish to go ashore you must ob-

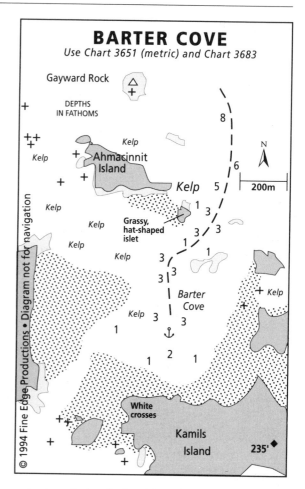

Entrance to Barter Cove (left of island)

tain permission beforehand. (Make inquiries in Kyuquot.) A member of the Kyuquot Band told me that the band's concern for the sanctuary of Ahmacinnit Island is so great that if a yacht were stranded on the island they could not come to its rescue!

Using the light at Gayward Rock as a reference point, carefully enter Barter Cove close east of a hat-shaped islet off the southeast point of Ahmacinnit Island (locally called Deadman Island). Avoid the shoals to both the east and west. In northwest gales a slight swell and a 1- to 2-foot chop can be felt here, but a single hook with large scope will hold your boat into the wind quite comfortably.

Anchor anywhere in the bay in 1.5 to 3 fathoms with good swinging room. The sand-mud bottom has good holding.

Kamils Anchorage

Charts 3682, 3683: anchor: 50°00.2' N,
127°23.6' W

Kamils Anchorage...in the middle of Mission Group, is approached from the south by Favourite Entrance. The anchorage is only suitable for small craft; local knowledge is required. A narrow passage leads NE to Barter Cove, which is shallow. (p. 275)

Kamils Anchorage, an overnight favorite of fishermen in fair weather, is close to the fishing grounds and gives visual contact with outside conditions. The numerous scenic reefs and the constant interaction of the swells is the main cruising attraction here.

The north entrance from Barter Cove can be used only in high water; the south entrance, shown on the chart as Favourite Entrance, is unmarked and requires careful judgment. In southerly weather, Kamils could be a rough anchorage

Small boats are said to take anchor in 5 to 6 fathoms.

Kyuquot Bay

Chart 3682; anchor: 49°59.25' N, 127°17.47' W

Kyuquot Bay, on the SW side of Union Island, is entered between Racoon Point and White Cliff Head. Its SE part is encumbered with islets and rocks and the bay is open SW.(p. 276)

Kyuquot Bay, a favorite of sportfishing boats, cruising boats and sea kayakers, is an excellent destination. Offshore rocks and reefs diminish the prevailing swell, but this bay is exposed to the south. If weather conditions start to deteriorate, it's a relatively short run to well-protected Walters Cove or Dixie Cove.

Almost any nook in this beautiful, wild bay is a candidate for small boats to drop their hook for a short stay. Good anchorage in fair weather can be taken on the east shore of the bay just north of the islets

Anchor in 5 fathoms over a mixed bottom of undetermined holding power.

"Trail Creek Cove"

Chart 3682; anchor: 50°02.6' N, 127°128.9' W

Half a mile west of the southern tip of Surprise Island, tucked behind a peninsula near the outlet of Trail Creek, there is a calm, quiet bay that offers fair-weather protection for one or two boats.

Enter slowly and watch for uncharted rocks visible above and below water. A few pilings south of the creek, on the western shore, mark the ruins of an old cannery.

Anchor in either of two small bights on the cove's eastern side in 3 to 5 fathoms over a mixed bottom of mud, shell and kelp. Holding is good, but swinging room is limited.

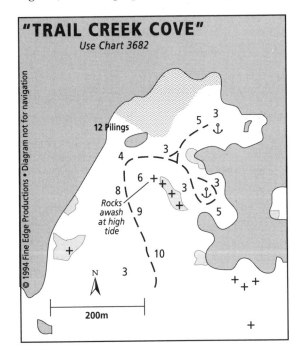

Surprise Island

Chart 3682

From Trail Creek Cove a narrow passage leads to the north side of the Surprise Island, now more appropriately called Stump Island.

Entrance to "Cove East of Jansen Lake"—stay to the left

Leaving "Cove East of Jansen Lake"

Kayakers and small runabouts frequently use this passage when going between Fair Harbour and Walters Cove.

You can carefully traverse this passage in minimum depth of about 2.5 fathoms and take conditional anchorage along the shore or in the deeper bay at the north end. Trees that used to cover the island were extensively hand-logged; if you examine the cuts on the stumps, you can see that many of the trees were felled to drop directly into the saltwater.

"Cove East of Jansen Lake"
Chart 3682, anchor: 50°06.2' N, 127°16.4' W

This small cove, 1 mile north of Chamiss Point and a half-mile northeast of Jansen Bay booming area, offers a calm, quiet place to spend some time alone. Landlocked in all directions, the cove should be secure in most if not all weather conditions.

An old rusting donkey, almost hidden in the second growth on the north side of the cove, is evidence of equipment once used to log this area. The creek on the northwest shore leads to a small lake a quarter mile inland.

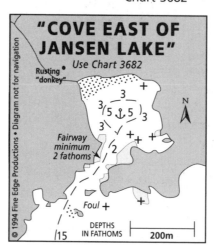

The entrance to this secluded cove is encumbered with underwater rocks and requires caution. The best way to enter is to hug the west shore, avoiding the foul shoal that extends from the peninsula on the eastern side. Stay west until you pass over a 1-fathom shoal (perhaps less at zero tide) avoiding two light-colored rocks along the western shore. The cove has a flat bottom that ranges between 2.5 and 4 fathoms.

Anchor near the center of the bay in 3 fathoms. The bottom is a mixture of gravel and mud. We had some difficulty setting the anchor; be sure yours is well set.

Kashutl Inlet
Chart 3682

Kashutl Inlet is a wide, deep inlet with a lot of logging activity and not much to interest visiting yachtsmen. Monteith Bay, Easy Inlet to the west and Wood Cove at the very head of the inlet are all reported to offer shelter to small craft; however, the water is relatively deep and logging or mining operations spoil the scenery for pleasure vessels.

Hankin Cove

Chart 3683; anchor: 50°06.6' N, 127°13.6' W

Hankin Cove, 1.5 miles north of Moketas Island, is a well-sheltered cove with an easy entrance. Remarkably protected from all quarters, it's a good anchorage to head for when the weather starts to deteriorate. Keep your eye peeled for birds and seals that like the drying shoal to the southwest.

Entrance to Hankin Cove

Although the log dump and booming operation formerly operated here are gone, the hillsides to the east have been devastated by old clear-cuts; several eroding roads crisscross the torn-up slopes. Trees were removed down to the very high tide line, and all that remains is slash everywhere. Nature is trying to make a comeback in this cove, and in time it will be a charming spot, however, the devastation in this cove contrasts greatly with the beautiful old growth trees on the islets and peninsula to the west.

In times of bad weather when clouds cover the ridge and mist hangs low, you hardly notice the scarring on the hillsides; and with your anchor well set you will be snug and comfortable here. The best anchorage is deep in the cove, north of the islet shown in the diagram.

Anchor in 4 fathoms over a soft mud bottom. Use a light touch when you set your anchor, giving it a chance to dig deep; it will hold well once it's in place.

Tahsish Inlet

Chart 3682

Tahsish Inlet to the northeast is a deep fjord with steep, high sides. Two major rivers—the Tahsish and Artlish—drain the upper inlet. Both have extensive drying flats and are steep to the edge. The eastern shore has been extensively logged, and there are booming grounds off the south side of the Artlish River.

Yaku Bay is a protected anchorage with a drying flat at its west end. Quite deep, it is used only by locals who have adequate ground tackle. The bottom is undetermined.

Fair Harbour

Chart 3682; position: 50°04' N, 127°07' W

Fair Harbour, a landlocked inlet, is too deep and steep for convenient anchorage. A public wharf and float are located at the eastern end. The road that serves Walters Cove and the entire Kyuquot Sound ends here. There is a parking lot and a boat-launching ramp. Many sea kayak expeditions start from here. A causeway

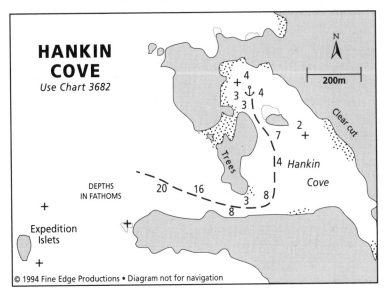

HANKIN COVE

Use Chart 3682

N

200m

4

3 ⚓ 4

3

2

7 +

Clear cut

Trees

|4 *Hankin*

Cove

3 8

8

DEPTHS IN FATHOMS

20 — 16

+

Expedition Islets

+

© 1994 Fine Edge Productions • Diagram not for navigation

Old growth rain forest

Fair Harbour—road's end

*Above: Entrance to Dixie Cove
Below: Entrance to inner bay, Dixie Cove*

with a sizable log bridge connects to the road that follows the Kaouk River to the east. The ruins of an old logging operation and a rusting LST litter the shore.

There is enough fetch in Fair Harbour for wind waves to build up. Otherwise, it is well protected. Anchorage can be taken in deep water at either end of the harbor in a mud bottom with good holding in all but east to southeast winds.

Dixie Cove

Chart 3682; anchor: 50°03.2' N, 127°12' W

Dixie Cove is one of the most picturesque, scenic and well-sheltered coves for small vessels on the West Coast. Its shores are covered with magnificent old growth trees whose limbs brush the water at high tide, giving you the feeling you are truly *inside* the rain forest. It's a remarkable place that should be preserved as it is!

You can tell no waves disturb this cove, because there is no driftwood or debris on shore. The low saddle to the northwest sometimes lets the wind howl across it, but that shouldn't disturb your anchor; it will just serve as a reminder that you are still on the Pacific side of Vancouver Island! The outer cove has room for several good-sized yachts.

Anchor in 8 fathoms in mud bottom with good holding.

The inner bay of Dixie Cove is easily entered through the narrows to the west. The narrows are about 80 feet wide with 3 fathoms over the shoal.

Anchor in 3 to 7 fathoms over wide, flat, mud bottom with good holding.

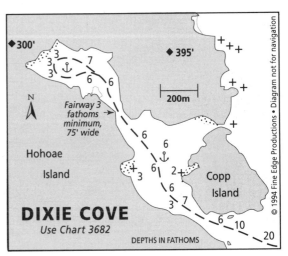

Amai Inlet
Chart 3682

Amai Inlet is a narrow, deep and scenic fjord with a striking precipice on its north side. Its high peaks with bare grey rock give it an alpine appearance. Once a logging area, the environment in the inlet is now recovering. Near its western entrance, 1 mile north of Balcom Point, we found what we consider a striking anchorage for small boats.

"Petroglyph Cove"
Chart 3682; anchor: 50°01.5' N 127°10.7' W

Petroglyph Cove is the name we've given this unusual and little-known spot at the extreme west side of Amai Inlet. Locals told us that the cove has no known name and that it is too small to enter, and although we found no writ-

Above: Entrance to "Petroglyph Cove"
Below: View of landlocked entrance from inside "Petroglyph Cove"

ten reference to it, we thought it an excellent anchorage for small craft. It is protected from all weather and is scenic as well. Like Dixie Cove, Petroglyph Cove is surrounded by beautiful old growth.

The central attraction here is a series of small petroglyphs etched in the vertical cliff on the north side of the narrows. These animal glyphs appear to have been done from a boat at high tide. The cove calls for more exploration, as well as protection for it historic and recreational values.

Easterlies that blow down Amai Inlet and out through the low saddle to the west should cause little concern if you set your anchor well. In strong southeast winds Dixie Cove may have less fetch, but the shoreline here indicates it is a calm anchorage.

Nearly landlocked, the cove has a uniform flat bottom of between 3 and 5 fathoms. A small islet inside the south entrance forms a small beach and lagoon that provides a good dinghy landing.

The water temperature here (68°F) was the highest we measured in Kyuquot Sound! The only drawback we could find to this cove was that weather radio broadcasts were difficult to receive.

The entrance is about 40 feet wide and steep; we found no rocks or problems. The water is so clear you can see bottom all the way

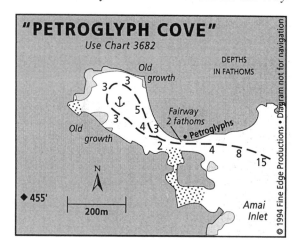

through the narrows at a minimum depth of about 2 fathoms.

Anchor in 3 fathoms over a bottom of soft mud and decaying matter. A light touch is needed in setting your anchor, but holding is good when it is well set.

Cachalot Inlet
Chart 3682

Although Cachalot Inlet is a petite, classic fjord of unusual beauty, the southern shore is falling victim to chain saws and will need time to heal before it can reach its recreational potential. Like Amai Inlet, Cachalot lies in an east-west line. Storm fronts that veer from east to southeast roar down the steep slopes of both inlets, creating difficult conditions for your anchor rode.

Volcanic Cove
Chart 3682; position: 49°58.6' N, 127°13.9' W

Volcanic Cove is a tiny, narrow nook with possibilities for one small craft only. The head of the bay is clear-cut; it is fouled with kelp and a heavy nylon line is stretched across the cove at the 2-fathom line. This appears to be an indifferent anchorage.

Overhanging rock containing petroglyphs

McLean Cove
Chart 3682; anchor: 49°58.3' N, 127°14.1' W

This cove offers some temporary anchorage. It dries for the most part, and the rocky shoreline has been clear-cut to the water's edge. There is a tiny, well-protected kayak beach on the west corner.

Anchor in 3 fathoms inside outer rock. Bottom and holding are undetermined.

Rugged Point
Chart 3682; anchor: 49°58.2' N, 127°14.6' W

Close east of the north tip of Rugged Point there is a series of beautiful sandy beaches

Volcanic Cove with cable across water

McLean Cove

extending to Robin Point in a half-mile semi-circle. This beach and the south side beaches of Rugged Point form Rugged Point Marine Park. The east end is an excellent kayak beach and a dinghy can easily be landed anywhere along its length in prevailing moderate northwest weather.

An old cabin on shore provides temporary shelter for park visitors, and a well-developed trail leads from there about 350 yards south to the open beach facing Clear Passage; there's a pit toilet located 75 yards behind the cabin on the trail.

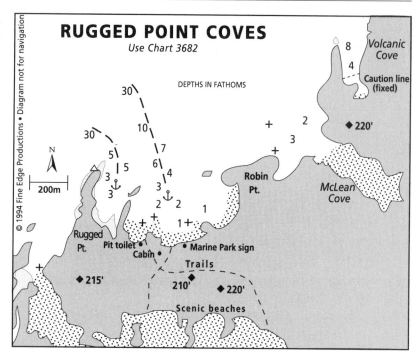

Some large Douglas fir and spruce have blown down here, and their massive but shallow root systems, which reach 25 feet in width, are quite impressive.

At low tide the sand on the flat outer beach reveals a striking, alternating black-and-white pattern. The scalloped sand beaches, with rocky arms that push out toward the Volcanic Islets, are most picturesque. Note that powerful southeast and southwest storms have driven huge logs up into the line of vegetation.

Rugged Point with Barrier Islands in background

Don't miss the opportunity to explore these beaches!

The anchorage at Rugged Point is open and somewhat exposed. Caution: The beach is shallow for a long way out into the cove, and during an outflow wind at night you could find yourself on a shallow lee shore with 1- to 3-foot chop!

Anchor in 2 fathoms over a packed sand bottom with good holding.

Clear Passage

Chart 3682; "M38" buoy: 49°58.23' N, 127°15.03' W

> *Clear Passage is only suitable for small craft and local knowledge is required.* (p. 277)

Proceeding from Kyuquot Sound to Esperanza Inlet, you can take the outside route or a smoother, more interesting inside route through Clear Passage.

The outside route—preferred any time visibility is poor—can be found by proceeding 2.5 miles out from Rugged Point. Pass entrance buoy "M38" to port before turning southeast-ward and stay west of the Barrier Islands.

Clear Passage to the south stays inside the Barrier Islands a bit longer. It is clear most of the way with a flat bottom (except at the north and south entrances), and this route can be an easy trip in benign weather. The prevailing swells that foam and surge over the charted rocks and reefs give you advance warning of any hazards.

The strategy for entering from the north is to stay close to Rugged Point, locate Grogran Rock (a 23-foot pinnacle) and nearby underwater rocks marked by attached kelp beds; steer a course between them in a minimum fairway of about 10 fathoms. For a less-demanding northern entrance head southwest from Rugged Point for about a mile, then turn south, passing

Grogan Rock, Clear Passage

equidistant between Nipple Rocks and the Volcanic Islets to the south in a minimum depth of about 12 fathoms; the fairway for this route is slightly wider.

Grassy Islets are a good area for kayak exploration. The islet marked (51) feet has a small landing beach on its protected southeast side. Thousands of birds thrive here, including tufted puffins, pigeon guillemots and stormy petrels.

The south entrance has a couple of possibilities for exiting. Although some boats pass north of McQuarrie Islets, I prefer to pass close to known obstacles rather than to guess where unmarked and unseen obstacles may lie. To exit at the south end of the Barrier Islands, I pass close east of McQuarrie Islets and the rock that dries 15 feet, and west of the rock and shoal, which dry 8 feet just to the northeast of McQuarrie Islets. Swell, as well as kelp, identify these port-side marks.

The fairway has 7 fathoms and a flat bottom. This particular route gives you protection from swells a little longer than the more northerly exit and doesn't have as nasty a lee shore. Since Tatchu Rocks on the southeast side of this entrance are marked with breakers, you can spot the dangers on your port side.

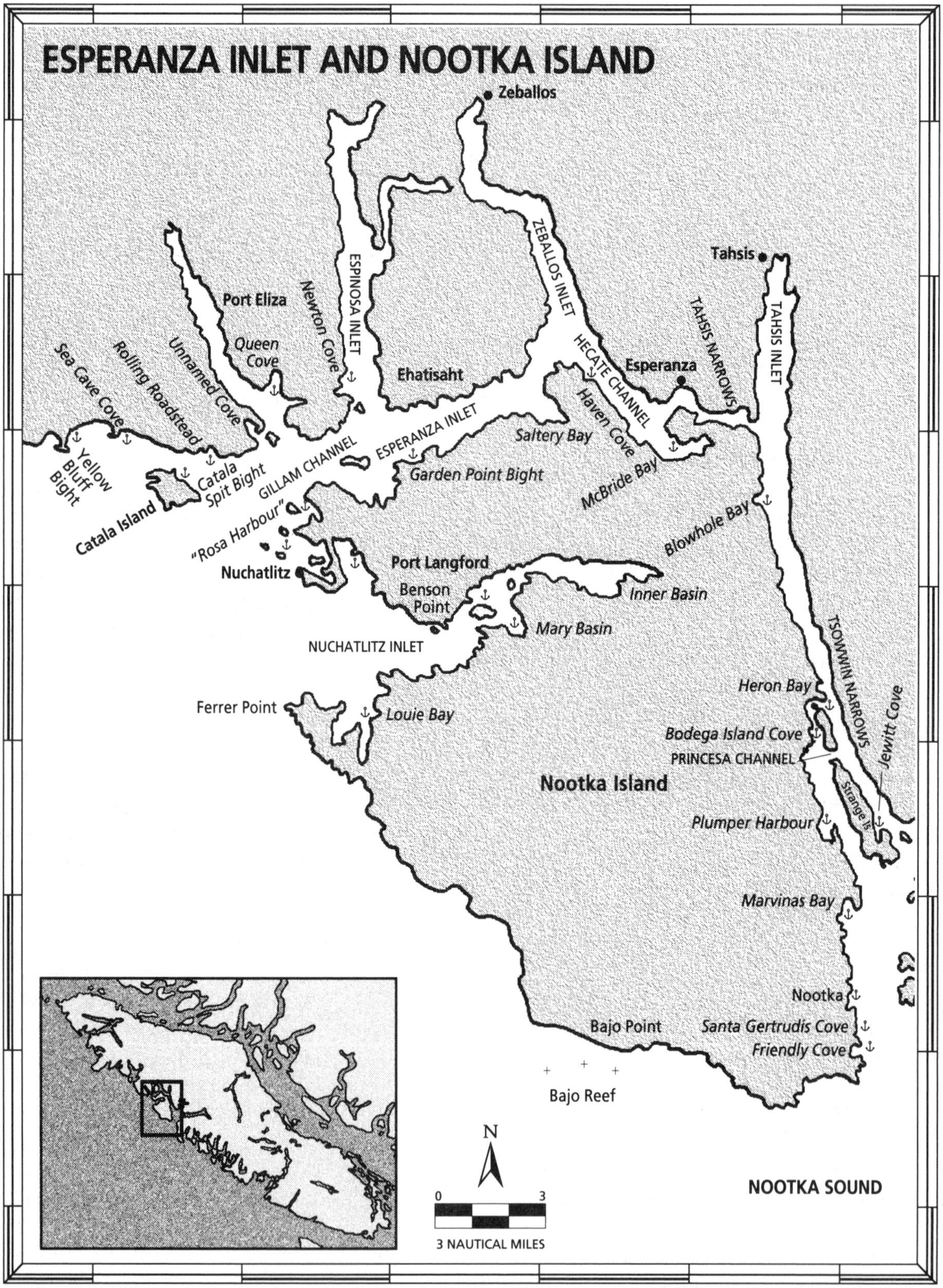

ESPERANZA INLET AND NOOTKA ISLAND

Zeballos

Tahsis

Port Eliza

Queen Cove

ESPINOSA INLET

Newton Cove

ZEBALLOS INLET

Ehatisaht

HECATE CHANNEL

Esperanza

TAHSIS NARROWS

TAHSIS INLET

Unnamed Cove

Rolling Roadstead

Sea Cave Cove

Yellow Bluff Bight

Haven Cove

Saltery Bay

ESPERANZA INLET

GILLAM CHANNEL

Catala Spit Bight

Garden Point Bight

McBride Bay

Catala Island

"Rosa Harbour"

Nuchatlitz

Blowhole Bay

Port Langford

Benson Point

Inner Basin

Mary Basin

NUCHATLITZ INLET

TSOWWIN NARROWS

Heron Bay

Jewitt Cove

Ferrer Point

Louie Bay

Bodega Island Cove

PRINCESA CHANNEL

Strange Is.

Nootka Island

Plumper Harbour

Marvinas Bay

Nootka

Bajo Point

Santa Gertrudis Cove

Friendly Cove

Bajo Reef

N

0   3

3 NAUTICAL MILES

NOOTKA SOUND

© 1994 Fine Edge Productions • Diagram not for navigation

13
Esperanza Inlet and Nootka Island

As you proceed south along Vancouver Island, the coast from Kyuquot Sound seems to be an unending line of high, steep mountains. Off Tatchu Point you soon realize that the mainland coast turns abruptly east and the coast you see ahead is really that of Nootka Island, the largest island on this coast. It is a thrill to see Nootka and recall all the history associated with the area.

Esperanza Inlet heads east, connecting a series of calm channels that lead around Nootka Island all the way to its southeast point at Friendly Cove. Except for entrance buoys, the inlet probably looks exactly as it did 200 years ago when European sailing ships first began exploring the region.

Tatchu Point to Estevan Point
Charts 3662, 3640

> The coast between Tatchu Point (49°51' N, 127°09' W) and Estevan Point, 37 miles SE is indented by Esperanza Inlet, Nuchatlitz Inlet and Nootka Sound. Caution—Mariners are warned that there is likely to be an indraught into these large inlets, especially during strong winds from SE to SW. This part of the coast should, therefore, be given a wide berth. (p. 277)

On their way south from Tatchu Point, most cruising boats prefer the route that takes them behind Nootka Island. The route from the north enters Esperanza Inlet, continues along the north coast of Nootka Island through Tahsis Narrows to Tahsis Inlet, then heads south to Friendly Cove. Although this route is longer, it allows a more comfortable, scenic cruise. Just east of Tatchu Point there are a number of fine coves to explore, starting with one we call Yellow Bluff Bight. The village sites of Nuchatlitz and Nuchatlitz Inlet also have their own remote charm. Please remember that all lands marked IR on charts are private lands belonging to native bands, and prior permission is required if you want to go ashore. Please respect all native sites.

If you are in a hurry, you may want to stay outside Nootka Island. If so, watch for Inner Bajo Reef and Bajo Reef off the southwest side of Nootka Island. Bajo Reef light and whistle buoy lie just inside the 20-fathom curve, and their position—49°33.80' N, 126°50.00' W—is useful as a way-point.

Esperanza Inlet
Chart 3663; entrance buoy "MD": 49°47.12' N, 127°02.80' W, Middle Reef light buoy "M41": 49°48.10' N, 127°02.30' W

> Three channels lead through the dangers in the entrance to Esperanza Inlet...Gillam Channel...North Channel...west approach. (p. 296)

The best route to use if you enter Esperanza Inlet in reduced visibility is via Gillam Channel. Its entrance buoy "MD," and the port hand Middle Reef light buoy "M41" give you good checkpoints. In stable weather with good vis-

Entrance to "Yellow Bluff Bight"

ibility, small boats can take a shortcut using the "west approach" and head east through Rolling Roadstead. The motor vessel, *Uchuck III,* that delivers supplies and passengers to the area frequently uses this route.

"Yellow Bluff Bight"

Chart 3663; anchor: 49°51.47' N, 127°06.90' W

> *...west approach to Rolling Roadstead. The channels between these dangers are narrow, intricate and require local knowledge.* (p. 296)

Yellow Bluff, the name for the large sand spit 1 mile east of Tatchu Point, is not listed in *Sailing Directions.* The bight east of the spit, which we call Yellow Bluff Bight, is an excellent temporary anchorage for a short rest stop if weather and sea conditions allow it.

Yellow Bluff Bight is a beautiful shallow bay with a wide sand and pebble beach. It gives enough protection from northwesterlies that little swell is felt in stable weather. From Yellow Bluff Bight it is easy to study conditions around the offlying rocks and reefs of the High Rocks area directly to the south.

Entering Yellow Bluff Bight from the south (the west approach) should be done only in good visibility and after you have identified the marked reefs and rocks. Specifically, you should not attempt the route shown in the diagram unless you identify Halftide Reef, Ob-

struction Reef and the rock that lies one-quarter mile south of High Rocks. The reefs of High Rocks and extensive kelp beds that surround them quickly knock down prevailing northwest swells. The fairway is straight with a flat bottom. In southerly winds or in limited visibility, you should avoid this route altogether and locate the entrance buoys to Gillam Channel, using them to enter Esperanza Inlet.

Extensive kelp beds surrounding the reefs are full of sea life, and in favorable weather you can easily land a dinghy or kayak on the reef and explore the mussels, barnacles and flora. The islets between here and Rugged Point are home to the tufted puffins, among other unusual birds. You can comb the beach and explore the small cove immediately west where

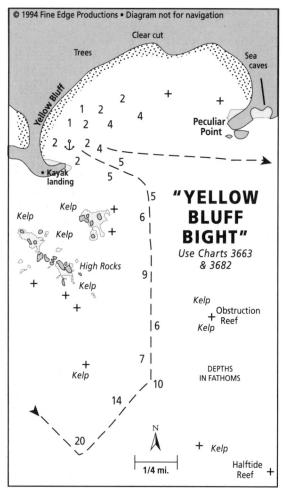

© 1994 Fine Edge Productions • Diagram not for navigation

"YELLOW BLUFF BIGHT"
Use Charts 3663 & 3682

DEPTHS IN FATHOMS

1/4 mi.

there is a logging camp The best landing spot on the beach is inside the point. You can also explore the sea caves 1 mile to the east near Particular Point.

There is plenty of swinging room here for several boats; we had no evidence of rocks on our echo sounder except for those marked with kelp on the east side of the bay. (Dan DeVault, long-time resident of the area, was surprised to find 3- to 9-foot rocky reefs off the sandy bottom one year when he was diving here.) If you set a small stern anchor toward shore, you can keep rolling to a minimum. If weather or sea conditions change, it is wise to leave and look for more protection farther into Esperanza Inlet, such as at Queen Cove.

Anchor in 2 fathoms over a bottom of soft gray mud and sand with good holding.

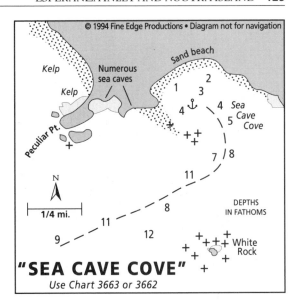

"SEA CAVE COVE"
Use Chart 3663 or 3662

"Sea Cave Cove"

Chart 3663; anchor: 59°51.64' N, 127°04.62' W

A half mile east of Peculiar Point is a small, unnamed bight in the coastline with offlying rocks and kelp. This spot, which we call Sea Cave Cove, offers limited protection in favorable conditions. The attraction here is that it's an easy dinghy row to a series of caves (both sea caves and walk-in caves) as well as interesting tide pools. Like Yellow Bluff Bight to the west and Rolling Roadstead to the east, there is no protection in Sea Cave Cove from southerly weather or seas, and you should be prepared to leave if conditions change.

Anchor near shore in 3 fathoms. The bottom is mud and sand with good holding.

Rolling Roadstead

Chart 3663; anchor: 49°50.86' N, 127°02.34' W

Anchorage for small vessels can be obtained in Rolling Roadstead about 0.5 mile NW of Entrance Reef in 27 feet (8.2m), sand and shell, or between Entrance Reef and Double Island in about 8 fathoms (15 m), sand. A swell is usually present. (p. 297)

Rolling Roadstead, the first available protection for vessels entering Esperanza Inlet via

Above: "Yellow Bluff Bight"—High Rocks in background. Below: "Sea Cave Cove"

Campsite—"Catala Spit Bight"

Gillam Channel, is a large, flat, shallow area between Catala Island and the coast of Vancouver Island. Entrance Reef, marked with buoy "MJ," bares on an 8-foot tide or less and you can enter the area easily in poor visibility with good radar targets. The least swell is found in the east part of the bay. For a more intimate and scenic anchorage, small vessels might consider a location we call Catala Spit Bight (see below).

"Catala Spit Bight"
Chart 3663; anchor: 49°50.62' N, 127°02.67' W

Temporary anchorage can be taken at the north end of Catala Island close in at the southeast corner of the spit. We refer to this spot as Catala Spit Bight. The water is deeper here than the chart indicates, and it is a good place to enjoy fishing and exploring. There's great driftwood along the pebble beach and good primitive campsites for kayakers. Since it's easy to land a dinghy or kayak here, this area is a favorite among sportfishing boats and kayakers.

Catala Spit Bight offers fairly good shelter in the summer, but not in stormy weather. At the first sign of a rapidly falling barometer, you should head for Rosa Harbour or Queen Cove.

Anchor in 1 to 2 fathoms close to the beach over a sand bottom with fair holding.

Nuchatlitz Inlet
Chart 3663

If you are not in a rush to enter Esperanza Inlet and the idea of solitude and beauty sounds attractive, head into Nuchatlitz Inlet and take some time to poke your bow into the anchorages along the way. Nuchatlitz village, on the northern side of the inlet, as well as some of the nearby coves, are seldom visited. The peaks of Nootka Island, most of which rise over 2,000 feet, form a splendid backdrop for anchorages in the area.

Entering Nuchatlitz Inlet, you can pass on either side of Nuchatlitz Reef, which lies in the center of the entrance. Be sure you make positive identification of all hazards, however, to avoid high anxiety or grief. Nuchatlitz Reef breaks the Pacific swell in several places, but much of it is underwater on a 12-foot tide. The northern entry is marked by buoy "M42" (indicated on Chart 3663) and Pin Rock, which

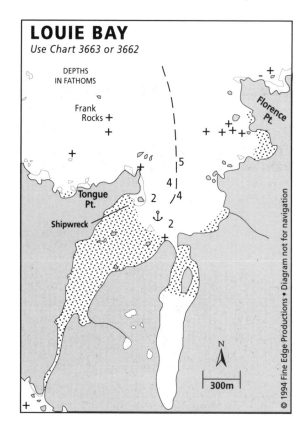

bares on a 10-foot tide and breaks rather dramatically most of the time. Set your course to about 092° magnetic and take Justice Rock on either the port or starboard hand. The southern entry passes south of Danger Rock and north of South Reef and Frank Rocks.

Louie Bay

Chart 3663; anchor: 49°44.77' N, 126°56.09' W

Louie Bay, entered between Tongue Point and Florence Point, has drying reefs off both entrance points. It is only suitable for small craft and local knowledge is required. (p. 300)

If you study Louie Bay on the chart it appears to hold promise for cruising vessels. Other than sightseeing, however, its usefulness to yachtsmen is limited. Both the western and southern bays have drying mud flats and can be explored only by dinghy, and then only by careful

Above: Entrance to Louie Bay
Below: Wreck at Louie Bay

Approach to Mary Basin

attention to tidal action. The outer bay receives a lot of northwest swell, although it offers protection in heavy southerlies. Small craft, though, would be more secure inside Mary Basin to the east.

You may want to go ashore to examine the remains of a ship near Tongue Point—the vessel that foundered near Ferrer Point was cut up and hauled here by tractors in an attempt to salvage its metal.

Temporary anchorage can be taken midway between two islets south of Tongue Point in about 2 fathoms, over a bottom of mixed mud, rock and kelp. Since tidal action is strong here at times, holding power is somewhat questionnable.

Mary Basin

Chart 3663; anchor: 49°46.86' N, 126°50.10' W

Mary Basin, between Lord Island and Narrows Island, provides anchorage in about 4 fathoms (7m), mud. It was reported (1987) that a wreck with its mast visible at LW is in the south end of Mary Basin, east of Lord Island. (p. 300)

Mary Basin is well protected and secluded and has plenty of swinging room for a number of boats. It is worth the effort to get here if you like peace and solitude. East of Florence Point the water shoals for over a mile to a constant 4 fathoms, creating an entrance bar to Mary Basin, the classic sign of a fjord. When there are strong westerly swells and wind, ebb conditions on the bar can be dangerous. The wreck mentioned in *Sailing Directions* was a troller that capsized in a heavy winter southeaster. It has since been salvaged and removed from Mary Basin.

A few crab-pot floats and some ugly clear-cut scars on the north side is all that reminds you that man has passed through here. Mary Basin is a good anchorage if you want to watch the tidal rapids in the narrows or visit the sea caves to the west of Benson Point.

For the best protection and a more intimate setting, try the southern part of the bay, east of the small island and a drying isthmus near the mud flats off Laurie Creek. If the spot is taken, you can anchor in the northwest corner of the basin and be out of sight.

Anchor in about 3 fathoms, south side, or 4

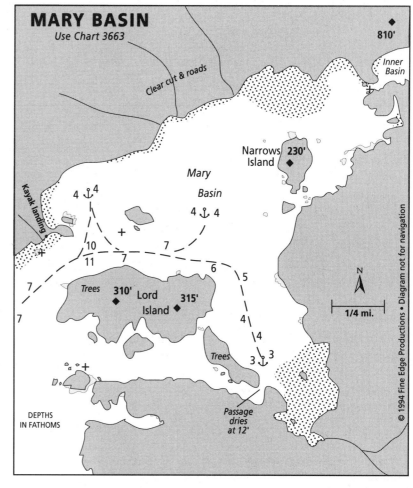

fathoms northwest side; the bottom is soft clay and clam shells. The holding is good, but you'll have to wash the mud off your anchor, chain and line.

Mary Basin—inner basin

Anchor site, Mary Basin

Inner Basin

Chart 3663; entrance: 49°48.0' N, 126°49.5' W

Inner Basin, at the head of Nuchatlitz Inlet, is entered through a narrow passage, only suitable for small craft. Local knowledge is needed. Tidal streams run with strength through the passage. Fishing boundary markers are on the north and south shores in the entrance to Inner Basin. (p. 300)

Inner Basin is a narrow, steep fjord with a difficult entrance and depths of 30 fathoms. Little is known about its possibilities for cruising boats. One story has it that Peter Puget got sucked through its narrows on an incoming tide as he was exploring in a small boat.

Port Langford

Chart 3663; anchor: 49°48.76' N, 126°56.67' W

Port Langford, entered between Colwood Rocks and Belmont Point, is not recommended as a anchorage as it is exposed to SW and the holding ground is poor. (p. 300)

Port Langford is a large north-tending bay located between the site of Nuchatlitz village and Nuchatlitz Inlet. Despite what *Sailing Directions* says, you can find good protection from prevailing northwesterlies during the summer at the northwest end of the bay, referred to by some locals as Troller Refuge. There are two small beaches nearby. You can enter the bay with ease, and once you're inside there is ample swinging room. If a low pressure front approaches or a surge from the south begins, Mary Basin offers better protection. Small craft can find moderate pro-

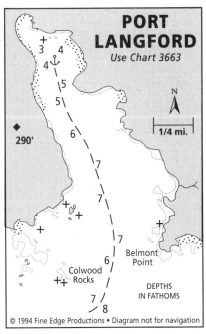

tection from easterlies a half mile north of Belmont Point behind the rocks in a small, shallow cove. The shoreline east of Belmont Point to Benson Point has many sea caves and unusual rock formations.

Entrance to Nuchatlitz Channel, light on right

Nuchatlitz

Chart 3663; Nuchatlitz light: 49°49.22' N, 126°58.83' W; anchor: 49°48.55' N, 126°57.54' W

Nuchatlitz...is approached from the south side of Esperanza Inlet through a narrow and tortuous channel between Rosa Island and Nuchatlitz light... Local knowledge is advised. (p. 297)

Unusually scenic and dynamic, the maze of rocks, islets and low islands off the northwest coast of Nootka Island are the historical home of the Nuchatlitz Band. The houses shown on the chart are in ruins and the wharf is gone, but several hardy individuals still live in this picturesque place. The land—native reserve, private and crown land—is used for oyster farming and as a getaway for solitude seekers.

Although the band has moved to Reserve land near Zeballos to be closer to work and conveniences, many individuals return to Nuchatlitz for summer visits. It is important to obtain permission if you wish to

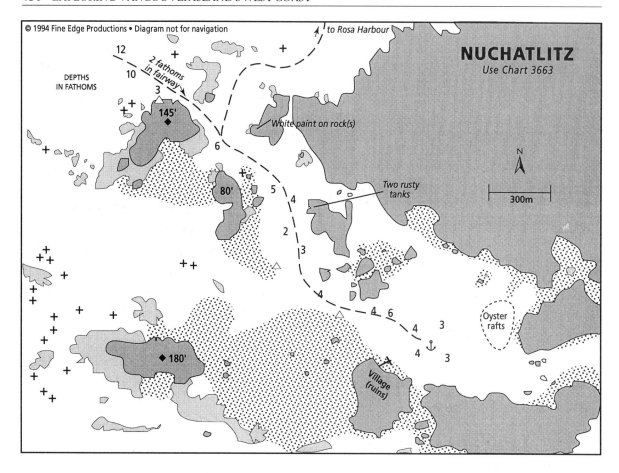

© 1994 Fine Edge Productions • Diagram not for navigation

to Rosa Harbour

NUCHATLITZ
Use Chart 3663

12
10
DEPTHS
IN FATHOMS
2 fathoms in fairway
3
145'
White paint on rock(s)
6
80'
5
Two rusty tanks
4
2
3
N
300m
3
4
4
6
Oyster rafts
4
3
180'
4
3
Village (ruins)

visit any Reserve lands or private areas.

This is a good place to explore by dinghy, but if you go ashore remember to take nothing but photos and leave nothing but footprints. Dan DeVault, a partner in the oyster operations who lives here in a picturesque house he built in 1977, told me, with tongue in cheek, to write that "the natives are hostile and it's a bad place to anchor!"

Although the wind can howl at times, once you tuck behind the islets you can find quick relief from weather and seas. Study Chart 3663 carefully before you enter. It's so narrow that trollers have to raise their stabilizers before entering.

The entrance to Nuchatlitz is narrow, shallow, intricate and encumbered with numerous rocks, reefs and shoals. The small white light on a pillar on the north side of island (145) marks the west side of the entrance. Stay close to island (145), avoiding the reefs and rocks to the east. Slowly cross the 2-fathom bar, then head toward two rusting tanks on the island directly ahead. When buoy "M46" is open to the south, turn and pass over a 2- to 3-fathom shoal, keep-

South entrance to "Rosa Harbour"

View northwest from "Rosa Harbour"

ing the buoy to starboard. Hold this course for about 100 meters, then turn southeast, passing buoy "M48" to starboard into the central bay. Well protected, the bay is nearly flat with a depth of 3 to 6 fathoms.

Anchor in 3 fathoms off the site of the abandoned village. The bottom is mud with good holding.

"Rosa Harbour"

Chart 3663; anchor:
49°49.71' N, 126°58.56' W

Named by locals, Rosa Harbour is not mentioned in *Sailing Directions.* This bay, located on the east side of Rosa Island is considered by local fishermen to be a good anchorage with easy access and protection from most wind, especially southerlies. Since they like to leave their stabilizers down, please give fishing boats plenty of room.

You can approach Rosa Harbour easily from the north through Esperanza Inlet, or carefully from the south by a narrow route from Nuchatlitz Channel, as indicated in the diagram.

If you enter from the south, white paint on the rocks helps you locate the correct channel. Keep a sharp lookout for underwater surprises and avoid the rock near the middle of the bay.

Small craft can find good protection from westerlies and southerlies close to shore, where there is very little swell.

Anchor in 5 fathoms off the small beach. Bottom and holding power are undetermined.

"Unnamed Cove" Northwest of Harbour Island

Chart 3663; entrance: 49°51.5' N, 126°59.5' W

From seaward, the first cove on the north side of Esperanza Inlet a half mile northwest of Harbour Island, may seem to offer protection for a pleasure boat, but it is not recommended. The entrance is encumbered with dangerous drying reefs and underwater rocks that have not been adequately charted. You'll be better

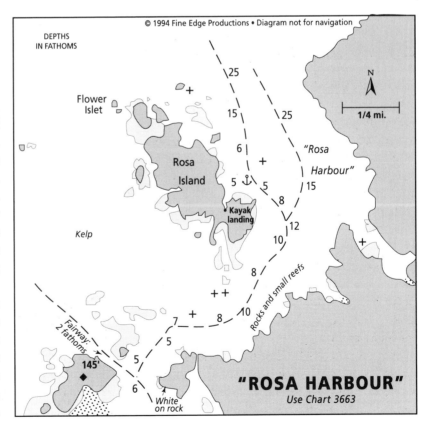

© 1994 Fine Edge Productions • Diagram not for navigation

DEPTHS IN FATHOMS

Flower Islet

Rosa Island

Kayak landing

Kelp

Fairway: 2 fathoms

145'

White on rock

"Rosa Harbour"

Rocks and small reefs

N

1/4 mi.

"ROSA HARBOUR"
Use Chart 3663

off in Queen Cove or Rosa Harbour.

If you want to check it out by dinghy or sportfishing boat however, there is a fairway of sorts that leads against the west wall until you approach a reef. Then you should turn sharply right and cross over a poorly defined bar to the east wall, and from there to the bitter end.

The best all-around protection in Esperanza Inlet is the anchorage in Queen Cove, 2 miles to the northeast. False Channel offers a small shortcut to Queen Cove and has a deep fairway; favor the Harbour Island side of the channel. Two sets of charted rocks are on the southwest side of Harbour Island, and they should be avoided.

Port Eliza
Chart 3663

> *Anchorage can be obtained about 0.5 mile from the head of Port Eliza in 12 to 17 fathoms (22 to 31 m), mud bottom.* (p. 299)

Port Eliza is a deep, narrow, scenic fjord filled from Eliza Island northward by a logging operation. An excellent anchorage for cruising boats can be found in Queen Cove on the east side of the Port Eliza entrance.

Queen Cove
Chart 3663; anchor: 49°52.72' N, 126°58.90' W

> *Queen Cove, NNE of Channel Reef, has a narrow entrance with a least depth of 15*

Queen Cove

> *feet (4.6m) but is easy of access. It is almost land-locked.... Anchorage for small vessels can be obtained in Queen Cove in about 7 fathoms (13m), mud bottom.* (p. 297)

Queen Cove is a major stopping place for cruising boats because it offers all-weather protection and scenic surroundings. There is no sign of swell in Queen Cove, and there is room for several boats. Cabin ruins and signs of man-made improvements are being overgrown with rain forest. A small landing and primitive campsite are located at the north end of the cove. Property at the north end of the cove and around Park River has recently been sold and is private.

Although the entire cove is good for anchoring, a spot off the small bight on the southern islet is the best. Anchor between a rock with an iron ring on it and a rock awash at high water

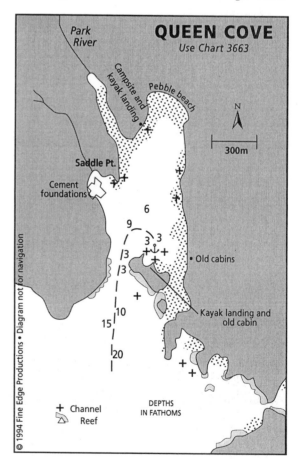

Wreck, Queen Cove

100 meters to the east. The bottom is mud with good holding. If strong westerlies are blowing outside, you may experience a slight southerly breeze in here. This is the most protected anchorage for many miles, and if foul weather is expected it's a good destination.

Espinosa Inlet

Chart 3663; entrance: 49°52' N, 126°55' W

Espinosa Inlet is the second of three inlets that tend north from Esperanza Inlet. Although the mountains surrounding it make it quite scenic, it is primarily used by logging and oyster farming operations and is too deep to afford small craft anchorage. The fairway inside Otter Is-

Entrance to Newton Cove

lands at the south entrance to Espinosa is over 20 fathoms, not 4 fathoms as the chart indicates.

Little Espinosa Inlet branches north then east off the main inlet. Where the inlet turns east there is a causeway with 2-foot clearance at highwater on the shoal midway in the inlet. The bay is a popular oyster farming area. Newton Cove offers the only anchorage for cruising boats in Espinosa Inlet.

Newton Cove

Chart 3663; anchor: 49°52.49' N, 126°56.46' W

Newton Cove...is small, free of dangers, and affords temporary anchorage for small craft. (p. 299)

Newton Cove, on the southwest corner of Espinosa Inlet, has a private log boom breakwater on its north side and offers some protection. The water is deep, however, and there is

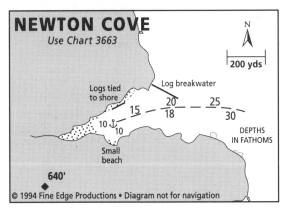

very little swinging room. Since the area is used to store log booms and to load big barges, it can be noisy. You can find an alternative anchoring site in the middle of Esperanza Inlet on the south side, just east of Garden Point. Since the 10-fathom curve is just 60 to 75 feet from shore, a stern line ashore is useful.

Anchor in 10 fathoms near the head of the cove.

Above: Inside Newton Cove, looking northeast
Below: "Garden Point Bight"

"Garden Point Bight"
Chart 3663; anchor: 49°50.85' N, 126°53.54' W

> *Anchorage for small vessels can be obtained in the bay east of Garden Point in 16 fathoms (29 m) with good holding, mud bottom.* (p. 297)

The only place shallow enough for small craft anchorage in the inner reach of Esperanza Inlet is on the south side just beyond Centre Island on a shelf at the outlet of Brodick Creek just east of Garden Point. From mid-channel, steer for the light-colored mud flat just east of the two islets; then head southeast to a point 100 yards from the light-colored rocks east of the mud flat. Note that this is a rather exposed anchorage and the mud shelf shoals rapidly.

Garden Point has a small beach behind the two islets, and it could make a good kayak haul-out spot. A large logging and booming area located a mile east of Garden Point in the next cove creates a lot of smoke and noise.

Anchor in about 6 fathoms. The bottom is mud and good holding.

Ehatisaht
Chart 3663; entrance: 49°52.4' N, 126°52.0' W

> *Ehatisaht, 0.7 mile east of Graveyard Bay, is an abandoned, overgrown Indian Village with no visible remains.* (p. 297)

The famous Ehatisaht totem that greeted visitors to Esperanza Inlet is no longer located here; thickets are about all that remain. The totem was moved to a Victoria museum, and a replica was given to the local band, most of whom now reside near Zeballos. After some discussion about where they should raise the replica—at Ehatisaht or near Zeballos—the band decided on the latter. Shortly after it was raised the totem blew down. The band decided that the only response to such a bad omen was to chop up the replica, which they did.

Ehatisaht is a an open roadstead with a steeply shoaling shore; therefore it has little anchoring possibilities. It is, however, is a good place to land a dinghy or kayak.

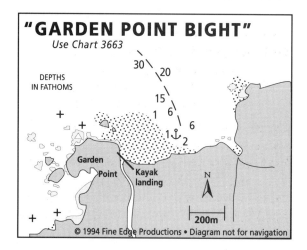

Zeballos Inlet

Chart 3663; public dock: 49°58.72' N, 126°50.67' W

> *Zeballos Inlet leads north from the east end of Esperanza Inlet. Its shores are rocky and steep-to; depths are too great for anchorage.* (p. 297)

Zeballos, the interesting village at the very end of Zeballos Inlet, caters to the logging industry and other commercial operations. Its boom-bust history includes several gold-mining cycles. The village offers supplies, services and communication. There is a public wharf with public floats (some with power and fresh water) for small craft. Some cruising boats prefer the conveniences of Zeballos to those of Tahsis (maybe due to the proximity of its pub and museum!). A dirt road north connects Zeballos to the main Vancouver Island highway. Although *Uchuck III* of the Nootka Sound Service no longer offers regular service to Zeballos, it will stop there by special arrangement. Float planes are available for hire. The Provincial Ministry of Forests maintains a float, picnic area with tables, and a campground on the south shore, 1.5 miles west of the Zeballos Inlet light.

Hecate Channel

Chart 3663; entrance 49°3.5' N, 126°47.0' W

> *Hecate Channel connects the east end of Esperanza Inlet to Tahsis Narrows. The fairway is deep and free of dangers.* (p. 297)

Hecate Channel and Tahsis Narrows, at its east end, connects Esperanza Inlet to Tahsis Inlet, making possible the inside route to the south end of Nootka Island. High, vertical terrain and rocky outcroppings line the shores. There are no muskeg flats along here and there is good underwater visibility.

Haven Cove

Chart 3663; anchor: 49°52.85' N, 126°46.66' W

> *Haven Cove provides limited anchorage for small craft.* (p. 297)

Haven Cove, almost landlocked, is suitable only for very small boats, such as sportfishing runabouts. It offers fair all-weather protection. There is little swinging room due to the shoaling mud flats on all shores. Just west of a large bald rock that has a pipe mounted on it, there is a small 2-fathom hole where you can anchor.

A small shoal that extends northwest off this bald rock, and another that extends from the spit to the northwest, make the entrance quite narrow.

Anchor in 2 fathoms, mud, shell and grass bottom with good holding. One or more stern lines ashore may make this cove secure enough for a small boat.

Entrance to Haven Cove

Saltery Bay

Chart 3663; entrance 49°52.0' N, 126°48.5' W

> *Saltery Bay, SW of Steamer Point, is too deep for anchorage.* (p. 297)

Saltery Bay is open to the northwest, and although it appears to be strategically located, depths vary from 30 to 50 fathoms over most of the bay and are too great to be of much interest to cruising boats. Westerly chop penetrates well into Saltery Bay.

Marginal anchorage can be found close along shore near Saltery Creek off a gray pebble beach at the head of the bay. Bottom and holding are undetermined.

Esperanza

Chart 3663; fuel dock: 49°52.33' N, 126°44.41' W

Esperanza, on the north shore of Hecate Channel, is a religious retreat. It is not connected by road to other settlements. The Nootka Sound Ferry calls at frequent intervals. (p. 297)

Esperanza, the home base of the Nootka Mission, is run by warm, friendly people who say, "The coffee's always on." The complex, which sits on a lovely grassy site, includes a set of sparkling white buildings that are beautifully maintained. Originally founded in 1937, the mission once ran a hospital here for loggers, fishermen and natives and now uses the center for environmental education and spiritual retreats. It is run under the auspices of the Shantymen organization founded in eastern Canada in 1908. (Shantymen takes it name from the time when loggers lived in shanties.)

The fuel dock, privately owned by the mission, is located at the southeast side of the complex and is easy to approach; depths alongside

Nootka Mission, Esperanza

the dock are adequate for the biggest yachts or sailboats. (Formerly an Esso station, the fuel dock was "debranded" to reduce liability.) The station takes cash, Visa or Master Card. An autotel telephone can be used in case of emergency. Good-tasting water that comes from a creek 1,800 feet up-canyon is available at the dock.

Whether northbound or southbound, all cruising boats pass within a few yards of Esperanza. The staff of the mission, who know Nootka Sound and its residents well, are a treasure of local knowledge. We recommend that you buy their cookbook, which is a storehouse of good, old-fashioned recipes suitable for cruising as well as home.

The hospital float north of the fuel float is available for tie-up.

McBride Bay

Chart 3663; entrance 49°51' N, 126°44' W

McBride Bay is a deep water bay used principally by logging operations; its shores are heavily logged. In summer weather, the inner bay warms up enough for good swimming and waterskiing.

Tahsis Narrows

Chart 3663; entrance: 49°52.0' N, 126°42.6' W

Tahsis Narrows connects Hecate Channel to Tahsis Inlet and has a minimum width of 0.1 mile in its fairway. Two shoals lie in the middle of the fairway; the least depth over them is 32 feet (9.9 m). Tidal streams in Tahsis Narrows are weak. (p. 297)

The area around Tahsis Narrows was a traditional hunting and gathering grounds of the local Mowachahts and other native peoples. The towns of Tahsis and Gold River offer re-supply possibilities for cruising boats, and their lumber and paper mills are serviced by large ocean-going vessels.

Nootka Mission fuel station, Esperanza

Tahsis Inlet
Chart 3663

Tahsis Inlet, extends 15 miles (from Salter Point) in a north direction. Its shores are steep-to, rocky and mountainous, and depths in most places are too great for anchorage. The fairway is narrowed to less than 0.15 mile wide at Tsowwin Narrows, 6 miles north of Salter Point. Tidal streams at Tsowwin Narrows attain 2 to 3 knots; elsewhere they are considerably weaker. The flood sets north and the ebb south. (p. 303)

Tahsis
Chart 3665; public dock: 49°54.70' N, 126°39.62' W

Tahsis is located 3 miles north of Tahsis Narrows at the head of a deep and beautiful fjord with towering red volcanic peaks. Several rivers and creeks flow into the bay and create large mud flats. The scenic inlet is a U-shaped valley, indicating deep glaciation. Tahsis, the traditional winter home of the Mowachahts of Friendly Cove, is now home to a large lumber mill complex.

The village, with a population of 1,000, has a hospital, hotel, post office, and several stores. A bank previously located in Tahsis has closed. A private marina with fuel dock is located on the western shore, south of the sawmill. As the year-round home to a number of local boats, the marina is usually crowded. The public

Upper Tahsis Inlet

wharf and float for small craft, located farther south, is generally used for loading and unloading. The inlet is exposed to southerlies, and anchorage in the deep bay is not recommended. Several log boom breakwaters provide some shelter for areas close ashore. Keep clear of the sea plane float at the public wharf. Large cargo vessels, as well as the Nootka Sound ferry, *Uchuck III*, call regularly at Tahsis.

Some cruising supplies and services are available here; a laundromat and restaurant are located about a mile north of the docks on the east side of the Tahsis River. The town is connected by dirt road to Gold River, then by paved road to Campbell River.

Blowhole Bay
Chart 3663; entrance: 49°7' N, 126°40.3' W

Blowhole Bay, 3.5 miles north of Tsowwin Narrows, has a jetty, float, log dump and a logging camp on its south side. (p. 303)

Blowhole Bay offers some protection in the north end of Tahsis Inlet, although locals say it can be blustery, as its name suggest. It is taken

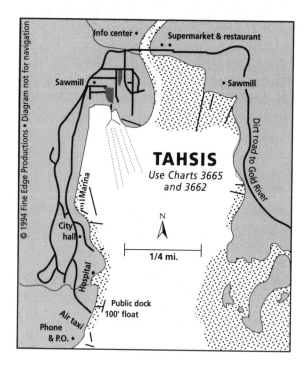

© 1994 Fine Edge Productions • Diagram not for navigation

Info center •
Supermarket & restaurant
Sawmill
• Sawmill
Dirt road to Gold River

TAHSIS
Use Charts 3665 and 3662

Marina
N
City hall •
1/4 mi.
Hospital
Public dock 100' float
Air taxi
Phone & P.O. •

up largely by private logging and booming operations and is of little interest to cruising boats. Two large, white fuel tanks are located at the head of the bay, and most of the surrounding area has been clear-cut. Watch for logs and deadheads afloat.

Nootka Sound Ferry, Uchuck III

Uchuck III is a converted mine sweeper that you frequently see passing through Tahsis Inlet on its weekly schedule from Gold River to Tahsis and Kyuquot. Its home port is Gold River. In addition to delivering equipment, supplies and passengers, *Uchuck III* also picks up and drops off kayakers by prior arrangement.

Above: Uchuck III.
Below: Entrance to "Heron Bay"

It's fun to watch as the kayaks are unloaded. With a sailor to assist, the kayak—with its paddler installed in its cockpit!—is loaded onto a pallet on deck, hoisted up and over the side and set in the water alongside the hull. In the process, the assisting sailor, still standing on the pallet, is lowered into the water almost enough to get his pants wet, while the paddler simply paddles off.

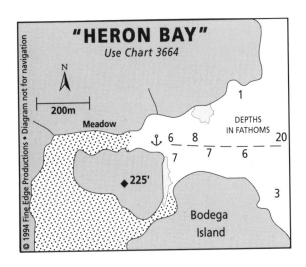

"Heron Bay"

Chart 3664; anchor: 49°44.74' N, 126°38.22' W

Heron Bay is the name locals use for the unnamed cove formed by the north end of Bodega Island and an indention in Nootka Island. This is the first intimate spot you come to as you head south in Tahsis Inlet, and it offers good northerly or southerly protection. There is an unnamed islet marked (225) and a drying mud flat at the head of the cove. At high tide levels water floods into the Kendrick Inlet to the south.

Anchorage can be found between the islet and the north shore, but because the mud bank shoals rapidly, you should use a stern line to restrict swinging room.

Anchor in 6 fathoms. The bottom is a combination of mud, shells and grass with good holding.

Princesa Channel
Chart 3665

Princesa Channel leads between Strange and Bodega Islands into Tahsis Inlet. It is very narrow, encumbered with rocks, and only suitable for small craft. Local knowledge is needed. (p. 302)

Princesa Channel is used by southbound cruising boats, as well as the *Uchuck III*, as a shortcut or to find protection in Kendrick Inlet. It is not advisable to use Princesa Channel without consulting large-scale Chart 3665, since the narrow channel can be quite dangerous when current is running.

A northbound current in Tahsis Inlet will set a slow craft northward directly onto the charted below-water rock 100 feet north-northeast of the Princesa Channel light. If you are southbound, do not head directly for the Princesa Channel light; instead, before you turn west, stay off (east) 100 yards or so until you approach the shoal on the north side of Strange Island. Chart 3665 indicates a dangerous rock reported in 1972 with an approximate position of 200 feet north-northeast of the light. I feel that its probable position is 100 feet, which means that if the current is flowing north you must stay *very close* to the light itself, remaining ever alert to a northward set.

There is a fairway with a least depth of 3 fathoms in the channel itself; one underwater rock lies 150 feet west of islet (119).

Looking south from "Heron Bay"

"Bodega Cove"
Chart 3664; anchor: 49°44.10' N, 126°38.19' W

Bodega Cove is how we refer to the unnamed cove at the end of Kendrick Inlet on the west side of Bodega Island. Wonderfully protected, the cove is scenic and intimate for small craft anchorage. The water here, which reaches 67°F or more in late summer, is good for swimming. This is a fun spot to explore by dinghy and watch for wildlife—bear like to poke around the cove's west shore.

Favor the east shore as you approach the narrows between Bodega Island and Nootka Island; a rocky reef extends south from Nootka

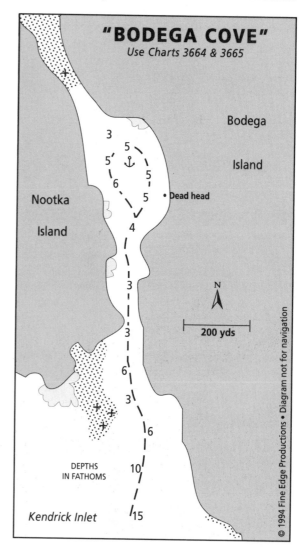

"BODEGA COVE"
Use Charts 3664 & 3665

Bodega Island

Nootka Island

Dead head

DEPTHS IN FATHOMS

Kendrick Inlet

200 yds

© 1994 Fine Edge Productions • Diagram not for navigation

Approaching "Bodega Cove" from the south

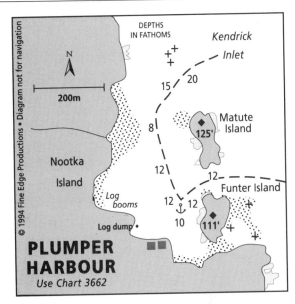

Island for about 400 yards. The entrance is narrow with an irregular bottom, but depth in the fairway is 3 fathoms. The bay is flat and has ample room for several small cruising boats.

Anchor in 5 fathoms; the bottom is mud with good holding.

Plumper Harbour
Chart 3664; anchor: 49°41.53' N, 126°37.80' W

Anchorage, with good shelter , can be obtained in 12 fathoms (22 m) in the middle of Plumper Harbour. (p. 302)

Plumper Harbour, a well-sheltered but busy logging area, makes a good anchorage for larger cruising boats that can anchor in deep water. The log booming operation here, complete with numerous float houses, can be quite noisy. Avoid the rock that lies a quarter mile north of Matute Island.

Anchor in mid-bay in 11 to 15 fathoms, mud bottom with good holding.

Looking south from "Bodega Cove"

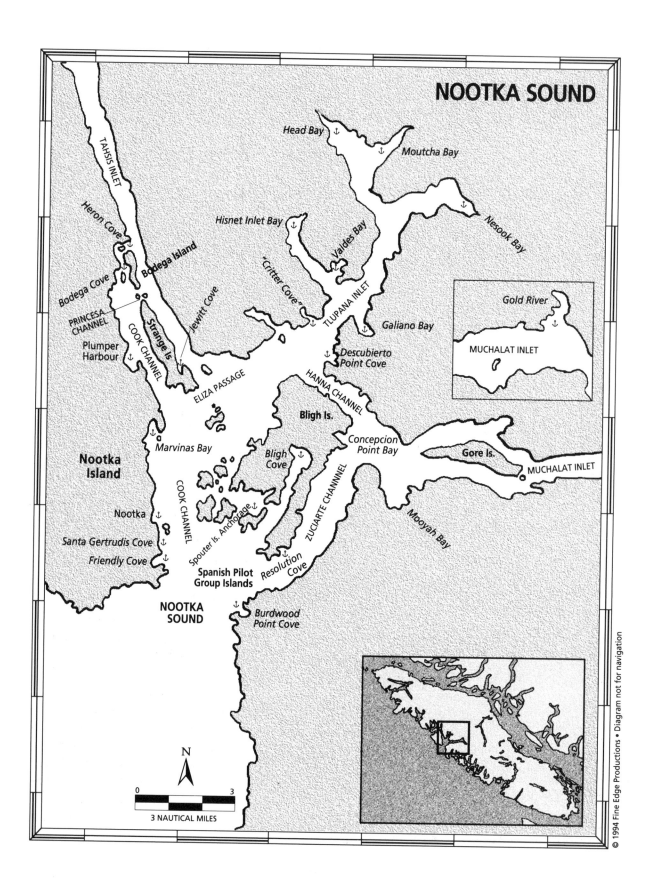

NOOTKA SOUND

Head Bay

Moutcha Bay

Nesook Bay

Hisnet Inlet Bay

Valdes Bay

"Critter Cove"

TAHSIS INLET

Heron Cove

Bodega Island

Bodega Cove

PRINCESA CHANNEL

Plumper Harbour

Jewitt Cove

Strange Is.

COOK CHANNEL

ELIZA PASSAGE

TLUPANA INLET

Galiano Bay

Descubierto Point Cove

HANNA CHANNEL

Bligh Is.

Marvinas Bay

Bligh Cove

Concepcion Point Bay

Gore Is.

MUCHALAT INLET

Nootka Island

Nootka

Santa Gertrudis Cove

Friendly Cove

Spouter Is. Anchorage

Spanish Pilot Group Islands

Resolution Cove

ZUCIARTE CHANNEL

Mooyah Bay

NOOTKA SOUND

Burdwood Point Cove

Gold River

MUCHALAT INLET

N

0   3

3 NAUTICAL MILES

14
Nootka Sound

Nootka Sound, with its Friendly Cove, holds a unique place in the recorded history of the Northwest. This is where Perez, Cook, Bodega y Quadra, Vancouver and others played out a drama that broke the Spaniards' grip on the Northwest, establishing the "freedom of the seas" doctrine.

Friendly Cove was the traditional summer home of the Mowachahts First Nation and their famous chief, Maquinna. Archaeological studies in the cove have shown that natives lived here for several thousand years before Europeans began their local explorations.

In 1778, Captain James Cook—the first recorded European to enter Nootka Sound—used Resolution Cove, 3.5 miles east of Friendly Cove, as a location for repairing his two ships *Resolution* and *Discovery*. Plaques placed on shore at Bligh Island commemorate this event.

As you enter Friendly Cove, there is a granite marker on Monument Islet on which Quadra and Vancouver's names were carved. The names, which were still visible in the 1970s, are now worn away.

Surprisingly little has changed in Nootka Sound in the last two centuries, and as you explore this area you will be treading on largely unchanged ground.

Mowachaht Hereditary Chief Larry Andrews recently commented on those *changes:* "We had all the territory we needed; we had free rent and paid no taxes; we had all the fresh food we wanted for the taking; we had women and slaves to care of us. And White Man came along and thought he could improve on that!"

Friendly Cove
Chart 3664; anchor: 49°35.67' N, 126°36.93' W

> *Friendly Cove, NW of San Rafael Island, affords limited anchorage to small craft.* (p. 300)

Friendly Cove, of moderate size and rather shallow, offers fair protection in summer with only a small swell in prevailing northwest winds. During summer months, a double-log float extending about 100 yards from shore is set up below the gray house. The float that belongs to the Mowachaht Reserve can be used for a small fee. Water is sometimes available on the float.

The author (left) with
Mowachaht Hereditary Chief Jerry Jack

Master carver Sanford Williams, Friendly Cove, shows his latest designs.

*New altar,
Friendly Cove Church*

With the exception of the light station on San Rafael Island, the land in Friendly Cove belongs to the Mowachaht Band, and you should obtain permission to cross it before you enter. A landing fee is collected for dinghies and kayaks. Visitors should land on the log float or the beach nearby and pay the fee before walking to the lighthouse or visiting the Mowachaht Reserve lands. (A small float located at the foot of the lighthouse is for rescue service only.)

Caretakers for the reserve—and the band's only full-time residents—are Ray and Terry Williams and their family, who live in a two-story house on shore. (The gray house mentioned above is being converted to a carving shop for the Williams' talented son, Sanford.) They will advise you on where you may go, and they'll share some of the area's history with you. Since the Williams have no way to dispose of trash, they ask that all visitors carry away everything they bring in.

The village formerly located here was known as Yuquot ("Where winds come from all directions"). The "Governor's" totem, raised in 1929 just north of the Williams residence, blew over during a winter storm of 1994.

A white church built in 1956 to the west of the landing beach contains several plaques as well as some fine stained glass windows commemorating significant historical events since the arrival of Europeans. The windows, a gift from the Spanish government, depict the natives' conversion to Catholicism and the signing of the Nootka Treaty between England and Spain by Captains Quadra and Vancouver.

In August 1993, after the church was handed back to the Mowachahts, a ceremony was held in which several colorful replica totems were installed in place of the altar as part of an elders' campaign to restore traditional values to local lands.

West of the church, the beach facing the sea is composed of small, polished stones that "sing" as the surf washes over them. From this lovely beach, you have a good view of the outer coast. Several primitive campsites are located at the beach's north end not far from the lake that was historically the center of communal life and was used for pre-hunt whaling ceremonies. The trail from the old village site passes burial grounds and continues farther west along the shore. The numerous grave sites in the Nootka area, including this burial ground, are sacred and should not be entered.

Mowachaht headquarters is now located in Gold River, and for administrative purposes, they have joined with the Muchalahts, who live at A'haminaquus at the outlet of Gold River.

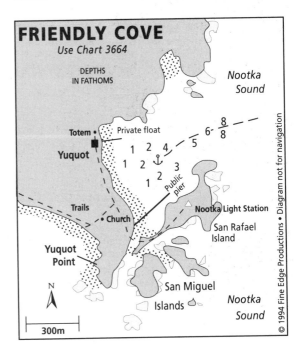

The public wharf on the south side of the beach is currently closed awaiting repairs and has no float. San Rafael Island, site of the Nootka Light Station, is connected to Nootka Island by a rock causeway that gives some protection to the cove. The causeway, damaged during a 1994 winter storm, may not last much longer.

Nootka Light Station, one of the most picturesque along Vancouver Island's outer coast, makes an interesting little side trip for boaters. It is open to visitors between 9:00 a.m. and 5:00 p.m. (or by invitation); children must be accompanied by an adult. The current light keepers, Ed and Pat Kidder—who have spent the last 23 years here—keep the area spotlessly trimmed and cultivated. During summer months, visitors can enjoy brightly colored dahlias and roses that bloom around the complex. When

they have a free moment, Ed or Pat will answer your questions and give you a tour. For a marvelous 360-degree view of the sound and ocean (weather permitting) you may want to climb the four flights of ladders to the top of the lighthouse.

The beacon—housed at the top of the lighthouse—sweeps the cove every 12.5 seconds, 24 hours each day. During low visibility or foggy weather, its foghorn puts out a distinctive moan, much like a two-note pipe organ the size of the QE II. It sounds for ten seconds and is silent for fifty. Its powerful horn contrasts dramatically with foghorns to the north, like Addenbrooke's off key choir boy or Boat Bluff's tired hound dog. Two 20 kW diesel engines provide power to the light station. A backup battery system takes over in case of power failure.

Nootka Light Station monitors Channels 6

Friendly Cove

Above: Outer beach, Friendly Cove
Below: Nootka Light Station, Friendly Cove

and 68. Channel 82 is used for Coast Guard business.

Manned light stations provide a valuable service to cruising yachtsmen and commercial fishing boats, a human touch sorely missing in these days of automation. We hope the Canadian government will continue to support these stations.

Anchor in 3 to 4 fathoms over a flat sand and mud bottom with good holding. Boats with shallow draft usually anchor close to shore in about 1 or 2 fathoms so they can get to shore easily.

Some yachts find holding power in Friendly Cove less than satisfactory and move to Santa Gertrudis Cove for better protection and holding.

Santa Gertrudis Cove ("Dawleys")

Chart 3664; north anchorage: 49°36.23' N, 126°37.01' W; south anchorage: 49°36.13' N, 126°37.19' W

Santa Gertrudis Cove, 0.5 mile north of Friendly Cove, is encumbered in its entrance by an islet, above-water rocks and a drying rock; inside it offers sheltered anchorage for small craft. (p. 300)

Santa Gertrudis Cove, known locally as Dawleys, after a family who once lived here, is an attractive small cove that offers a solitary alternative to Friendly Cove. Protection here is good from all quarters, and the view is scenic and quiet, but maneuverability and swinging room are tight.

The cove was named after the small ship that Englishman John Meares built in Friendly Cove (the *Northwest America*). After a dispute with England in 1789, the Spanish confiscated the *Northwest America* and renamed it *Santa Gertrudis.*

Care must be taken on entering the cove, especially on a summer afternoon when the sun shines directly from the west. A mid-channel drying rock just below the surface can be particularly difficult to locate with the sun in your eyes. Enter at dead-slow and post alert lookouts on your bow.

Anchor in 3 to 4 fathoms in either the northern or western part of the bay (the northern is slightly deeper). The bottom is mud.

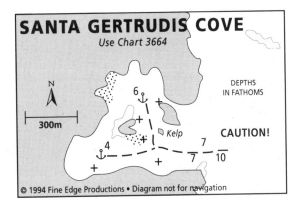

Nootka Fish Camp

Nootka

Chart 3665; resort: 49°37.43' N, 126°37.30' W

> *Nootka, 0.3 mile west of the north Saavedra Island, is the site of a sport fishing resort. (p. 302)*

Nootka is a modern, attractive fishing resort whose skiffs you see running about through the sound. The resort, as well as several private homes, are built on a peninsula that was formerly the site of a pilchard plant. The resort is located on the south side. The wharf on the north side is in disrepair, and there are numerous pilings in the small cove.

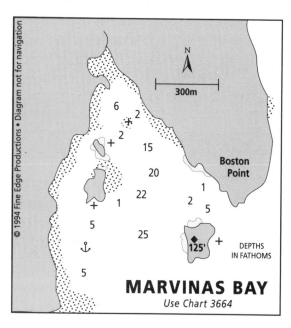

© 1994 Fine Edge Productions • Diagram not for navigation

N

300m

6
2
2
15
Boston
Point
20
1
22
2
1
5
5
25
125'
DEPTHS
IN FATHOMS
5

MARVINAS BAY
Use Chart 3664

Although temporary anchorage can be taken on either side of the peninsula, there is little space, and the bottom off Boca del Infierno Bay is irregular.

The tiny narrows at Boca del Infierno Bay have a spectacular tidal fall that should be given adequate clearance. Unwary individuals who enter in skiffs discover a short while later that they are suddenly above a waterfall and can't see their way out! A dangerous rock is said to be in the narrows.

Marvinas Bay

Chart 3664; anchor 49°39.54' N, 126°37.37' W

> *Boston Point forms the east side of Marvinas Bay. A large cabin, with a float, is at the NW end of the bay. (p. 302)*

Marvinas Bay (site of the *Boston* massacre) is exposed to the south and is of little interest to cruising boats, except as temporary protection from northerlies, or if the more popular anchorages to the south are congested.

Anchor in 5 fathoms just north of the outlet of the unnamed creek on the west shore of the bay.

Jewitt Cove

Chart 3664; anchor 49°41.43' N, 126°36.07' W

> *Jewitt Cove, on the east side of Strange Island, affords anchorage to small vessels in 16 fathoms (29 m), mud bottom. (p. 303)*

Jewitt Cove offers good shelter from southerlies but only fair protection from northerlies. The 1.4-fathom shoal in the center of the cove's entrance may startle you, but it is of little danger and can easily be avoided.

The cove was named after John Jewitt, metalworker of the trading ship *Boston*. All but one of his fellow crew members were massacred at Friendly Cove in 1803. Jewitt became a slave to Mowachaht Chief Maquinna until his rescue two years later. This quiet cove is a good place to be anchored while you read Jewitt's *White*

Slave of the Nootka, an account of life with the Mowachahts that is certainly a classic tale.

Anchor in 6 fathoms just west of the tiny bight that contains two float homes. The bottom is mixed. Larger craft can anchor farther north in deeper water.

Tlupana Inlet
Chart 3664

> *Tlupana Inlet is entered between Descubierta Point (49°49' N, 126°30' W), which is fringed by above-water and drying rocks, and Hoiss Point, 2 miles WNW. Depths are great, and its shores are steep and rocky.* (p. 304)

Tlupana Inlet is a northeast trending fjord of deep water with scenic mountainous sides and rocky shores. An unusual feature visible for many miles at its north end is Quadra Saddle, formed by two high, barren peaks. With dirt road access at several points, the inlet is fast becoming a popular sportfishing area. Head Bay (at the head of the inlet) is a scenic locale dominated by a large logging operation and the dirt road from Tahsis to Gold River. The offshore is-

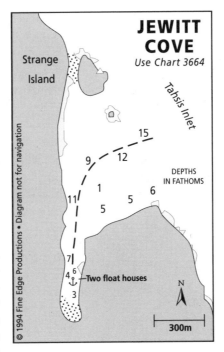

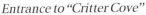
Entrance to "Critter Cove"

lets in the vicinity are particularly picturesque.

Moutcha Bay and Nesook Bay offer protection and anchoring possibilities under beautiful towering peaks, but they are seldom visited. (A new marina under development on the north shore of Moutcha Bay may change this.) With their large drying flats, these bays attract large quantities of fish and wildlife. There is a dirt road and boat launching ramp with a float located a half mile north of Galiano Bay. Civilization is beginning to make its mark on Tlupana Inlet—witness the clear-cut areas, numerous float houses and dirt roads—but it is still a beautiful area worth visiting.

"Critter Cove"
Chart 3664; anchor: 49°42.85' N, 126°30.62' W

Critter Cove, as it is known by locals, is the unnamed cove located behind the Critter Cove Marina 1 mile southwest of Argonaut Point.

Critter Cove Marina, in the outer entrance, is an attractive new sportfishing marina (July 1993) with floating cabins, boat dock and fuel dock. Owners Cameron and Dean Forbes have ambitious plans for a pub and expanded services. "Critter" is a nickname Cameron acquired playing hockey during his school years. He had a birthmark on his shoulder with hair growing out of it (since removed) that his teammates would rub for good luck before games. The name Critter stuck, and somehow it seems appropriate for this small, isolated, landlocked cove surrounded by thick rain forest. (You would expect to see little critters poking around on shore.) Despite two old work floats moored along the edge of the inner cover, the

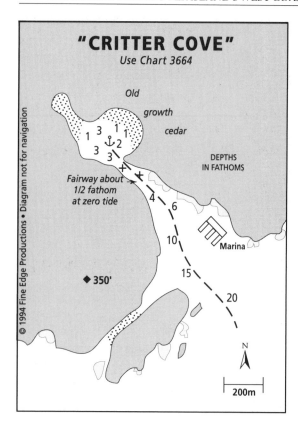

"Critter Cove," looking back out through entrance

Valdes Bay

Chart 3664; anchor SE corner: 49°43.88' N, 126°29.05' W

The small cove in the NE corner of Valdes Bay has a boom across its entrance and a sign on shore stating "Oyster Lease.(p. 304)

Valdes Bay is located on the north shore of Hisnit Inlet, 1 mile north of Argonaut Point. Although it is scenic, it is rather deep and currently too busy for a cruising anchorage. A number of float homes are located here, along with a yellow buoy that reads "Fish Hatchery."

Temporary anchorage can be found in the small southeast cove. The center islet has a

cove is quite lovely.

Entrance to the landlocked cove is narrow and shallow, but visibility through the water is good and you can see the bottom clearly. At zero tide there is about 4 feet of water in the fairway, so most cruising boats can negotiate it carefully at most tide levels. Caution: We did not find the two rocks shown in the entrance on Chart 3664, but the 4,000-foot-long plastic water line for the marina is visible on the bottom and you should not anchor over it. Inside the cove, the bottom appears flat for the most part—between 2 and 4 fathoms with no sign of rocks.

You can anchor with good all-weather protection in the center of the cove. There is enough room for several small boats. Inner cove water temperature reaches more than 66°F in summer.

Anchor in 3 fathoms over a sand, mud and grass bottom with good holding.

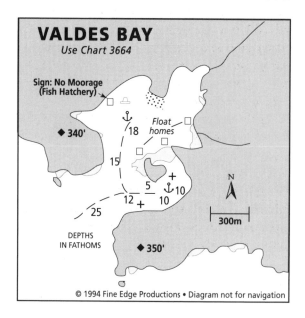

dangerous shoal protruding southwest off its western end.

Anchor in 10 fathoms over a mixed rocky bottom with not much swinging room. For more swinging room, anchor in the main bay between the float houses and the fish hatchery.

Valdes Bay

"Hisnit Inlet Bay"

Chart 3664; anchor: 49°45.15' N, 126°30.73' W

> *Anchorage near the head of Hisnit Inlet can be obtained in 11 fathoms (20 m), mud bottom.* (p. 304)

Hisnit Inlet is a small inlet that heads northwest from Argonaut Point. Except for the clearcut areas and a logging road on the northwest side, the bay is surrounded by picturesque old growth forest and a grassy shore. It is a quiet and restful place. It is said that a limestone deposit nearby furnished some of the stones for the parliament building in Victoria.

Little in the way of logs enter the bay in storms, so shelter is greater than that indicated on the chart.

The inlet and bay are relatively easy to enter in foul weather under radar. Two rocks mid-channel halfway up the inlet are the only dangers (one rock dries at 2 feet), so you should favor the south shore here.

The bay at the head of the inlet is now quiet and has plenty of anchoring and swinging room. It offers good protection in most

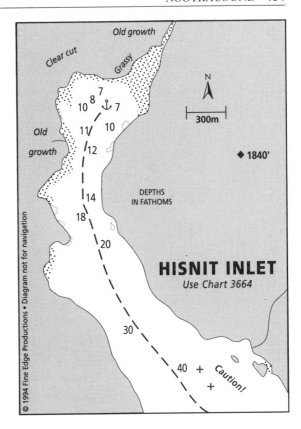

weather. Anchor in the center in 11 fathoms, or anywhere along shore in 6 to 8 fathoms, mud bottom with good holding.

Galiano Bay

Chart 3664; anchor: 49°42.30' N, 126°27.90' W

> *Anchorage in Galiano Bay can be obtained about 0.4 mile SSE of the island in 15 fathoms (27 m) mud. Holding is good but swinging room is limited.* (p. 304)

Galiano Bay looking north

Galiano Bay provides good protection from all weather in fairly deep water. The best anchorage is rather close in to the south end. The view is becoming somewhat suburban, encompassing a number of one-, two- and even three-story floating homes (some with airplane floats) as well as fish farms.

Anchor in 10 fathoms over a mud bottom with good holding.

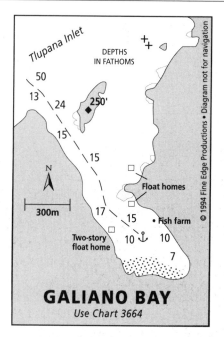

GALIANO BAY
Use Chart 3664

Head Bay

Chart 3664; anchor: 49°47.59' N, 126°29.78' W

Head Bay...affords anchorage in 15 fathoms (27 m) mud. (p. 304)

When the logging operation is not going full bore, this bay can be a quiet, out-of-the-way stop. Except for logging on the west shore, the area is pristine and beautiful.

Anchor in 8 fathoms off Canton Creek Outlet. The bottom is said to be rocky.

Moutcha Bay

Chart 3664; anchor: 49°47.00' N, 126°26.87' W

Moutcha Bay...affords anchorage in 16 to 19 fathoms (29 to 35 m) SE of a rock which dries 9 feet (2.7 m), off the north shore of the bay. (p. 304)

Moutcha Bay is situated at the base of the 2,000-foot-high Quadra Saddle and is quite picturesque.

Anchor in 14 fathoms off the outlet of Conuma River over a bottom reported to be mud. The head of the bay shoals rapidly, but you may be able to find a bench that allows shallower anchorage.

Nesook Bay

Chart 3664; anchor: 49°46.17' N, 126°24.24' W

Nesook Bay has a drying flat at its head over which flows the Tlupana River. Small vessels can obtain anchorage in 17 fathoms (31 m), mud bottom, north of a rock with 27 feet (8.2 m) over it, 0.2 mile off the east shore. (p. 304)

Nesook Bay lies at the foot of the south side of Quadra Saddle and is surrounded by high, sheer mountains.

Anchor in about 9 fathoms close to the northeast shore. Bottom and holding are undetermined.

"Descubierta Point Cove"

Chart 3664; anchor: 49°41.50' N, 126°29.25' W

The unnamed cove, 0.4 mile NE of Descubierta Point, offers shelter for small craft and has four float houses in it (1988). (p. 304)

Descubierta Point Cove, our name for this intricate three-part cove, is encumbered with rocks and reefs and has a well-logged eastern shore. Although there is a large sign at the entrance reading "Warning Blasting Area 7 a.m. to 5 p.m. Keep Clear," there are several work houses and float houses tucked between the islets.

Anchor in 3 fathoms; although it appears to offer protected anchorage, the cove's accessibility is unclear.

Muchalat Inlet

Chart 3664

Muchalat Inlet...extends about 14 miles east and then 3 miles SE. Depths are great and the fairway is 0.2 mile wide at its narrowest point. (p. 304)

Muchalat Inlet is another of the beautiful fjords of this region, with many peaks that tower 4,000 feet above the sea. At the inlet's eastern end is Gold River Harbour, the site of a large pulp mill and the roadhead for the paved thoroughfare that leads 9 miles (14 km) to the town of Gold River and 63 miles (100 km) to Campbell River. It is also the location of the A'haminaquus Indian Reserve, the combined home of the Muchalat and Mowachaht bands. Gold River public wharf is the home of the Nootka Sound ferry, *Uchuck III.*

Mooyah Bay

Chart 3664; entrance: 49°38.20' N, 126°27.00' W

> *Mooyah has an extensive mud flat at its head and booming grounds with a logging camp on its west side.* (p. 304)

We have not been in Mooyah Bay and do not know its cruising potential. The chart shows a small cove on the west side of the bay that looks interesting.

Gold River

Chart 3664; float: 49°40.73' N, 126°06.95' W

> *Gold River pulp mill and port facilities are on the west side of the entrance to Gold River.* (p. 305)

The port of Gold River consists of a public wharf (*Uchuck III* docks on the west side) where large boats unload on its south side. Two small floats for fishing boats are located on the east side; the outer dock on the east side is for float airplanes. The pulp mill has its own facilities for large cargo vessels.

The village of Gold River, a thoroughly new and pleasant "planned city," is 9 miles (14 km) north of the wharf and has a population of about 2,000. It has all the modern conveniences, including a medical clinic, doctors, dentist, shopping center, post office, radio station and several motels. The motels (such as

Gold River

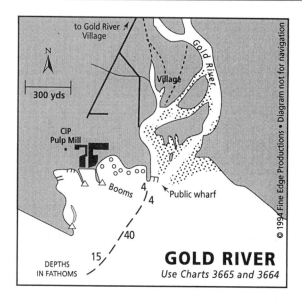

GOLD RIVER
Use Charts 3665 and 3664

DEPTHS IN FATHOMS

Ridgeview Motel) will provide free taxi service to the port for guests. Fuel can be obtained only at the town site; a small boat launching ramp lies just inside the river outlet north of the public float.

Since the wharf and float are congested at all times, rafting is necessary. Anchoring is out of the question: the bay is too deep, the river mouth shoals rapidly, and the pulp mill is a busy work area. Other than to pick up or drop off crew, Gold River offers little advantages to the average yacht.

When there is high river runoff with contrary winds and tides, an uncomfortable 2- to 3-foot chop is found close offshore.

Rock at entrance to Resolution Cove

"Concepcion Point Bay"

Chart 3664; entrance: 49°39.45' N, 126°29.30' W

This unnamed bay just below Concepcion Point on Bligh Island can offer temporary shelter, but it does not hold much interest for cruising boats. The outer bay is deep and exposed, and although the inner bay is shallow, it is clogged with log booms.

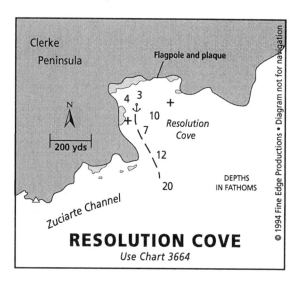

RESOLUTION COVE
Use Chart 3664

DEPTHS IN FATHOMS

Resolution Cove

Chart 3664; anchor: 49°36.42' N, 126°31.83' W

Resolution Cove, on the east side of Clerke Peninsula, is inconvenient as an anchorage.... It is of historical interest as the place where Captain Cook refitted his ships in April 1778. (p. 302)

This historic place, where white men first encountered the Northwest country and its natives, has changed little in the last two centuries. Only a flag pole and plaques on a rock give evidence that anyone has ever been here. The small beach at the head of the cove is choked with driftwood, and the trees are probably as dense and overgrown as they were when Cook sought refuge here for his ships.

The north shore is rocky, with one rock on a small shoal on close in. This is an exciting place to visit, but a little exposed for craft smaller than Cook's *Resolution.*

Anchor in 7 fathoms near the head of the cove with a mixed bottom of undetermined holding power.

"Bligh Cove"

Chart 3664; anchor: 49°39.04' N, 126°31.15' W

Ewin Inlet penetrates the south side of Bligh Island. (p. 300)

Bligh Island, which has peaks exceeding 1,000 feet in elevation, is still very natural (logged on the north side only). Off Bligh's western shore, the islands known as the Spanish Pilot Group offer much in the way of sportfishing, kayaking, dinghy sailing and exploring. The cove at the head of Ewin Inlet, which we call "Bligh Cove,"

makes a good base from which to visit the surrounding area. The island was named after William Bligh, master of the *Resolution* on Cook's third and fatal expedition in 1778. (Bligh later earned notoriety for the mutiny on his ship, *Bounty.)*

Located at the extreme northerly end of Ewin Inlet, Bligh Cove offers some of the best protection and scenic solitude in all of Nootka Sound. The head of the inlet has a few rocks and islets that totally block any wave action from the south. In summer, the water warms up well here (above 66°F), creating a favorable environment for red "bloom" (thick colonies of microorganisms).

Old growth forest surrounds the cove, and 3,000-foot peaks rise skyward a few miles to the east on the main island. The inlet has an easy

"Bligh Cove" looking south

approach with over 20 fathoms minimum in the fairway before it narrows and turns west. The fairway follows the middle of the channel and the shoal noted on the chart at the narrows appears to be quite small.

There is an natural underwater dike from the north shore to the islet where minimum depth is between 3 to 5 fathoms; the fairway is about 50 feet wide. Inside, the bottom is a relatively flat.

Anchor in 6 fathoms at the far northwest corner of the cove near a small float. There is plenty of swinging room, and the bottom is mud with good holding.

"Spouter Island Anchorage"
Chart 3664; anchor: 49°37.40' N, 126°32.97' W

Sailing Directions mentions that anchorage can be taken between Narvaez Island and

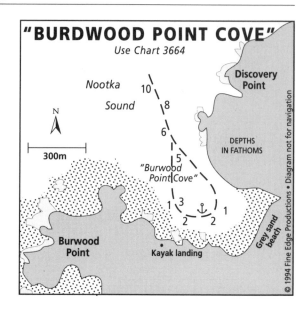

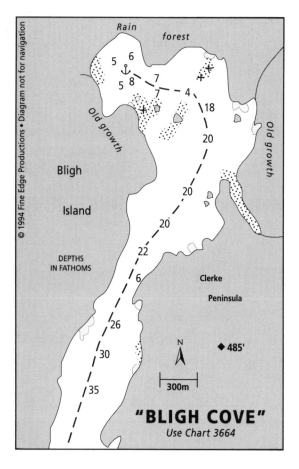

Vernaci Island in 23 fathoms. Although this may work for large vessels, small local vessels that want more protection from strong southerlies frequently use the bight on the north side of Spouter Island. This bight, which we call Spouter Island Anchorage, is still rather deep for convenient anchoring and it has a dangerous shoal on its northwest corner. It is mostly used during the winter for its easy access and good shelter.

Anchor in 11 fathoms close to shore (near a small float house). The bottom and holding are undetermined. A line to shore may help, since swinging room is limited.

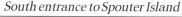
South entrance to Spouter Island

"Burdwood Point Cove"

Chart 3664; anchor: 49°34.80' N, 126°33.50' W

Burdwood Point Cove is the name locals have given to a moderate-sized cove across from Friendly Cove behind Discovery Point. The beach is a favorite camping spot for those in sportfishing boats and kayaks. Fishing off the rocks to the south is said to be quite good. You can easily land a dinghy on the beach and go for a walk.

While the cove is relatively well protected from southerlies, it is open to northwest winds. You can feel a slight swell in the cove, but dinghies and kayaks can be landed most of the time. The small beach to the west of the big gray sand beach has the least wave action and is suitable for kayaks. The shores off the kayak beach and farther west are fouled with small rocks, reefs and kelp beds.

Anchor in 3 fathoms in the southern end of the cove with a sand-mud bottom and good holding.

Above: Entrance to "Burdwood Point Cove"
Below: Campsite at "Burdwood Point Cove"

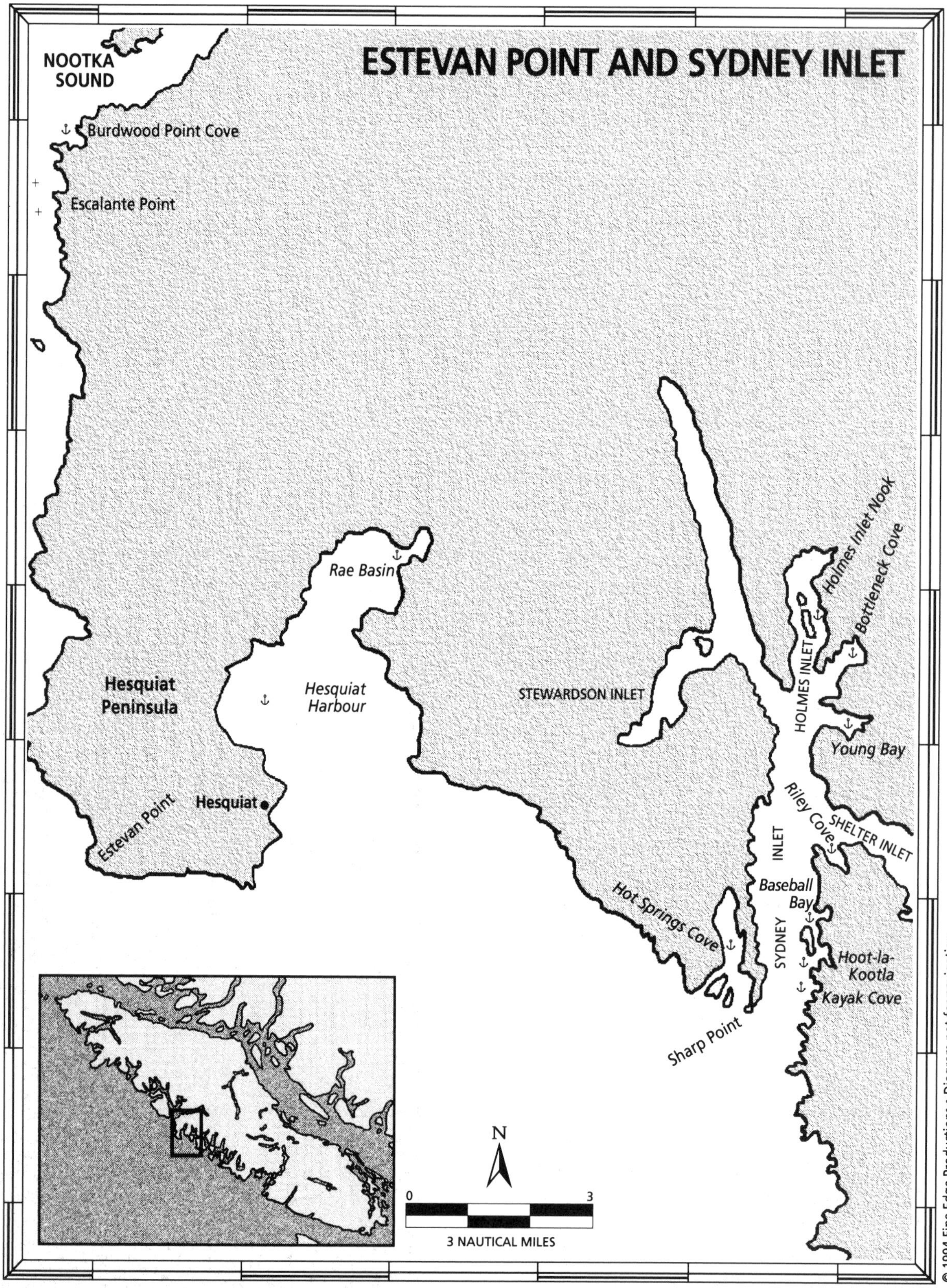

ESTEVAN POINT AND SYDNEY INLET

NOOTKA
SOUND

⌀ Burdwood Point Cove

Escalante Point

Rae Basin

Hesquiat
Peninsula

Hesquiat
Harbour

STEWARDSON INLET

HOLMES INLET

Holmes Inlet Nook

Bottleneck Cove

Young Bay

SHELTER INLET

Riley Cove

Estevan Point

Hesquiat •

Hot Springs Cove

SYDNEY INLET

Baseball
Bay

Hoot-la-
Kootla

Kayak Cove

Sharp Point

N

0   3

3 NAUTICAL MILES

15

Estevan Point and Sydney Inlet

Making the transition from quiet Nootka Sound to "swinging and swaying" Clayoquot Sound may be a shock to a skipper and crew who have become accustomed to cruising without seeing other boats.

Clayoquot and Barkley sounds have the most islands and the greatest number of anchoring choices for cruising yachts on the West Coast. They offer the conveniences found in tourist towns, but they also have the busyness and congestion that come with good connections to Vancouver Island's roads.

For the last few years Clayoquot Sound has been the focal point of an environmentalist movement to end the destruction of old growth forests and the practice of clear-cutting. Meares Island and the Kennedy River have been the sites of these protests.

A public relations office of MacMillan Bloedel, located in Tofino, includes educational materials and demonstrations for the public; your input is solicited. Direct your comments or questions to MacMillan Bloedel Ltd., P.O. Box 6300, Vancouver, B.C., V6B 4B5.

To contact the local environmentalists write Friends of Clayoquot Sound, P.O. Box 489, Tofino, B.C. V0R 2Z0.

The good news about the environment of the sound is that clear-cutting to high tide line is becoming a thing of the past, and more enlightened timber harvesting methods are being used now. This will start to make a difference in the aesthetics of Clayoquot Sound.

By the time you reach Sydney Inlet, you have covered over half the West Coast's "outside," but there are still more than half of the many secluded and intimate spots left to explore. To help your transition to civilization, we strongly suggest you visit Hot Springs Cove and check out these steaming pools and their world-class setting. Sydney Inlet has several fine places where you can delay your re-entry if time allows.

Looking down upon Hot Springs Cove

Examining a jellyfish

Estevan Point

Chart 3640; light: 49°23.00' N, 126°32.53' W

Estevan Point, the SW extremity of Hesquiat Peninsula, is low, wooded and fringed with a sand and boulder beach.
(p. 277)

Estevan Point, like Cape Cook on Brooks Peninsula, juts out into the Pacific and is considered a challenging passage. While rounding the point requires careful navigation, most cruising boats have no problems.

From Nootka Sound south, the shore is hostile, with rocks that extend more than a mile offshore. Escalante Rocks and Perez Rocks need to be avoided as you travel along a coast that rapidly flattens out and becomes featureless. Because Estevan Point is so flat, the shore is not well defined and it is difficult for small vessels to tell how far offshore they are. Fog can make the passage more hazardous, since the low, wooded point is a poor radar target (GPS is quite helpful here). The seas are sometimes confused off the point itself, but farther east, the northwest swells die off rather quickly, much like in Checleset Bay. As Captain Harold Monks, one of B.C.'s senior pilots says, "Give Estevan lots of room when it's angry."

A comparison of wind and sea data indicates a general lessening of wind at Estevan Point as compared to farther north. The average small boat can make the passage from Friendly Cove to Hot Springs Cove (28 miles) in a few hours in good weather. Hesquiat Harbour at the midway point offers shelter if the seas kick up.

Estevan Point Lighthouse, the tallest along the coast at 125 feet high, can be seen for 18 miles in clear weather. The lighthouse is over

85 years old. During the summer of 1908, concrete for the lighthouse was poured nearly continuously from a wood scaffold that reached to the top. The light was completed in 1909. Fired upon by a Japanese submarine in World War II, it has the distinction of being the only place in Canada ever under enemy fire.

Hesquiat Harbour

Chart 3640; entrance buoy "ME": 49°23.12' N, 126°25.80' W

> *Hesquiat Harbour is entered between Matlahaw Point and Hesquiat Point. Hesquiat Bar, across its entrance, protects the harbour to a great extent from the ocean swell; kelp grows in patches on the bar.... Anchorage is good.... During strong south or SW gales the sea breaks heavily on Hesquiat Bar but the anchorage is safe and landing can always be made in Rae Basin.* (p. 277)

Hesquiat Harbour is a large natural bay with a wide, shallow bar at its entrance. A small Indian village is located on the southeast point of the peninsula, and a church at the north end is prominent. A concrete breakwater at the south end of the settlement can be used by dinghies only. There are numerous shoals in the vicinity. A planked trail leads along the beach to the lighthouse 3.5 miles to the west, and it makes an interesting hike.

The shallow bar is 4 fathoms deep and 2 miles wide. During summer, many local fishing boats anchor on the bar itself, east of the settlement, and their anchor lights at night look to passing boats like a Christmas tree.

In southerly weather, crossing the bar can be dangerous. Boats wanting more protection can move to the northeast corner of the harbor behind Rondeault Point or tuck into tiny Rae Basin.

Anchor in 5 fathoms in the western part of the bay, north of the drying Anton Spit. There is plenty of swinging room. The bottom is mud with good holding.

Rae Basin

Chart 3640; inner basin anchor: 49°28.29' N, 126°24.17' W

> *Rae Basin...has two above-water rocks, one drying rock and a mud bottom; it is suitable only for small craft.* (p. 277)

At the outlet of the stream draining Hesquiat and Rae lakes, Rae Basin has a small nook that largely dries at low water. The inner basin east of the entrance rocks is well protected from winds and seas.

Rae Basin's name comes from the Rae Arthur family which homesteaded here in the early 1900s. Mrs. Rae Arthur, known as Cougar Annie, shot 63 cougars and survived three husbands.

Steep-sided 3,000-foot Mt. Seghers, 2 miles to the northwest, and high peaks just to the east, make this a cozy place with excellent views. When you enter the inner basin, stay close north to the shoal to avoid the drying entrance rocks. A logging road that crosses the stream makes a good place to stretch your legs.

Anchor in 4 to 5 fathoms outside the entrance, staying north of the large drying shoal, or inside the basin in 2 to 3 fathoms with mud and sand bottom. Swinging room is limited and a stern anchor is useful.

Hot Springs Cove— wharf and Bed & Breakfast

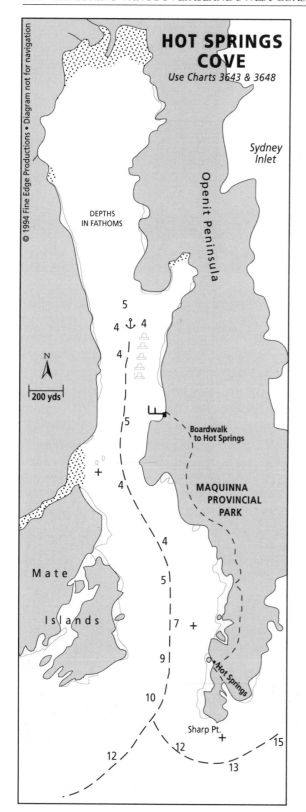

Boardwalk to Hot Springs

Hot Springs Cove

Charts 3643, 3648; anchor: 49°21.93' N, 126°15.95' W

Hot Springs Cove...entered between Sharp Point and Mate Islands, is a Public Harbour. A rock awash lies on the east side of the fairway about 0.3 mile north of Sharp Point. Drying rocks on the west side of the cove, close north of Mate Islands, narrow the fairway in this locality to barely 0.1 mile wide. (p. 278)

Hot Springs Cove has been a destination of choice for all West Coast cruising boats for generations. It has also become a popular attraction for Tofino tourists who arrive by sea kayak, float plane or high-powered runabouts. Its famous natural outdoor hot springs are a 1-mile walk from the wharf along a scenic cedar-planked trail that passes through thick rain forest. The walk itself is a world-class attraction, while the bubbling hot water that flows through several pools on its way to the ocean offers unforgettable pleasures.

A public wharf with two long floats lies

half-way up the cove on the east side. In summer the public float is frequently crowded, and a fee is charged for boats staying longer than "1 hour and 59 minutes."

The hot springs, 250 yards north of Sharp Point on the west side of Openit Peninsula, are situated near a rough, rocky, small cove with no access. Maquinna Provincial Park, which stretches from Sharp Point to the wharf, is maintained in a rustic, undeveloped state except for pit toilets near the wharf and the hot springs. There are several picturesque, primitive campsites just south of the hot springs near a small kayak beach. The land for the park was given to the province in 1954 by Ivan Clarke, whose son Hugh now runs the store and marine ways at Ahousat.

Recently Dave, who lives aboard his sailboat, *Die Flyn*, became wharfinger of the public wharf. Dave is owner of the barge tied to the float, which operates as a bed and breakfast. The establishment offers limited supplies (mostly backpacking foods). No fuel or water are available on the dock. Drinking water is available on shore from a hand pump just north of the pier.

If the hot springs are to retain their natural, wild beauty, visitors need to respect their fragility. With the current increase of visitors, park authorities may upgrade standards and tighten restrictions on some common practices (such as nude bathing, primitive camping, etc.). The park is user-maintained, and when you visit it, you should observe the following rules: Use caution on the slippery boardwalk; stay on existing trails; remove all garbage; use no glass or soap in pool area; no pets beyond the wharf kiosk; no alcoholic beverages; and perhaps most important, no fires.

The unique split-cedar boardwalk dates back 60 years or more and is famous for its planks carved or painted with the names and dates of visiting ships. These planks attest to the long history of visiting yachts and crew members. Each year maintenance is done on the boardwalk, and work crews have been careful to retain the old planks when they improve or divert the trail.

This wharf and the village across the cove were destroyed in the 1964 tsunami. Norma, for many years unofficial caretaker of Hot Springs Cove, is no longer here, nor are her float house, store and famous floating garden. She has moved to "Baseball Cove" on the east side of Sydney Inlet.

Five public mooring buoys, located 200 yards north of the floats, are frequently used by fishing boats. The area close northwest of the buoys is a well-sheltered anchorage, 4 to 5 fathoms deep over a mud bottom.

Boardwalk carving of boat name

The ultimate soak, Hot Springs Cove

Sharp Point

Charts 3643, 3648; light: 49°20.87' N,
126°15.50' W

Boats heading south on a tight schedule usually leave Sharp Point and stay outside Flores Island, the fastest way to Tofino and points south. Those visiting Clayoquot Sound usually take the inside passage around the north end of Flores Island. In either case, avoid two dangerous rocks off Sharp Point. The first one is close off the point; the second is due south less than a quarter mile. Neither is marked by a navigational aid, but the close north rock breaks heavily with any swell running and gives you your first clue. Boats passing into Sydney Inlet can carefully pass between the two rocks in about 15 fathoms. On spring tides with strong ebb current and southerly winds the seas can be very steep and dangerous.

Sydney Inlet

Chart 3648

The entrance to Sydney Inlet is formed by Openit Peninsula on the west and Flores Island on the east. A white sand beach located on the west shore of Flores Island provides a lovely camping site for kayakers, while farther north two coves offer protection for cruising boats.

Sydney Inlet, north of the junction with Shelter Inlet, has several well-sheltered, secluded anchorages and is worth a stop for cruising boats.

"Hoot-la-Kootla," looking north

"Kayak Cove"

Chart 3648; entrance: 49°21.3' N, 126.13.7' W

Kayak Cove (sometimes called Crescent Beach by locals) is our name for the beautiful, nearly landlocked shallow cove 1.25 miles northeast of Sharp Point. While this cove is too shallow and foul for cruising boats, it is a natural for sea kayaks. The wide, white sandy beach offers a number of primitive campsites. On several occasions we have seen martens do their own "cruise" of the beach for food.

"Kayak Cove," Flores Island

When Hot Springs Cove is overrun, this peaceful, quiet beach provides a nice alternative campsite for kayakers. We found refuge here during one summer gale while we were on a sea kayaking expedition. We found this the best campsite west of White Sand Cove. A half mile south, "Pretty Pocket Beach" provides another kayak campsite, and although it is a lovely beach, it is more exposed to westerlies.

"Hoot-la-Kootla"

Chart 3648; anchor south: 49°21.69' N,
126°13.80' W; anchor north: 49°21.93' N,
126°13.72' W

The first anchorage inside Sydney Inlet lies 500 yards north of Kayak Cove and east of island (190). The name of the cove, Hoot-la-Kootla, is related to the Indian Reserve on the southeast shore. This cove is a picturesque fair-weather anchorage and a good alternative to Hot Springs Cove 2.5 miles away. While some southerly swell can be felt here, in stable weather you can find good shelter in either the northern end or the southern end off a small beach. The northern exit behind island (190) is foul, and cruising boats should avoid it.

Anchor in 2 to 3 fathoms, at the south end of the cove, over mud and sand bottom with good holding. In the north end of the cove, anchor in 3 fathoms at the north end of the cove over mud-gravel with good holding.

"Baseball Bay"

Chart 3648; anchor:
49°22.48' N, 126°13.60' W

Less than half a mile north of island (190) is another unnamed cove on Flores Island locally known as Baseball Cove. The name originated when a group of pilchard boats were anchored here in the early part of the 1900s, and one day the crews started throwing a baseball back and forth between their boats.

Norma's float, store and garden are located at the northeast end; the cove is marked by a small sign on the north entrance and by a flag on the first rock. Two rocks (just above water at high tide) must be avoided. Navigate cautiously, since the entrance is shallow and irregular with between 1 and 2 fathoms in the fairway on the north side of the first rock.

Anchor in mid-bay between the two drying rocks in 3 fathoms over a mud bottom.

Riley Cove

Chart 3648; anchor: 49°23.45' N, 126°13.37' W

Riley Cove, east of the point, affords good shelter for small craft. (p. 306)

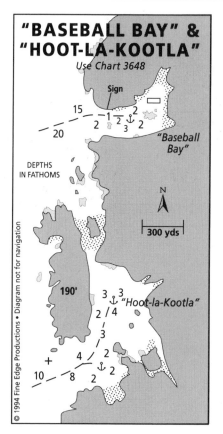

Riley Cove is located just east of Starling Point, at the northeast tip of Flores Island. It is secluded and well protected from southerlies, and no swell is felt here. Favor the west shore on entering Riley Cove; a shoal extends over halfway from its eastern point.

The name for the cove comes from Reese Riley who operated one of the first water taxis on the coast; he drowned off Rafael Point in the 1950s.

The southwest beach can be used by kayaks, although there is not much clear, flat ground for a campsite. This cove once harbored a herring plant and is a good place to explore.

Anchor in 2 fathoms, gravel and mud bottom, midway off the small pebble beach due west of a cement bollard on shore. A stern anchor or a line ashore is helpful in windy weather since swinging room is tight. Larger boats can anchor farther out in 6 to 8 fathoms as indicated in the diagram.

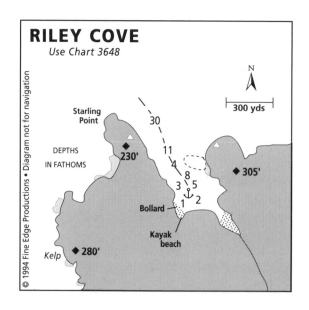

Beach, Riley Cove

Islet in Young Bay

Young Bay

Chart 3648; anchor: 49°25.68' N, 126°13.06' W

> *Young Bay, 2 miles north of Starling Point, affords secure anchorage for small craft.* (p. 306)

As Sydney Inlet narrows, it grows steeper with a more rugged alpine appearance. On the eastern shore there are several good anchorages.

Young Bay is the first of several remote and scenic anchorages in upper Sydney Inlet that offer a maximum of protection. The inner basin of Young Bay, locally known as East Bay is quiet, secluded, and surrounded by rain forest. You can often spot bear and deer on its southern shore. The islet near the north shore has cement and brick remains of one of the pilchard plants that thrived here years ago.

The entrance to Young Bay is straightforward: stay near the middle, avoiding shoals on either side and a rock on the north. Pass the islet on the south side.

Anchor in 8 fathoms in the center of the basin, or on the south side if you want more shallow water. Little wind penetrates this cove; in summer the water is a balmy 65°F.

Bottleneck Cove ("Coyote Cove")

Chart 3648; anchor: 49°26.77' N, 126°12.90' W

> *...Bottleneck Cove, at the head of Adventure Bay has a very narrow entrance.* (p. 306)

Located one mile north of Young Bay, Bottleneck Cove, locally known as Bottle Bay, is one of the best protected anchorages you will find anywhere. Its narrow entrance gives the inner basin complete protection.

According to a local yarn, the name is due to the fact that during Prohibition rum runners would run for this bay and quickly stash their booze on the overhanging rock entrance before they anchored. When the federal cutter arrived

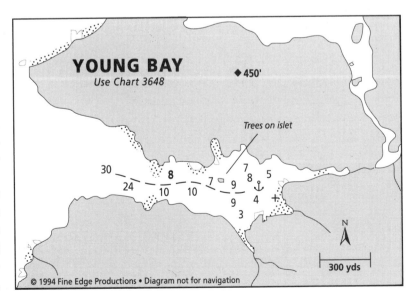

YOUNG BAY
Use Chart 3648

◆450'

Trees on islet

30
24
8
10   10
7   7
9
9
3
7   5
8
4
N
300 yds

© 1994 Fine Edge Productions • Diagram not for navigation

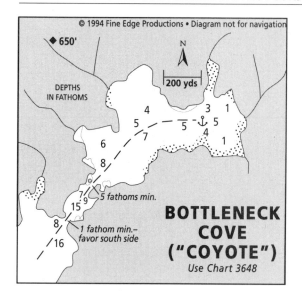

pears to be flat and without rocks. There is room for several boats to anchor without being too crowded. The wind and currents are so slight here that it seems a string could hold your boat over the anchor. The water, as high as 68°F in summer, is subject to a red bloom.

Anchor in 5 fathoms over mud bottom as indicated on the diagram. Holding is good, and in this cove it's hard to imagine ever having any strain on your anchor rode.

to inspect their boats, they would be found free of liquor.

This beautiful cove, with its old-growth cedar, quiet atmosphere and supreme solitude, was named Coyote after Don Watmough's sailboat, in which he explored the West Coast while preparing his book. Although Bottleneck Cove is described in *Sailing Directions,* it is not named on the chart.

When you enter, favor the right-hand (south) shore near the first narrows to avoid a small shoal located on the north side; then stay in mid-channel. The fairway is narrow, but has 4 fathoms minimum at its narrowest point and seems clear of dangers.

On the echo sounder the inner basin ap-

Entrance to Bottleneck Cove

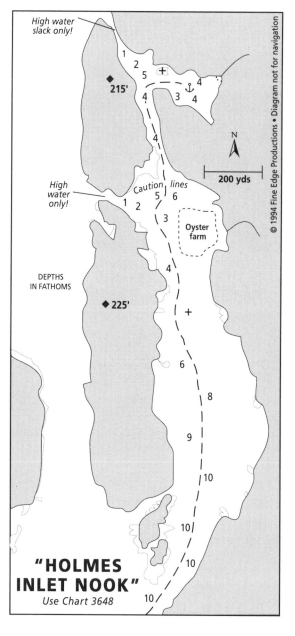

Holmes Inlet

Chart 3648; anchor: 49°26' N, 126°14' W

Holmes Inlet, narrow and scenic, ends in a dry-ing shoal. At its northern head there is a well-protected area known as Pretty Girl Cove. The water there is too deep for convenient anchor-age. The towering peaks on both sides of the in-let give it a truly alpine appearance. Trees, cov-ered with yellow lichen and light green mosses, line the steep, rocky shores.

"Holmes Inlet Nook"

Chart 3648; anchor: 49°27.72' N, 126°14.06' W

On the east side of the inlet, between island (215) and Vancouver Island, there is a small, unnamed nook that looks like it came straight out of Hansel and Gretel's Black Forest. This tiny cove offers total isolation from the outside world. For cruising anchorages the cove defines the term *intimate,* and we recommend it as a complete getaway for smaller boats.

As indicated in the diagram, the only safe entrance to Holmes Inlet Nook is from the south. The main bay, full of oyster floats and equipment, has an uneven, shallow bottom and requires careful navigation to avoid the various lines tied to shore.

The two entrances on either end of island (215) are shallow and feasible only for small boats at high water slack. The water is so warm here, it's frequently full of red bloom tide that prevents visibility below more than 6 inches of water. The northern exit, only 30 feet wide, has

Above: Holmes Inlet, north end of nook
Below: Anchor site, "Holmes Inlet Nook"

extending trees limbs that nearly fill the space. Because of the narrow restriction in the main part of Holmes Inlet, current flows past island (215) on the east side, making maneuvering difficult if you attempt to transit the northern narrows.

Anchor in 4 fathoms in the middle of the cove southeast of the drying rock. The bottom here is light mud, which requires a tender hand setting the anchor. Since swinging room is tight, you may want to set a stern tie to shore.

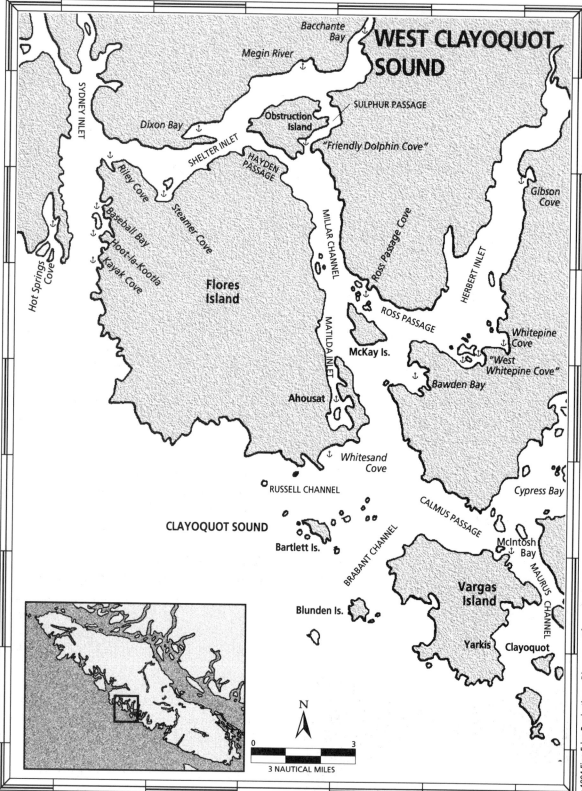

WEST CLAYOQUOT SOUND

SYDNEY INLET

Bacchante Bay

Megin River

Dixon Bay

SULPHUR PASSAGE

Obstruction Island

"Friendly Dolphin Cove"

SHELTER INLET

HAYDEN PASSAGE

Riley Cove

Gibson Cove

Baseball Bay

Hoot-la-Kootla

Steamer Cove

MILLAR CHANNEL

Ross Passage Cove

HERBERT INLET

Kayak Cove

Hot Springs Cove

Flores Island

ROSS PASSAGE

Whitepine Cove

MATILDA INLET

McKay Is.

"West Whitepine Cove"

Bawden Bay

Ahousat

Whitesand Cove

RUSSELL CHANNEL

Cypress Bay

CALMUS PASSAGE

CLAYOQUOT SOUND

Bartlett Is.

BRABANT CHANNEL

McIntosh Bay

MAURUS CHANNEL

Vargas Island

Blunden Is.

Yarkis

Clayoquot

N

0   3

3 NAUTICAL MILES

16

West Clayoquot Sound

West Clayoquot Sound offers cruising boats a calm inside passage via Shelter Inlet, Millar Channel, Calmus Passage, Maurus Channel, Heynen Channel, and Deadman Pass to Tofino. Boats that can linger will find a number of intimate getaways just off the beaten path.

The small-scale charts of this area look daunting for all the shallow water, however with careful navigation there is little need for concern. Those intending to visit Tofino should carefully consult Chart 3685.

Ahousat, a hub for exploring West Clayoquot Sound, makes a handy stop if you're running low on fuel and provisions.

Shelter Inlet

Chart 3648

Shelter Inlet, a transverse (east-west) passage on the north side of Flores Island, connects

Steamer Cove, looking east

Sydney Inlet to Millar Channel via Hayden and Sulphur passages. Little fetch builds ups during southerly storm winds here, and the water is generally calm during summer. The major refuges for small boats in Shelter Inlet are Steamer Cove at the west end, and Bacchante Bay at the extreme northeast end. Steep shores line this inlet and trees grow out of rocky ledges in unexpected places. Beautiful, tall cedars stand along the Megin River, and you can often spot scavenging bears and flocks of merganzers.

During a kayak trip in 1989 we encountered a basking shark at close hand (mid-channel north of George Island). Longer than our 21-foot double kayak, the sighting gave us quite an adrenaline rush and a fine burst of speed.

Steamer Cove

Chart 3648; anchor: 49°22.55' N, 126°11.45' W

> Steamer Cove can be entered on either side of George Islands; the west channel is the wider. It affords good anchorage in 17 to 19 fathoms (31 to 35 m), mud bottom. Small craft can find good anchorage, mud, in a cove in its SW corner. (p. 306-307)

Steamer Cove, named because of its agreeable shelter for old-time steamers, has an inner cove that offers good protection for small craft. While not particularly scenic, the cove has easy access and good radar targets in poor visibility, making it a serious refuge in foul weather. Its west side has been clear-cut and old logging

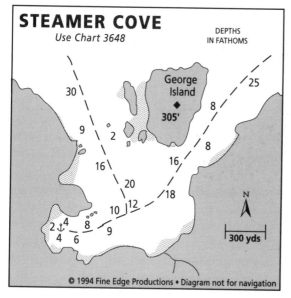

STEAMER COVE
Use Chart 3648

DEPTHS IN FATHOMS

George Island
◆
305'

© 1994 Fine Edge Productions • Diagram not for navigation

300 yds

operations are still evident, but the dirt roads close to shore offer you a chance to stretch your legs.

You can tuck up against the north side of the inner cove. Some large kelp on the bottom can make anchoring tricky, so be sure to set your anchor well.

Anchor in 4 fathoms over a sticky mud bottom with very good holding.

Dixon Bay
Chart 3648; anchor: 49°24.20' N, 126°10.15' W)

> *Dixon Bay...is too deep for anchorage though small craft can anchor near the head.*(p. 307)

Scenic Dixon Bay is located on the north shore of Shelter Cove. The bay is open to easterlies, and a low peninsula to the west offers little protection from westerly winds. The north shore is densely forested and steep, with a dark rocky bluff. At the far west end there is a pebble beach. Shoals at the head of the bay are rather small for long-term anchoring; however, this is a good place for a rest stop while you wait for favorable currents in Hayden Passage. There is a large fish farm just inside Dixon Point.

Anchor in 4 fathoms. The bottom is of unknown holding.

Hayden Passage
Chart 3648

> *Hayden Passage is used by coasting vessels. Shoal and drying rocks, at the NW end of the passage, extend up to 0.15 mile off the Obstruction Island shore. A group of above-water and drying rocks, at the SE end of the passage, extend about 0.1 mile off the Obstruction Island shore.* (p. 307)

Tidal streams in Hayden Passage can reach 2.5 knots, according to *Sailing Directions*; however, the chart indicates a 4.0-knot current. My experience is that this passage, which connects two different openings to the sea, is unpredictable. Don't be surprised if the current changes direction at far different times than those recorded for local high or low water, or if the direction of flood or ebb is not always that shown on the chart! Other than the identified rocks, you should have little difficulty, unless you are in a kayak.

Megin River
Chart 3648; anchor: 49°26.13' N, 126°05.00' W)

Megin River drains a large section of the north Clayoquot region and offers many recreational opportunities. The area has not been as heavily cut as others, and its scenic values are excellent. The broad, U-shaped Megin River Valley has a large stand of old-growth trees along its banks. The river offers good sportfishing, outstanding rafting and other recreational opportunities for those dropped upstream by float planes.

In calm weather temporary anchorage can be taken in 3 fathoms west of the house on the eastern point; this spot, off the rocky, narrow entrance to the Megin River, shoals rapidly and is subject to strong outflow currents. The eastern point is an Indian Reserve.

Anchor in 3 fathoms. Bottom and holding power are undetermined. You need to maintain an anchor watch.

Bacchante Bay

Chart 3648; anchor: 49°27.10' N, 126°02.10' W

Bacchante Bay...has a very narrow entrance encumbered by rocks on either side. The fairway is only about 300 feet (91 m) wide. It can be entered by small craft but local knowledge is needed. (p. 307)

Bacchante Bay is a miniature alpine fjord complete with a bar across its narrow entrance. Nearly landlocked, it offers very good protection and adequate swinging room for quite a few boats. This out-of-the-way, solitary place is an ideal cruising anchorage featuring excellent natural sights and wildlife. The call of the common loon breaks an otherwise complete silence. Steep granite walls line the bay, and trees grow out of ledges and rocky crevasses in the most unexpected places.

The entrance is hard to see until you are close aboard. A pointed entrance rock, about 18 feet above high water, is splashed with white paint or bird guano. Pass this rock to your port side. The position of a rock shown on the chart at the east side of the narrows is doubtful; favor the west shore upon entering. The fairway has a minimum depth of about 2 fathoms (not the 5 fathoms shown on the chart), and the bottom for the first 500 yards or so is a series of uneven ups and downs. After this, the bottom flattens out without any sign of obstructions. A gentle up-valley afternoon wind can be expected in heavy weather. As you approach the river delta, be sure to watch for rapid shoaling.

The federal Fisheries and Oceans, as well as locals, call this area Watta Creek after the creek that comes in on the east side of the bay.

The large, grassy area of the delta is worth exploring. You can navigate the river by motorized dinghy for about a half mile until you approach shallow rapids. Note that about 18 inches of the fresh river water flows seaward on flood on top of the saltwater, which in turn floods inward at between 1 to 2 knots. This interesting phenomenon can be observed easily due to gossamer threads of plant material in the water.

Anchor in 6 fathoms not far from the outlet of the river. The bottom is sand and mud with good holding.

Entrance to Bacchante Bay

Sulphur Passage

Chart 3648; position: 49°24' N, 126°04' W

Sulphur Passage...leads south along the east side of Obstruction Island to Millar Channel. It is encumbered with rocks but suitable for small craft. Local knowledge is necessary. (p. 307)

Sulphur Passage takes you around Obstruction Island following a scenic route; however, the

---

© 1994 Fine Edge Productions • Diagram not for navigation

Grassy

1 1 1
4 4
⚓ 5
6 6
8 / 8
9
8
7 / 8
6 / 5
+ / +
5 | 3
| 9

BACCHANTE BAY
Use Chart 3648

N

|300 yds|

Favor west shore

DEPTHS
IN FATHOMS

Watta Creek, Bacchante Bay

intricate nature of its passage requires careful navigation with alert lookouts. The crux of the problem is a constriction less than half a mile south of Belcher Point.

I have used the very small passage east of islet (115) and west of islet (135) with a minimum of about 3 fathoms (not 9 fathoms as indicated on the chart). With the current running, though, it was an experience of high anxiety and I do not recommend taking it. Locals say the far west side next to Obstruction Island, although not much deeper, is simpler; that is the route they recommend.

If you plan to anchor in the vicinity or need to wait for a change of current in Hayden Passage, the small unnamed cove on the southwest side of Sulphur Passage is a delightful find.

The southern entrance to Sulphur Passage has a minimum depth in its fairway of 6 fathoms. Favor the east side of the narrows for an easy entry or exit, but remain clear of the rock (3 feet above water) and the large kelp bed to the northwest off the east point of Vancouver Island.

"Friendly Dolphin Cove"
Chart 3648; anchor: 49°23.88' N, 126°05.48' W

Unnamed and largely unknown, this cove lies north-northeast of a 530-foot, cone-shaped peak on the south end of Obstruction Island. It is landlocked and offers good protection from all weather. The horizontal line of tree limbs along the shore at high water, as well as the absence of driftwood, indicates that these are calm waters.

I have taken the liberty to call this cove Friendly Dolphin after my trusty sailboat, *le Dauphin Amical*, (a Porpoise design ketch by William Garden of Victoria). In 1975, after my wife and I pitchpoled 800 miles WNW of Cape Horn, our crippled boat got us safely to land on the coast of Patagonia where we found the first sheltered anchorage from the seas of the

"Screaming Fifties. Friendly Dolphin Cove resembles that anchorage.

For ease of entry, scenic qualities, quietness and seclusion, Friendly Dolphin Cove is one of the best in Clayoquot Sound. The north shore has high cliffs, and old-growth rain forest surrounds the cove in all directions. The shore is steep-to, and there's no place to land. The current of Sulphur Passage does not enter here. Although Friendly Dolphin Cove is a bit deep for convenient anchoring, its southwest corner offers a good spot with room for several boats.

Anchor in 7 fathoms over a soft mud bottom with good holding.

"Ross Passage Cove"
Chart 3648; anchor: 49°20.06' N, 126°02.90' W

Ross Passage, between McKay Island and the mainland NE, is obstructed by islets and rocks. (p. 307)

Ross Passage is cluttered with islets which protect the cove we call Ross Passage Cove. You can find temporary anchorage here in fair weather, and the tree-covered islets offer good fishing, exploring and diving opportunities. Despite its central location, this area is relatively quiet.

Anchor in 4 fathoms over a mixed bottom with somewhat indifferent holding.

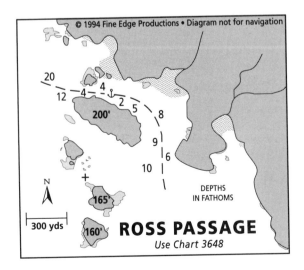

Matilda Inlet

Chart 3643

> *Matilda Inlet is sheltered by McNeil Peninsula and affords good anchorage.... Anchorage is available in Matilda Inlet in about 17 fathoms (31 m), mud bottom..... Marktosis, at the head of a shallow bay on the east side of Matilda Inlet, is an Indian Reserve with a population of 416 (1986).... No attempt should be made to approach Marktosis from Matilda Inlet unless in possession of local knowledge.* (p. 307)

Ahousat

Chart 3643: Ahousat fuel float: 49°16.94' N, 126 04.20' W

Ahousat, a settlement on the west side of Matilda Inlet, offers several services to cruising boats: a Chevron fuel dock, water on the float, a telephone at the head of the dock, a well-stocked store and a marine ways. The Ahousat store complex is owned by Hugh Clark, son of Mabel and Ivan Clark who donated Hot Springs Maquinna Park to the province 30 years ago.

Hugh and his family are a storehouse of local information. Overnight moorage at the dock is usually gratis if you purchase fuel or provisions. Power is available on the most southerly dock. The 40-foot-long marine ways has handled up to a 50-foot fishing boat. Any skipper or shipwright is allowed to do repair work here. A second-story restaurant and rooms-for-let are planned for the future.

The word Ahousat means "the people with their backs to the mountain." The inhabitants of Marktosis originally came from a village site located on Catface Point, below the high range of mountains to the east.

Ahousat General Store

Little local wind blows through here unless a southeaster of over 40 knots comes up, and it is so protected you can't even judge what the northwesterlies are doing. Matilda Inlet is located off the head of a large mud shoal at the north end of Gibson Marine Park. A primitive trail, marked with flags, leads to the warm springs and beautiful beach. There are no facilities at Gibson Marine Park.

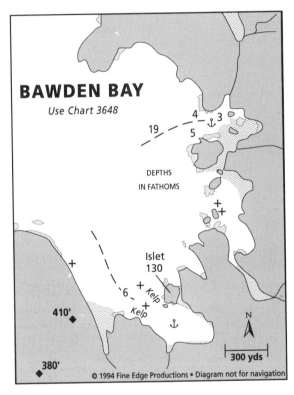

Anchor in 2 to 5 fathoms a half mile south of Ahousat float and fuel station. The bottom is a sand-mud mixture with good holding.

Whitesand Cove

Chart 3648; anchor: 49°15.04' N, 126°04.60' W

...Whitesand Cove lie[s] on the north side of the fairway. (p. 278)

Whitesand Cove and Gibson Marine Park have some of the most beautiful wide, sandy beaches in Clayoquot Sound. Popular with sea kayakers, the eastern part of the beach has sev-eral primitive campsites located along the shore. Landing on the beach is easy, except during southerly gales.

The bottom of the cove is shallow, flat and sandy. Because there is no protection from southerlies here, it is generally not considered a cruising anchorage. It does, however, make an excellent temporary rest stop if the weather is favorable. We recommend you go ashore for a stroll; you'll have a good time digging your toes into the fine white sand. Local fishing boats use the far west end as a convenient overnight anchorage in fair, calm weather.

Anchor in 1.5 fathoms against Kutcous Point, in a sandy bottom, with fair holding. There is plenty of swinging room, and a stern anchor can keep you facing into the residual swell, if it becomes rolly.

Bawden Bay

Chart 3648; inner north nook anchor: 49°17.03' N, 126°00.35' W

Bawden Bay...entered north of Clifford Point, affords anchorage in its SE part in 10 to 15 fathoms (18 to 27 m), mud. Allow sufficient space to clear the shoals lying 0.1 mile offshore in this part of the bay. (p. 307)

Bawden Bay, like Whitepine Cove, is used by larger cruising vessels looking for a protected anchorage.

The small cove in the southeast corner of Bawden Bay is said to be clear of dangers, but there are dangerous rocks in the middle of its entrance! We had difficulty locating one of the rocks awash on about a 7-foot tide, as well as a second awash on a 4-foot tide; a narrow passage leads between this and a similar rock to the southwest of islet (130). Chart 3648 is inadequate for such close navigation and further charting needs to be done, so at this time we do not recommend the southeast area of Bawden Bay. Although it is very secure, unless you enter at low water and in good visibility when the rocks can be identified, it is too risky.

The northeast corner of the bay is used regularly for transient anchorage.

Small craft can find protection in the northern nook, anchoring as shown in the diagram and tucked up well inside. Larger boats anchor just outside in 10 fathoms.

Anchor in 3 fathoms; the bottom is mixed and of undetermined holding power.

Gibson Cove

Chart 3649; entrance: 49°20' N, 125°58' W

Gibson Cove, 3 miles NNE of Binns Island, has below-water rocks off both entrance points; within the cove it is free of dangers and affords anchorage for small vessels. (p. 308)

We have not visited Gibson Cove. However, locals say they have found good shelter here, although it is rather deep. Good fresh water runs into the cove from the 3,000-foot mountains immediately to the east.

Starfish

Whitepine Cove

Chart 3648; entrance: 49°18' N, 125°57' W

Whitepine Cove affords anchorage for small vessels in 10 fathoms (18 m) near the edge of a drying bank at its head. Care must be taken to avoid Sutlej Rock and the two shoals, one with 15 feet (4.6 m) and the other with 26 feet (7.8 m) over it. (p. 308)

Larger cruising vessels use Whitepine Cove for anchoring; however, small craft will find a more protected and intimate shelter 1 mile to the southwest in what we call West Whitepine Cove.

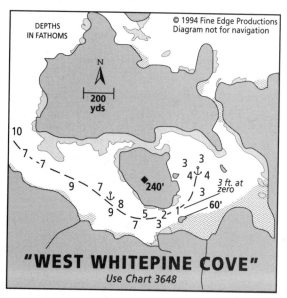

"WEST WHITEPINE COVE"
Use Chart 3648

"West Whitepine Cove"

Chart 3648; inner cove anchor: 49°17.88' N, 125°58.30' W

Sheltered anchorage for small craft, in 9 to 10 fathoms (16 to 18 m) mud, can be obtained in the cove south of the islets on the west side of the entrance to Whitepine Cove; entry should be made south of the west islet. Local knowledge is needed. (p. 308)

A quiet and secure unnamed anchorage for small craft is available in two places as indicated in the diagram. The inner cove, about as calm as any saltwater anchorage can be, is

Kayakers haul out on beach

worth the effort of a careful approach.

West Whitepine Cove, as we call it, is fully protected from all winds and seas; there is sufficient swinging room for several boats. The east side of the cove looks like a stump farm and contrasts unfavorably with the wooded islets to the north and west. Summer water temperatures reach 64°F, comfortable enough for a midday swim. This is a good spot to watch bears that walk the south and east shores. For a quiet, calm getaway, this is the place!

The inner cove, east of island (240), is entered close on the south side of island (240), north of islet (60). The least depth in the fair-way is only about 3 feet at zero tide, so plan to enter on half-tide or more. The fairway passes about 70 feet off the southeast side of island (240). Upon entering, favor island (240), avoiding a shoal that extends about 30 feet from shore. The rock on the east side of the cove, 150 feet south of a small peninsula, is awash at about a 6-foot tide; otherwise the fairway bottom is flat.

Anchor in 7 to 9 fathoms in the outer anchorage over a mixed bottom.

Anchor in 3 fathoms in the inner cove, mid-bay (avoiding shoals near shore). The bottom is mud bottom with good holding.

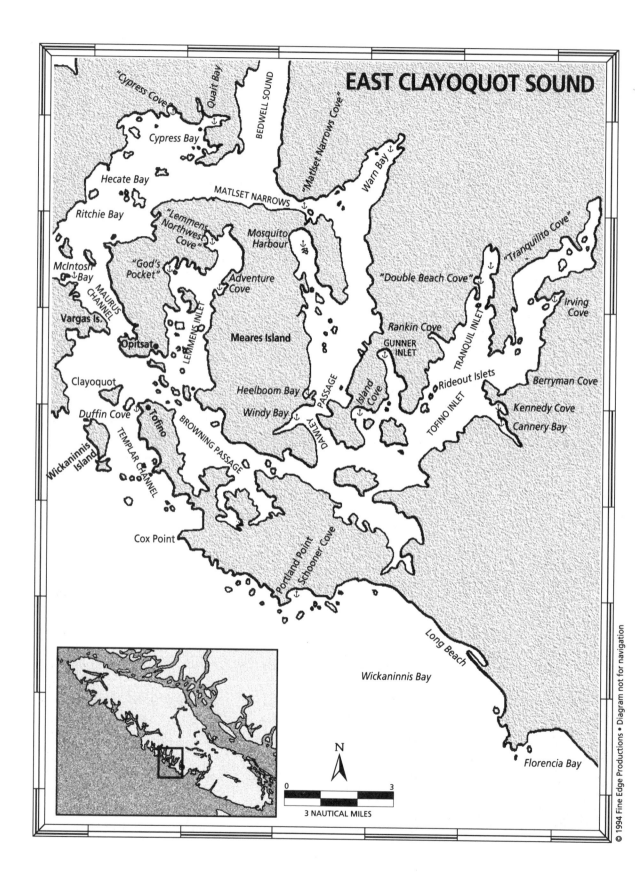

EAST CLAYOQUOT SOUND

"Cypress Cove"

Quait Bay

BEDWELL SOUND

"Matlset Narrows Cove"

Warn Bay

Cypress Bay

Hecate Bay

MATLSET NARROWS

"Tranquilito Cove"

Ritchie Bay

"Lemmens Northwest Cove"

Mosquito Harbour

"Double Beach Cove"

Irving Cove

McIntosh Bay

"God's Pocket"

Adventure Cove

Rankin Cove

MAURUS CHANNEL

Vargas Is.

LEMMENS INLET

Meares Island

GUNNER INLET

TRANQUIL INLET

Berryman Cove

Opitsat

Rideout Islets

Clayoquot

Heelboom Bay

Island Cove

Kennedy Cove

Duffin Cove

Windy Bay

DAWLEY PASSAGE

TOFINO INLET

Cannery Bay

Tofino

TEMPLAR CHANNEL

BROWNING PASSAGE

Wickaninnis Island

Cox Point

Portland Point

Schooner Cove

Long Beach

Wickaninnis Bay

N

0   3

3 NAUTICAL MILES

Florencia Bay

17
East Clayoquot Sound

Tofino, located in the center of Clayoquot Sound, is the first main town you encounter as you travel the West Coast of Vancouver Island from north to south; most cruising boats call here. Good restaurants and fine art galleries tempt your crew's wallet for the first time in hundreds of miles. As a skipper, you should remain alert to tricky shoals, fast currents and the hectic traffic of an active port. You need Chart 3685 (metric) to make an approach to Tofino or if you plan to transit Browning Passage or visit Lemmens Inlet. Don't be surprised by the numerous water taxis and fast runabouts that zoom around at all hours; there are numerous quiet kayaks as well.

Meares Island, just north of Tofino, is a wonderful place to visit or circumnavigate. An old native village, Opitsaht, is located across from Tofino. Middens 16 to 20 feet deep on Meares Island indicate the existence of early man in the sound. The name of the village means "people who live in the winter sun." Due to its southern exposure, when the winter sun does shine, Opitsaht has sunshine from morning till night.

Tofino Inlet, farther east and seldom visited by cruising boats, offers some fine, secluded anchorages. Because of concentrated logging activity here over the years, much of the bottom material throughout the area is a mixture of soft mud and decaying matter that requires you to set your anchor carefully in order to get it to hold well.

"McIntosh Bay"
Charts: 3648, 3649; anchor: 49°12.55' N, 125°56.44' W

Half a mile south of Morfee Island, the small cove located among a group of islets on the northeast corner of Vargas Island, is called McIntosh Bay by locals. A temporary fair-weather anchorage suitable for small boats only, it is a good place to go ashore and examine tidepools loaded with interesting creatures. There is a good landing spot and a campsite 300 yards to the southwest on Vargas Island.

Vargas Island, the only flat island in the sound, was homesteaded (pre-empted) in the early 1900s by settlers who hoped to make the entire island into a giant farm. However, 17 of their men died fighting in World War I, and

"McIntosh Bay"

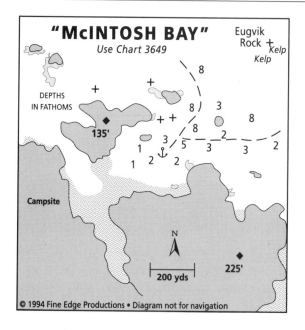

"McINTOSH BAY"
Use Chart 3649

Eugvik Rock

DEPTHS IN FATHOMS

Campsite

N

200 yds

© 1994 Fine Edge Productions • Diagram not for navigation

Tofino

Chart 3685 metric; public wharf: 49°09.29' N, 125°54.53' W

Tofino, on the north end of Esowista Peninsula, is a municipality with a population of 940 (1986). It has a hospital, post office (V0R 2Z0), stores, laundromat, liquor store, hotel and resorts. The village is served by broadcast radio station CBXZ which transmits on a frequency of 630 kHz from an aerial in 49° 09' 10" N., 125° 54' 20" W. It is the base for a Coast Guard search and rescue craft and has a Coast Guard heliport. (p. 280)

Tofino, situated at the end of the paved highway from Port Alberni, is a modern tourist

Above: Tofino kayak beach
Below: Kayakers ready for a journey

many of the remaining families gave up and banded together at the newly formed Tofino.

As an overnight anchorage, we don't recommend McIntosh Bay because it is rather exposed and you can feel the wake of every Tofino water taxi that passes inside Eugvik Rock. Use caution near Elbow Bank which is very shallow and has strong currents.

Anchor on a line midway between the 5-foot rock just south of the east end of islet (135) and the small point on the southeast end of Vargas Island.

Anchor in 2 fathoms east of the shoal, where you can get out of prevailing northwest swell. The bottom is sand with fair holding.

Deadman Pass, near Tofino

community. In addition to its many fine resorts and galleries, it serves as a supply center for other Clayoquot Sound villages and commercial operations. The public wharf, located 0.1 mile east of Grice Point, has a 121-foot-long float used extensively by water taxis and tour operators. This float provides the most convenient short-term moorage for cruising boats since it is just two blocks from the center of town. Telephones, as well as air taxi service, are available at the head of the wharf. The beach next to the wharf is used as a public launching area for kayaks. Tofino has scheduled bus and air service.

Cruising boats that remain at the downtown public wharf usually find this dock congested at all hours. Locally known as Whiskey Float, it is extremely noisy due to water taxis that come and go at all hours of the night. If you prefer quieter accommodations, try the marina or the small craft harbor. You can also pick up a buoy either at Duffin Cove or northwest of Arnet Island. Adventure Cove in Lemmens Inlet, 5 miles to the north, is the closest anchorage.

The small craft harbor, 0.5 mile east of Grice Point, has five floats with water and power, a public telephone, a tidal grid and facilities for dumping waste oil. A fuel dock west of the small craft harbor has fuel, water and propane. Weight West Marina, whose facilities are listed on page 326 of *Sailing Directions,* is located a quarter-mile east of the small craft harbor (0.2 mile west of Usatzes Point). Sailing vessels must be prepared to stop at the end of the floats because of a shallow riffle. A fast flooding tide over this riffle will find a deep-keeled vessel tipped over on its side, bouncing along as the tide comes in—a very unwelcome reception for an unsuspecting mariner.

Tofino public wharf and water taxi float

There is nothing half as much fun as poking about in boats

Caution: Strong 2- to 3-knot currents flow through Duffin Passage along the edge of town, making docking tricky. There are extensive tidal flats and shoals in the vicinity.

Tofino was named by Galiano and Valdez, Spanish navigators who explored the coast in the summer of 1792. Tofino was the name of a Spanish hydrographer.

Meares Island
Charts 3685 metric, 3649

Meares Island is of special interest both to environmentalists and local native bands. It has become a symbol in the movement for preserving old-growth timber. Although parts of the island were logged in the distant past, Meares Island offers strong scenic values and is popular for cruising boats and sea kayaks.

The site of historic Adventure Cove in Lemmens Inlet is worth a visit if you have time for nothing else.

Deadman Pass, the main route north and south out of Tofino, has heavy traffic. It is very narrow with a least depth of 2 fathoms. Stay carefully to the right-hand side of the fairway when transiting, and hold a steady course inside the well-buoyed channel. Don't be alarmed when water taxis pass a few feet away from your boat at full speed.

Lemmens Inlet
Charts: 3685 metric, 3649

Lemmens Inlet, entered east of Stockham Island, penetrates Meares Island and is shallow in its south part. It is only suitable for small craft; local knowledge is needed. (p. 309)

Lemmens Inlet is an attractive cruising ground with several well-protected coves. As you enter and exit, keep in mind the level of the tide and strength of the current. Because extensive

Adventure Cove, Meares Island

shoals in the region are filled with crab-pot floats, you need to watch carefully to find the channel between them.

Entrance: Close to the east side of Stockham Island, set a course of about 020° magnetic for island (140)—labeled (48) on the metric chart. As you approach island (140), favor the Meares Island shore on your port to try to avoid the most congested float areas. When you are 200 yards south of island (140), alter your course to pass close along the eastern shore using a heading of about 026° magnetic, which should take you directly abeam Columbia Islet at Adventure Cove. Keep an eye on your depth sounder and take corrective action if your readings indicate a depth less than that given for the fairway—it should be about 3 fathoms at zero tide. (Caution: Substantial current may set you on either side of course.)

The high, snow-covered peaks visible to the north are located beyond Bedwell Sound within the boundaries of Strathcona Park.

Adventure Cove
Chart 3649; anchor: 49°12.17' N, 125°51.14' W

(Adventure Cove, shown on the chart, is not mentioned in *Sailing Directions*.)

Adventure Cove is the historical site of Fort Defiance. Robert Gray, captain of the American

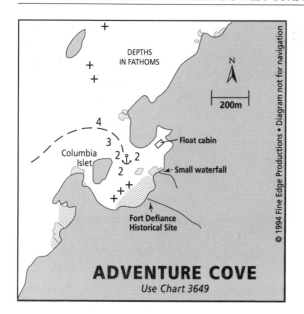

DEPTHS IN FATHOMS

N

200m

© 1994 Fine Edge Productions • Diagram not for navigation

4

3

2

2

2

Columbia Islet

Float cabin

Small waterfall

Fort Defiance Historical Site

ADVENTURE COVE
Use Chart 3649

fur trading vessel, *Columbia Rediviva*, wintered over in this cove in 1791. (Gray's greatest achievement was the discovery of the Columbia River, named after his vessel.) Although trees and bushes have taken over most of the forest, you can still see signs of the stockade.

The site of Fort Defiance was rediscovered by Ken Gibson of Tofino, who wrote: "After two years of searching, it was my pleasure in the summer of 1966 to unearth the site of Fort Defiance in a deserted little cove overgrown with cedar trees. The remains had layed [sic] untouched for nearly 175 years. It was here, that Captain Gray, the first American to circumnavigate the globe with the Stars and Stripes, built the 45 ton Sloop *Adventure*. Here they cleared away the forest growth and erected a log house, behind which they built two chimneys with hand-made bricks originally purchased and brought from Boston."

Fort Defiance and its 135 surrounding acres were established as an Archaeological Site December 9, 1967. An archaeological dig was performed by a team from the University of Victoria in 1968.

Three small streams drop directly from high peaks above and empty into the east side of the cove. Two are shown on the accompanying diagram; the stream just north of what we call "Christmas Tree Islet" has a small, conveniently located waterfall just above high water where old sailing ships probably filled their water caskets.

Adventure Cove is a well-protected scenic anchorage. Columbia Islet is high and breaks any west wind. In a strong northerly you may want to tuck up against the small float house in the north end of the bay. In foggy weather Adventure Cove is so quiet you can hear the foghorn on Lennard Island, 6.5 miles away.

Anchor in 2 fathoms over a wide area of the cove. The bottom is mud, sand and pebbles with good holding.

"Lemmens Northwest Cove"
Chart 3649; anchor: 49°13.43' N, 125°51.50' W

Near the head of Lemmens Inlet, an unnamed cove to the west offers good protection. This

Solitude in Adventure Cove

quiet, scenic place, which we call Lemmens Northwest Cove, is a good base from which to explore the head of the inlet. (Don't confuse this cove with the small, foul one immediately to the north.)

The entrance to Lemmens Northwest Cove lies between the east side of islet (130) and several drying rocks to the east. Do not enter without identifying these rocks. The fairway has a minimum depth of about 4 fathoms.

Pass about 50 yards off islet (130), midway to the rock to the east, which dries on an 11-

foot tide. There are two or more rocks 20 yards from islet (130) awash on a 7 to 8-foot tide.

Inside Lemmens Northwest Cove the bottom is fairly flat and secure. In summer, the water can reach 65°F and is warm enough for swimming, barring red tide (bloom) or jellyfish.

Anchor in 5 fathoms over a wide area with plenty of swinging room. The bottom is a mixture of mud and decaying matter with good holding.

"God's Pocket"

Chart 3649; anchor: 49°12.82' N, 125°53.10' W

God's Pocket is the local name for the bay on the far west side of Lemmens Inlet at the east base of Lone Cone Peak. Lone Cone Peak (2,470 ft.) and Catface Range to the northwest are the most distinguishing features in this immediate area.

God's Pocket has an easy approach and is secure and well protected. A lush, unspoiled rain forest covers the rocky shores and extends all the way to the summit of Lone Cove Peak. One mile to the south of God's Pocket on the south side of Lagoon Island there are remnants of a fish weir made of boulders by early native peoples.

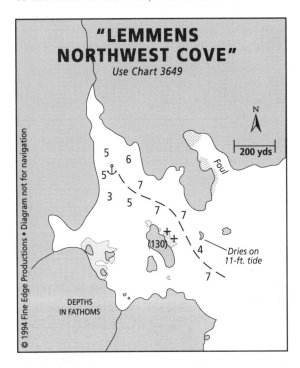

"Lemmens Northwest Cove"

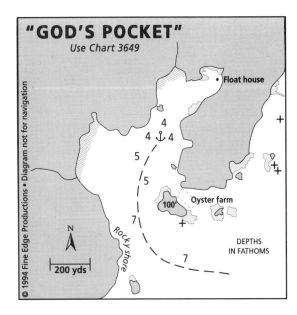

Entrance to "God's Pocket," Meares Island

The entrance to this cove has no obstructions, but an oyster farm completely occupies the space from islet (100) to its northern point. Enter south of islet (100). Small jellyfish seem to like this cove where water hovers around 64°F in summer.

Anchor in 4 fathoms in soft mud mixed with decaying matter. You will need to set your anchor with a soft touch, but once it is set, holding is good.

Ritchie Bay

Chart 3649; south bay anchor: 49°13.63' N, 125°53.98' W; north nook anchor: 49°14.11' N, 125°53.64' W

> *Ritchie Bay, ESE of Yellow Bank, has rocky shores and affords good anchorage in 6 to 10 fathoms (11 to 18 m). Rocks off the north entrance point are usually marked by kelp and a rock with less than 6 feet (1.8 m) over it lies 0.8 mile ENE of Robert Point.* (p. 309)

Ritchie Bay is a wide, open, somewhat protected roadstead where both larger and smaller boats can anchor.

The southeast corner of the bay, out of the current, is shielded from most winds.

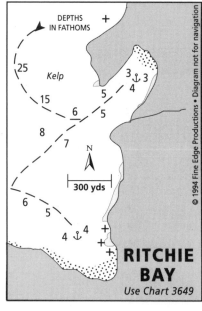

DEPTHS IN FATHOMS

25 *Kelp*

300 yds

© 1994 Fine Edge Productions • Diagram not for navigation

RITCHIE BAY

Use Chart 3649

Anchor in 4 to 5 fathoms over a flat bottom of sand and mud bottom with good holding.

The northeast nook offers good protection for small craft from northeast to southeast winds and is usually calm. Since Ritchie Bay is open to the southwest, it's not a good spot in which to sit out a gale.

The little nook is intimate and off the beaten track. There are two small landing beaches at its head with a small shoal that extends into the bay about 60 feet; otherwise its shores are steep-to. Be sure to have your binoculars handy, since eagles and loons seem to like this area.

Anchor in 3 fathoms; the soft gray mud bottom has good holding if you set your anchor with a gentle touch.

Hecate Bay

Chart 3649; entrance: 49°15' N, 125°56.5' W

> *Hecate Bay...is easy of access, well sheltered, free of dangers and one of the best anchorages in Clayoquot Sound with depths of 8 to 10 fathoms (15 to 18 m).* (p. 309)

Contrary to the opinion of *Sailing Directions*, we feel that the major timber operation centered in Hecate Bay spoils it for cruising boats. Large barges and timber-hauling vessels load under bright lights all night long, and their noise can be heard for miles around.

Small craft can find better shelter in the little cove at the far north end of Cypress Bay or inside landlocked Quait Bay.

The eastern portion of Cypress Bay is home to several large marine farms. You can pass east of the nearby islands, slowly and carefully staying clear of the oyster and fish farms. (If you happen to pass

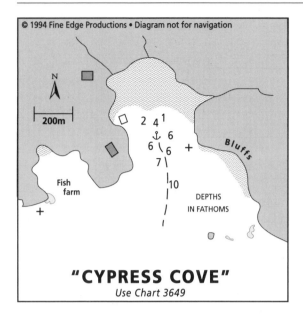

"CYPRESS COVE"
Use Chart 3649

the marine farms at feeding time, you might be interested to watch their technique of feeding the fish by means of fire hose nozzles.)

"Cypress Cove"
Chart 3649; anchor: 49°16.83' N, 125°52.93' W

> *Cypress Bay...affords good anchorage in 12 fathoms (22 m), about 0.5 mile off its NW shore.* (p. 309)

Small boats can take advantage of a more pleasant anchorage than that listed for Cypress Bay in *Sailing Directions*—an unnamed cove we call Cypress Cove. Located at the extreme north end of Cypress Bay, its access is relatively straightforward. Take caution, however, because the head of the bay shoals rapidly.

Although this cove offers good anchoring, it doesn't have much in the way of privacy. (If you want a nearly pristine, landlocked cove try Quait Bay, a mile to

the southeast.)

Anchor in 4 fathoms over a sand and mud bottom with good holding.

Quait Bay ("Calm Creek")
Chart 3649; anchor: 49°16.57' N, 125°51.05' W

> *Quait Bay...has a narrow entrance, obstructed by an islet; it is only suitable for small craft and local knowledge is needed.* (p. 309)

Quait Bay, known locally as Calm Creek, is a remote cruising anchorage with excellent protection from all weather. It is quiet and has excellent views in all directions. No swells of any kind enter the bay, and it has a flat bottom with plenty of swinging room for a number of boats. Summer water temperature is about 6 4°F, five degrees warmer than the channel outside.

The near-vertical summit of Mt. Quimper (4,215 ft.) rises ruggedly to the northeast. Undisturbed rain forest covers the shores, making this solitary anchorage a favorite of loons, tufted puffins and turnstones. An inhabited cabin sits on the north shore, and a marine farm operates here as well.

Enter Quait Bay by carefully navigating either side of entrance islet (185). Depths are less than those given on Chart 3649, so use extra

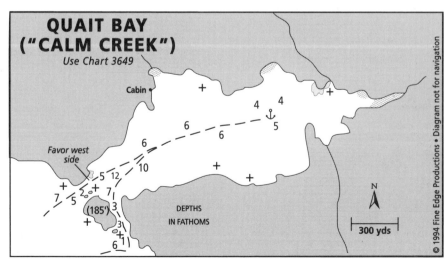

caution. Although the fairway east of islet (185) is the deeper of the two entrances, it is more difficult to navigate.

West Entrance: Although this passage is wider, several drying and underwater rocks next to islet (185) narrow its entrance. Favor the west mainland shore in a minimum fairway depth of about 1.5 fathoms at zero tide.

East Entrance: Stay well southeast of islet (185), avoiding its adjacent rocks. Cross over against the mainland bluff before turning inbound. Once you are past the underwater rocks, the fairway is flat with a least depth at zero tide of about 2.5 fathoms.

There are several detached rocks close to shore in the bay.

Anchor in 4 fathoms at the east end of Quait Bay over a mixed bottom of mud, clam shells and grass. Holding is good.

Above: South entrance to Quait Bay
Below: Inside Quait Bay, looking at north entrance

Bedwell Sound
Chart 3649

Bedwell Sound...has high rugged shores and is inconveniently deep for anchorage. Small vessels can obtain anchorage 2 miles north of Rant Point, about 0.2 mile off the west shore, in 22 fathoms (40 m) or 4 miles NNE or Rant Point in 12 to 16 fathoms (22 to 29 m), about 0.1 mile SE of a conspicuous bare 8 foot (2.4 m) high islet. (p. 309)

Bedwell Sound is one of the most beautiful, classic fjords on the West Coast of Vancouver Island, and although it is too deep for small boat anchorage, it's worth cruising to the head of the inlet to take in a glimpse of its beauty. The peaks to the east rise nearly a mile above sea level, and those in Strathcona Park to the north are often snow-covered throughout the summer months.

Use caution as you approach Bedwell River delta, where it shoals rapidly from 30 fathoms to 1 fathom in a couple of boat lengths!

The southeast entrance to the inlet has been denuded of trees, and old logging roads have left ugly cuts along the shores of the sound.

Matlset Narrows
Chart 3649; entrance: 49°14' N, 125°48' W

Matlset Narrows...leads from the south end of Bedwell Sound into the north end of Fortune Channel. The fairway has a minimum width of 0.15 mile. Foul ground usually marked by kelp, extends from the south shore west of an islet off the end of a small peninsula.... Tidal streams of about 4 knots can be expected at spring tides in Matlset Narrows. Strong tide-rips occur at times in the vicinity of Maltby Islets. The flood sets east and the ebb sets west through the narrows. (p. 309-310)

Matlset Narrows is one of three rapids you encounter in circumnavigating Meares Island. While all three run at about the same speed, they are not of major concern to well-

Entrance to "Matlset Narrows Cove"

powered cruising boats. Sea kayakers, however, need to time their transits appropriately.

"Matlset Narrows Cove"

Chart 3649; anchor: 49°13.98' N, 125°47.38' W

The small, unnamed cove we call Matlset Narrows Cove lies on the south shore of the narrows to the west of islet (165). It is frequently used for refuge by sea kayakers caught in unfavorable current. You can easily land a dinghy

on the small islets and beaches.

Small craft can use this picturesque cove as temporary anchorage for a lunch stop, for sportfishing or to watch the rapids. The cove has foul ground with extensive kelp on its west shore (watch for a current set here) and a small 2.5-fathom bar across its entrance. Just past the bar there is a 3- to 4-fathom hole not shown on the chart.

Once you are inside the cove, you leave turbulent water and can take temporary anchorage in its center. Keep an anchor watch in case conditions should change.

Anchor in the 3- to 4-fathom hole over a mixed bottom.

Warn Bay

Chart 3649; anchor: 49°15.45' N, 125°44.70' W

Warn Bay, at the north end of Fortune Channel, affords anchorage near its head in 19 fathoms (35 m), mud bottom. (p. 310)

Warn Bay has beautiful, high peaks to its north

"Matlset Narrows Cove," looking east

and east. In fair weather, some cruising boats find temporary anchorage just west of islet (165). Anchor in 5 fathoms, bottom and holding are undetermined. Larger vessels can anchor to the east of islet (165) in 18 fathoms, mud bottom.

Mosquito Harbour

Chart 3649; anchor: 49°3.05' N, 125°47.66' W

Mosquito Harbour, north of Wood Islets, affords anchorage in 6 fathoms (11 m) about 0.4 mile south of Blackberry Islets.... Approaching Mosquito Harbour from north give Plover Point a berth of about 0.3 mile then steer to pass south of Hankin Rock and north of the islets north of Dark Island. Alter course to pass west of Hankin Rock and the shoal north of it, but note the 18 foot (5.5 m) shoal off Wood Islets. After passing these dangers steer a mid-channel course.... Entering Mosquito Harbour from south vessels can pass west of Kirshaw Islets and the Wood Islets keeping midway between their west sides and the shore west of them. Note the 15 foot (4.6 m) shoal on the west side of the passage abreast the north end of the north Wood Islet. (p. 310)

Mosquito Harbour is a large natural harbor that affords good protection in most summer weather. (Because of possible chop here, Windy Bay to the south is a better choice if strong southerlies are expected.) *Sailing Directions* makes the entry appear difficult, but boats with a shallow draft will find little in the way of problems. Since the bottom of the entrance is uneven, however, your echo sounder may act like a yo-yo at times, giving you moments of consternation.

The bottom inside Mosquito Harbour is shallow and flat; there is room for many boats. The islets in Fortune Channel are fun to explore by dinghy or kayak. The shoaling cove southeast of Blackberry Islets is used as a camp site for kayakers.

One of the largest sawmills in British Columbia was built in Mosquito Harbour in 1906 by the Sutton Lumber Company of Seattle. Their 36-foot long bandsaw quickly cut nearly 6 million board feet of lumber. In one load, the sailing vessel, *Earl of Douglas*, took 4 million board feet of clear cedar around Cape Horn to New York.

Anchor in 4 fathoms on the north side of Blackberry Islets, mud bottom, with good holding and lots of room.

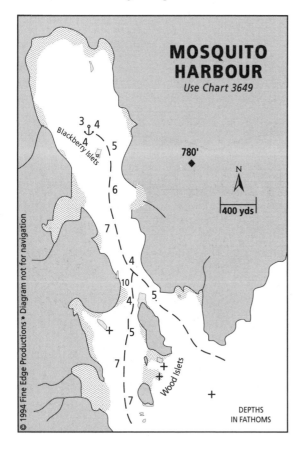

Mosquito Harbour

Heelboom Bay

Chart 3685 metric; anchor: 49°09.27' N,
125°47.73' W

> *Heelboom Bay, on the north end on the
> west side of Dawley Passage, has drying
> rocks extending from its west entrance
> point.*(p. 310)

Small and secluded,
Heelboom Bay offers
good protection in all
but northeast weather.
It's a picturesque place
worth exploring. The
name of the bay comes
from a giant log-load-
ing spar tree and heel-
boom assembly used
during the 1950s to
build log rafts and load
barges.

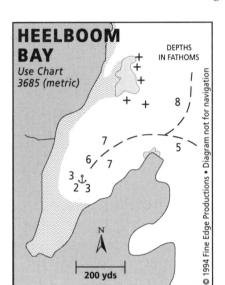

If you are entering
the bay from the north,
stay east of the bar and
rock that extend more
than halfway across the entrance. The bay
shoals rapidly, and you must be careful not to
swing into it at low tide.

Anchor in 5 fathoms. The bottom is sand,
mud and pebbles with good holding.

Dawley Passage

Chart 3685 metric; entrance: 49°09' N,
125°48' W

Dawley Passage has a flood current
(southbound) and ebb current (northbound) of
about 3 knots at spring tides. The water coming
out of Tofino Inlet splits just north of Indian
Island. Some of it goes north through Dawley Passage; the rest goes west through Tsapee
Narrows. The water passing through Dawley
takes a route to the ocean that is three times
as long.

You can safely pass on either side of Lane
Islet.

Windy Bay

Chart 3685 metric; anchor: 49°08.31' N,
125°49.00' W

> *Windy Bay...is 1 mile NW of Baxter Islet.*
> (p. 310)

Windy Bay has been under-appreciated as a
cruising anchorage. Conventional wisdom ig-
nores this beautiful place,
downplaying its cruising potential.
Tree limbs extending to the waterline, as well as a lack of driftlogs
along shore, indicate that little chop
ever develops here.

As its name implies, the bay is
subject to winds that zing across a
low pass heading east toward Fortune Channel. If you like the secure
feeling of being tethered into the
wind, tucked up against a windward
shore, and if you like to hear the
wind whistling through your rigging,
this is place!

A granite wall rises dramatically
on the north side of Windy Bay at a
45° angle to Sea Peak (1,365 ft.), one of the most
precipitous peaks along the West Coast. Beautiful old cedars grow along the creek at the
head of the bay, and crooked, windswept trees
bend and sway along rocky ledges. From inside
the bay there is nothing man-made in sight.
The view of the high sawtooth peaks through

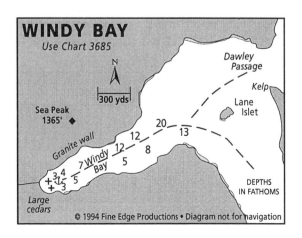

Rocky shore

the opening to the northeast is spectacular. When the wind dies and fog sets in, the Lennard Island foghorn resonates eerily inside the bay. Anchor in 4 fathoms mid-channel near the outlet to the creek. Stay outside the row of detached rocks close to shore, favoring the granite wall. The mud bottom provides good holding.

Tofino Inlet
Chart 3649

Tofino Inlet is a center for both logging and environmental interests, but because it is off the beaten path, it is seldom visited by cruising boats. Offering many well-protected and picturesque coves, the inlet may reclaim its place someday as a major scenic attraction. A healing process has begun, and already some of the logging scars are filling in.

The high, rugged peaks to the east make an imposing backdrop for this tranquil and deep inlet.

Island Cove, Gunner Inlet, "Tranquilito Cove" and the outlet of the Kennedy River offer the best anchorages.

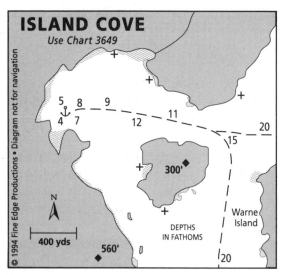

Island Cove

Chart 3649; anchor: 49°08.80' N, 125 45.80' W

> *Island Cove...provides good anchorage but its south entrance is obstructed by rocks and is not recommended.* (p. 311)

It's difficult to understand how *Sailing Directions* determined the above warning. We entered Island Cove under radar in thick fog and anchored without difficulty. The passage between Warne Island and island (300) is clear. If you favor island (300) to avoid a minor shoal, you can easily make a turn west into Island Cove, avoiding the problem of having to locate two rocks in its southern entrance.

Half a mile wide and almost entirely surrounded by land, Island Cove has steep sides and a flat bottom. It is well protected and has plenty of swinging room. Its south shore has been clear-cut, but its north and eastern sides are covered with virgin forest.

Anchor in 8 fathoms in the center of the bay, mud bottom with good holding. In southeasterly weather you can increase your protection by tucking in behind the small peninsula on the south side and anchoring in 4 fathoms.

Gunner Inlet

Chart 3649; inner basin anchor: 49°10.08' N, 125°44.45' W

> *Gunner Inlet...affords good anchorage to a small vessel in 9 fathoms...(16 m) east of the rock that dries 3 feet (0.9 m) and to the SSE of the 1 foot (0.3 m) high rock.* (p. 311)

The inner cove of Gunner Inlet offers good protection. Once heavily clear-cut to the water's edge on its northeast side, the inlet is beginning to recover.

Larger vessels can anchor according to *Sailing Directions*. Smaller vessels can carefully make their way to the head of the inlet and anchor in the shallow, more protected inner basin that has a grassy, pebble beach.

The route to the inner basin requires identifying and avoiding the rocks indicated on the chart. Start by favoring the east shore. The key aid to navigation lies on the east side midway up the inlet—a white rock that bares at 1 foot above high water. This rock defines the start of the S turn that takes you to the west side of the inlet. You'll often find yourself sharing this inlet with seals that like to bask on the rocks. Summer water temperature in the inner basin is over 67°F!

Anchor in 2 fathoms, mud bottom with good holding.

Rideout Islets

Chart 3649; position: 49°09' N, 125°43' W

Rideout Islets are a picturesque group of rocks and islets that provide shelter and interesting surroundings. Temporary anchorage for exploring the area can be found northwest of

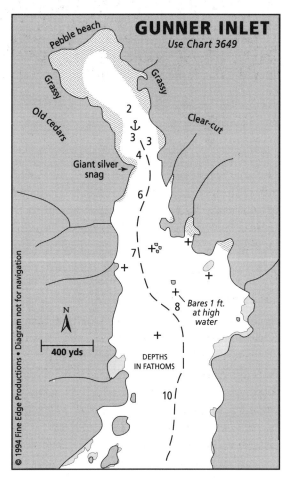

McCall Island. A marine farm is located here.

Anchor in 4 fathoms near the float house. The bottom is undetermined.

Rankin Cove

Chart 3649; entrance: 49°10.5' N, 125°42.3' W

Rankin Cove...has a booming grounds, a logging camp, A-frame, float, launching ramp and a private mooring buoy. (p. 311)

Although Rankin Cove is of moderate size and offers good protection, its busy logging operation deems it of little interest to cruising boats. It is choked with logging equipment and booms, and should be used as an emergency shelter only. Tranquil Inlet to the immediate north provides good alternative anchorage sites.

Tranquil Inlet

Chart 3649; entrance: 49°11' N, 125°41' W

Tranquil Inlet was written off in the past by cruising yachts, but the good news now is that chain saw activity has ceased and second growth is slowly taking over its shores. Calm waters have once more returned, allowing the inlet to redeem its name.

The inlet, guarded by Rankin Rocks, has several underwater rocks on its east side; it is wide and clear mid-channel.

Midway up the small inlet, two peninsulas nearly close off the fjord. Favor islet (186) as you pass over an 8-fathom shoal. One mile north there is a wonderful petite cove that makes a great cruising destination.

Entrance to "Tranquilito Cove"

"Tranquilito Cove"

Chart 3649; anchor: 49°12.23' N, 125°39.93' W

Unnamed on the charts, the spot we call Tranquilito Cove certainly delivers on the name. It provides excellent protection in all weather—even williwaws. It is almost landlocked, so chop is minimal.

The water here measured 70°F in September, making it the warmest we have found for swimming along the entire West Coast of Vancouver Island. There was no sign of red bloom or jellyfish at the time.

The edges of Tranquilito Cove are steep, and two or three small boats can find room to anchor. The north shore is a bold granite bluff where cedar grows along the ledges. The south shore has dense rain forest, and sea grass grows in the water to a depth of 1 fathom.

The southeast point, where we spotted a black bear and promptly named the point for the bear, has a shoal extending about a third of the way across its entrance.

Anchor in 4 fathoms near the center of the cove over a

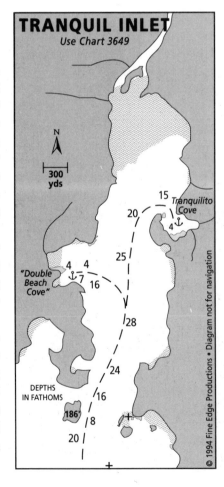

TRANQUIL INLET

Use Chart 3649

N

300 yds

15 Tranquilito Cove

20

4

25

"Double Beach Cove"

4 4

7

16

28

24

DEPTHS IN FATHOMS

16

186

8

20

© 1994 Fine Edge Productions • Diagram not for navigation

bottom of soft mud with twigs and grass. There is good holding when you set your anchor carefully. Locals warn that there may be submerged logs in the vicinity of both Tranquilito and Double Beach Cove.

If someone beats you to this paradise, consider anchoring across the bay near the west shore in what we named Double Beach Cove.

"Double Beach Cove"
Chart 3649; anchor: 49°12.02' N, 125°40.70' W

Double Beach Cove is our name for the unnamed cove on the west side of inner Tranquilito Inlet. This cove, wide and of easy access, offers good protection. We gave it this name because you can land on either of two beaches. The back of the bay, unfortunately, has been heavily logged.

Anchor in about 4 fathoms off the south beach over a somewhat uneven bottom. Holding is undetermined.

Head of Tofino Inlet
Chart 3649

As you proceed northeast, the head of Tofino Inlet becomes more alpine, and the tree-covered islets have steep, rocky edges. The upper inlet is nearly landlocked by these islets, and wind and seas seldom penetrate its upper reaches; however, the water is too deep for convenient anchoring.

Summer water temperatures continue to rise the farther in you go, sometimes reaching 70°F—even in 60 fathoms mid-channel! Barring the presence of jellyfish, you can easily treat yourself to a swim here.

"Tranquilito Cove"

Irving Cove

Irving Cove

Chart 3649; anchor: 49°11.47' N, 125°37.66' W

Irving Cove offers the best hope for protected anchoring in the upper part of Tofino Inlet. An attractive setting, the cove is filled with dark granite islets shaped like knobs and domes where stunted cedar trees miraculously find bits of earth to cling to.

The chart shows a well-protected nook 4 fathoms deep in the northeast corner of Irving Cove, as well as a deep water entrance to the inner cove. We could not verify this information under the conditions existing at the time of our visit, however.

There are many uncharted rocks below the water that defy entry without the proper angle of sunlight. The outer cove is too deep for small boat anchorage. A bald rock mid-channel has a number of cables attached to it, as if it had been used to hold stern lines at one time.

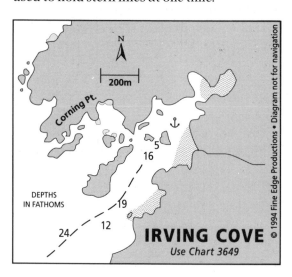

This cove looks like it could be a good base from which to explore the region. If you have any local knowledge, please share it with us.

Berryman Cove

Chart 3649; entrance: 49°09.10' N, 125°40.00' W

> *Berryman Cove...has a log loading facility with a float and an A-frame on its east side. A logging road follows the east shore north to Irving Cove.* (p. 311)

Although Berryman Cove offers shelter in southerlies, it is filled with logging operations and is of little interest to cruising boats.

Kennedy Cove ("Brewster's Bay")

Chart 3649; anchor: 49°08.74' N, 125°40.10' W

Kennedy Cove appears on Chart 3649. However, *Sailing Directions, p. 311,* say that Kennedy Cove is off the mouth of the Kennedy River, itself—the reverse of the chart. Coast Guardsmen at Tofino Search and Rescue say the chart has the correct names as far as they know. Some locals call Kennedy Cove, Brewster's Bay (after the founder of the cannery who later became a premier of B.C.); other locals call it Back Bay.

The area immediately north of the outlet of the Kennedy River is shallow. Since this is a favorite hideout for the great blue heron, you may set off quite a squawking when you enter.

Anchor in 2 fathoms at the north end of the cove, just south of a rocky point. The bottom is sand and mud bottom with good holding.

Cannery Bay

Chart 3649; anchor: 49°08.36' N, 125°40.27' W

The Kennedy River, Vancouver Island's largest, drains Kennedy Lake. A nearly landlocked bay lies directly off the outlet of the river. The south side of the bay offers good protection from all weather and is an excellent place to stay while you explore the mouth of the river.

Cannery pilings, the remains of the Kennedy River Fishing Company, can be seen on

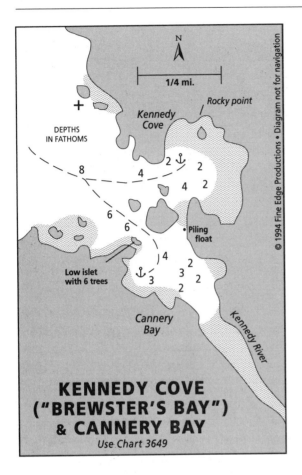

N

1/4 mi.

DEPTHS
IN FATHOMS

Kennedy
Cove

Rocky point

+

8

4

2

4

2

6

6

2

Piling
float

4

Low islet
with 6 trees

3

3
2

2

2

Cannery
Bay

Kennedy River

© 1994 Fine Edge Productions • Diagram not for navigation

**KENNEDY COVE
("BREWSTER'S BAY")
& CANNERY BAY**
Use Chart 3649

narrow and shallow, requiring you to do careful dead reckoning to keep track of your position. Many of the shoals are marked by kelp or sea grass; however, it is not wise to attempt a passage without the large-scale Chart 3685 and an alert crew.

You can choose either of two preferred routes back to Tofino. The first takes you close west of Morpheus Island, then south of Stockman Island and from there through Deadman Pass. The second takes you north toward Stone Island, then south of Arnet Island into Duffin Passage. Avoid Neil's Rock, located 400 feet northeast of the reef found on the north side of Strawberry Island. (Because the rock recently sunk a scow-load of equipment, it is now known as Neil's rock.)

A third route that uses the narrow passage between buoys "Y33" and "Y34" is not advised because so many visiting boats get into trouble in the vicinity's shifting shoals and bouldery bottoms. Since there may be an uncharted rock on the south side of the shoal off the marina west of Usatzes Point, it is advisable to hug the marina when you pass through here.

Duffin Cove

Chart 3685 metric; anchor: 49°09.08' N, 125°54.72' W

Duffin Cove, located just south of Grive Point and Tofino, is a moderately well-protected cove with little swell. It is close to town, but far enough around the corner to give you a preview of outside weather if you're planning to head out. Duffin Cove has many homes, and at night its shallow shoreline is well defined by their lights.

You can pick up one of four public mooring buoys here. When the buoys are full, you can anchor inside them in 1.5 fathoms.

From Duffin Cove, Templar Channel leads south in a gentle curve to Lennard Island, with its light, foghorn, and the open coast beyond. For local knowledge of Templar Channel, please see next chapter.

the north side of the bay. The cannery's vessel, *Kenfalls* (skippered by Capt. Harold Monks, Sr.), had a record catch of over 2500 sockeye on its initial set.

The entrance to the bay is narrow but not difficult or hazardous if you navigate carefully.

Anchor in 2 fathoms outside the line of sea grass, over a sand and gravel bottom with mixed holding.

Browning Passage

Chart 3685 metric

Browning Passage via Tsapee Narrows completes the route of your circumnavigation back through Duffin Passage to Tofino.

Tidal streams at spring tides reach 4 knots at Tsapee Narrows and 5 knots between Riley and Morpheus islands.

The fairway through Browning Passage is

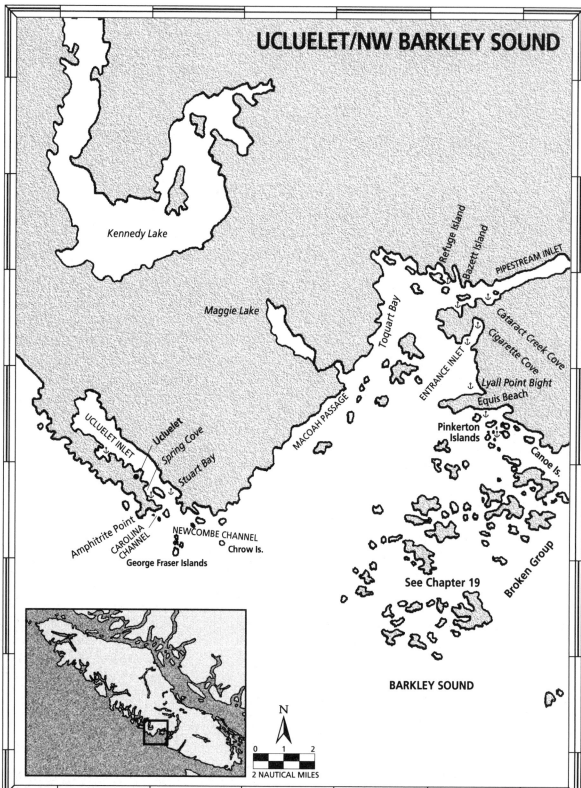

UCLUELET/NW BARKLEY SOUND

Kennedy Lake

Maggie Lake

Refuge Island

Bazett Island

PIPESTREAM INLET

Toquart Bay

Cataract Creek Cove

Cigarette Cove

ENTRANCE INLET

Lyall Point Bight

Equis Beach

Pinkerton Islands

UCLUELET INLET

Ucluelet

Spring Cove

Stuart Bay

MACOAH PASSAGE

Canoe Is.

Amphitrite Point

CAROLINA CHANNEL

NEWCOMBE CHANNEL

Chrow Is.

George Fraser Islands

See Chapter 19

Broken Group

BARKLEY SOUND

N

0 1 2

2 NAUTICAL MILES

18

Ucluelet:
Northwest Entrance to Barkley Sound

Barkley Sound, the largest and most southerly of the West Coast's five great sounds, is also the most popular for recreation. It is connected to Vancouver Island's highway system via Ucluelet on its northern edge and by Port Alberni to the east. Bamfield, on its southern border, is also connected by dirt roads. The most important connection for many individuals, however, is the ferry service provided by the 60-year-old motor vessel *Lady Rose,* which calls at the islands, coves, resorts and commercial operations, traveling between Port Alberni, Ucluelet, the Broken Group and Bamfield on a regular basis.

Ucluelet is the dominant fishing center on this part of the coast, and its well-protected inlet serves as a major refuge and outfitting center for both cruising and commercial boats. You know when you are nearing civilization because VHF radio traffic increases, AM-FM radio reception improves dramatically, and small sportfishing boats swarm like mosquitoes.

Along the northern shore of Barkley Sound there are several island groups and hidden coves that receive little attention from cruising boats. If you have adequate time, you may want to visit some of the sound's more hidden and less congested places.

When you leave Tofino and head south to Ucluelet, you need to exit Templar Channel carefully. While the passage is not difficult, it requires good piloting at both ends. In late summer, coastal fog can set in for days at a time, limiting travel to a few hours a day. If you are skilled in using radar (and GPS) you can go from Tofino to Ucluelet in near zero visibility.

Entrance to marina, Ucluelet

Some cruising boats without radar closely follow a buddy boat that is equipped with radar, but it is safer to wait until the fog lifts.

The following list of aids to navigation should help you transit Templar Channel as you leave Tofino, and Carolina Channel as you enter Ucluelet:

"Y3" buoy: 49°08.76' N, 125°55.38' W

"Y2" buoy: 49°08.01' N, 125°55.52' W

"Y1" can: 49°07.62' N' 125°55.32' W

Lennard Island Lighthouse: 49°06.64' N, 125°55.33' W

Amphitrite Point Lighthouse: 48°55.28' N, 125°32.38' W

"Y42" buoy: 48°54.72' N, 125°32.54' W

"Y43" buoy: 48°55.18' N, 125°31.67' W

"Y46" buoy: 48°55.68' N, 125°31.20' W

Templar Channel
Chart 3685 metric

> *Templar Channel, the SE channel leading into Clayoquot Sound, is entered between Lennard Island and Frank Island (49°06' N, 125°54' W); seas break across the entrance in heavy weather. Caution—Templar Channel is shallow in its north part and no vessel drawing more than 4 m (13 ft) should attempt it without local knowledge.* (p. 279)

Leaving Tofino southbound via Templar Channel, you take a curving route to the west side of the channel to avoid a 4-foot shoal located 0.6 mile southwest of Duffin Cove. Head initially to the southeast to pass close east of light buoy "Y3," south-southwest of Felice Island. From here, locate light buoy "Y2" bearing 165° magnetic at 0.75 mile. A direct line from "Y1" to "Y2" will take you over a shoal that has about 10 feet depth at zero tide. Favoring half the distance to the Wickaninnish shore, the least depth is about 22 feet.

Pass close west of buoy "Y2." Locate buoy "Y3," then bear 136° magnetic at 0.4 mile. From a position 200 yards southwest of buoy "Y2", turn southeast and pass close east of buoy "Y1"

in a least depth of 18 feet. From a point 200 yards southwest of buoy "Y1," set a course of about 140° magnetic, which takes you 0.2 mile east of Tonquin and Lennard islands, and out into the open coast.

Lennard Island
Chart 3685 metric; lighthouse: 49°06.64' N, 125°55.33' W

> *Lennard Island...lies at the south end and in the centre of the approach to both Father Charles and Templar Channels. Nob Rock and Surprise Reef, together with several drying reefs, extend NW from the island.... Lennard Island light (134), on the SE side of the island, is shown from a white tower with a red band at the top.... The fog signal consists of two blasts on a diaphone every minute.* (p. 279)

Should you leave on a foggy morning, the buoys in Templar Channel make good radar targets, and the Lennard Island light and foghorn give you good reference points.

Deep-sea dragger out of Ucluelet

Templar Channel to Amphitrite Point

Charts 3685 metric, 3640, 3603 metric, 3646 metric

The coast between the entrance to Templar Channel...and Amphitrite Point, 18 miles SE, should not be approached closer than 2 miles because of off-lying dangers. (p. 280)

Since the coast from Tofino to Ucluelet is frequently shrouded by summer fog (especially in the morning), you need to plan your passage carefully. There is no single large-scale chart showing this 18-mile stretch, so you must select a course based upon charts with the 1:150,000 scale. The main hazard is the Gowlland Rocks, both above and under water, near 49°04' N, 125°51' W. It's good strategy to pick up the 20-fathom curve south of Lennard Island, follow it to just south of Florencia Islet, then move out to pick up the 50- to 60-meter curve until you are off Ucluelet entrance. This way, you stay clear of the rocks and reefs along the shore. In foggy weather you may encounter a number of commercial and sportfishing boats that regularly ply these waters regardless of visibility.

If the weather is good as you cruise down the coast, you can see beautiful Long Beach to the east, a major landmark in the area. The 6-mile-long white beach is a favorite tourist attraction for people visiting Pacific Rim National Park. In fair weather and unrestricted visibility, you can close the coast at Schooner Cove to take a close-up look. Wickaninnish and Florencia bays are used extensively by small sportfishing boats, but both bays are generally too exposed to offer much anchoring potential for cruising boats.

Schooner Cove

Chart 3640; anchor: 49°03.93' N, 125°48.63' W

Schooner Cove, between Portland Point

Old buddies rendezvous in a secluded cove

and Box Island, affords some shelter from west winds for small craft. (p. 280)

Temporary anchorage can be taken in Schooner Cove in the lee of Portland Point during fair weather. The best entrance to Schooner Cove is south and east of islet (205).

Anchor in 2 fathoms over a white sand bottom. Holding is unknown.

Amphitrite Point

Chart 3646 metric; light: 48°55.28' N, 125°32.38' W

Amphitrite Point...the NW entrance point to Barkley Sound, is the SW extremity of Ucluth Peninsula and the site of Tofino Coast Guard radio station VAE and the Vessel Traffic Services Centre.... Amphitrite Point light (135) is shown at an elevation of 15 m (50 ft) from a white tower, 6 m (20 ft) high. It has an emergency light and a heliport. The fog signal consists of one blast on a horn every 20 seconds. (p. 281)

In foggy weather, you must approach Amphitrite Point with caution since the coast is rugged, the water is deep and the bottom is irregular. Fishing boats don't generally use their foghorns, relying instead on radar to avoid collision.

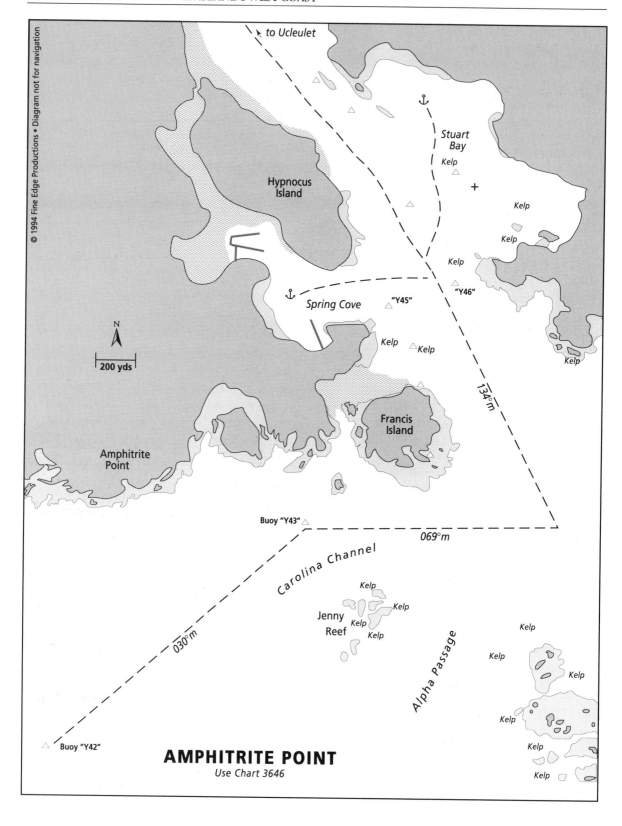

© 1994 Fine Edge Productions • Diagram not for navigation

to Ucleulet

Stuart
Bay

Hypnocus
Island

Kelp

Kelp

Kelp

Kelp

Kelp

"Y46"

N

Spring Cove

"Y45"

200 yds

Kelp

Kelp *Kelp*

134° m

Francis
Island

Amphitrite
Point

Buoy "Y43"

069° m

Carolina Channel

Kelp

Kelp

030° m

Jenny
Reef

Kelp

Kelp

Alpha Passage

Kelp

Kelp

Kelp

Kelp

Buoy "Y42"

Kelp

Kelp

Kelp

AMPHITRITE POINT
Use Chart 3646

Carolina Channel

Charts 3646 metric, 3671 metric;
entrance buoys (from *Light List*)—
bouy "Y42": 48°54.72' N, 125°32.54' W;
buoy "Y43": 48°55.18' N, 125°31.67' W;
buoy "Y46": 48°55.68' N, 125°31.20' W

Carolina Channel, close SE of Amphitrite Point, is the channel most frequently used by vessels of light draught, in calm weather, approaching Ucluelet Inlet from seaward. In bad weather, when a long swell rolls in from seaward, it becomes dangerous as several rocks and shoal patches lie in the fairway. Francis Island is joined to the SE end of Ucluth Peninsula by a drying bank.

Directions.—Enter Carolina Channel with Francis Island light structure ahead, bearing 058°, passing close north of light buoy "Y42" and close south of light buoy "Y43". When the summit of the south Beg Island bears 097°, steer for it on that bearing until the east extremity of Francis Island is abeam then round that island at a distance of 0.2 mile and enter Ucluelet Inlet. (p. 281)

Carolina Channel is the only well-marked channel into Ucluelet. The channel is small, and in foul weather waves breaking on Amphitrite Point and Jenny Reef to the east can give you white knuckles. Because Ucluelet is home to several hundred fishing boats, the entrance can sometimes be quite congested. *Sailing Directions* provides inadequate information for foggy weather when Francis and Beg islands are obscured.

We recommend the following strategy:

Follow a course to bring you dead-on to the flashing red whistle buoy, "Y42." Make a positive visual identification, then head for buoy "Y43" using a heading of 030° magnetic to take you close on the port hand to the flashing green bell-buoy, "Y43." Once again, make a positive visual identification, then take a heading of 069° magnetic for exactly 1 mile (a point off the southeast corner of Francis Island).

Round north to 134° magnetic and proceed up Ucluelet Inlet to the first starboard buoy, "Y46," and then to Ucluelet, keeping the red markers close to your starboard side.

It is imperative to make a positive visual identification of buoys "Y42" and "Y43." There may be one or more commercial fishing boats entering and exiting the channel at the same time, and since their radar images are similar to those of the buoys, careless identification could cause you to make a costly mistake.

As you approach buoy "Y43," you can hear the surf, see the foam and feel the reflected waves off the point. In addition, the Amphitrite Point foghorn is deafening, adding to any apprehension you may already feel. "Y43" is

The Canadian Princess *in Ucleulet*

placed close to shore to help you avoid dangerous Jenny Reef, 300 yards southeast of buoy "Y43." Use your foghorn frequently and proceed slowly. Although GPS gives you verification of your radar position, do not trust it to take you directly to "Y43" accuracy is not great enough in these tight quarters. When you pass an outbound fishing boat in the fog, avoid frequent changes of course and stay with a heading that gives the other boat adequate clearance.

Under adverse weather conditions, Carolina Channel should not be attempted on an ebbing tide; Felice Channel (48°54' N, 125°30' W) is the better channel for vessels

Old whaling vessel, Ucluelet
Below: Ucluelet Harbour

approaching Ucluelet Inlet from seaward. Under poor visibility consider Trevor Channel (48°50' N, 125°10' W), which is well marked with navigation aids and is not as encumbered with hazards.

Ucluelet Inlet

Chart 3646 metric

> *Ucluelet Inlet is entered between Francis Island and the Beg Islands, about 1 mile ESE. The NE shore of the inlet, for about 1 mile within the entrance, has a number of above-water, drying and sunken rocks lying off it, and the fairway in this vicinity is marked by several buoys and beacons.* (p. 281)
>
> *Anchorage can be obtained in 15 to 25 m (49 to 82 ft) about midway between the rocky area NW of Sutton Rock and Lyche Island. Small craft can obtain anchorage in Stuart Bay and Spring Cove, and*

> *in other areas where depths are suitable, taking care to avoid the above-mentioned submarine pipelines and cables.* (p. 284)

Swells quickly lose their punch as you pass Francis Island, and summer fog frequently dissipates as you move up the inlet. Although the first long public float on the west side is several blocks from town, it is a good place to tie up while you provision. The second public wharf and float is usually a bit congested with large fishing boats, and the outer float is reserved for float planes.

There are two public mooring buoys just south of Lyche Island, and an additional three mooring buoys 0.3 mile northwest of Lyche Island off the entrance to a small boat harbor. Small vessels can take anchorage between the latter three mooring buoys and the western shore, or anywhere to the north.

The boat harbor has a number of floats (fee required) close to conveniences and it is quite well protected. The *Canadian Princess*, permanently docked here, is used as a resort.

Fishing boats sometimes anchor in either Stuart or Spring coves. In stable weather they stay outside the harbor behind George Frazer Islands, where there is reportedly good anchorage as long as there is no wind or swell from the southeast or southwest.

Spring Cove

Chart 3646 metric; anchor: 48°55.64' N, 125°31.74' W

> *Spring Cove is entered south of Hyphocus Island.... The public float, in the SE corner of the cove, is 49 m (161 ft) long with a least depth of 2 m (7 ft) alongside. Several private floats and a B.C. Packers fish camp and floats are in the NW corner of the cove.* (p. 284)

Cruising boats can anchor west of the center of Spring Cove, being careful to avoid fishing boat traffic.

Anchor in 2 fathoms, mud bottom with good holding.

Stuart Bay
Chart 3646 metric; anchor: 48°56.06' N, 125°31.33' W

Stuart Bay, on the NE side of the inlet and east of Hyphocus Island, affords anchorage to small craft. Several rocks, awash and drying, lie in a chain extending SE from the NW entrance point of Stuart Bay. (p. 284)

A fairly quiet anchorage can be found inside the shoal markers of Stuart Bay (avoiding Native Rock) with plenty of swinging room.

Anchor in 2 to 3 fathoms with a gravel and mud bottom and good holding.

Port Albion
Chart 3646 metric

The Port Albion dock is condemned and landing is not advised. The area is used by sport-fishing boats.

Ucluelet
Chart 3646 metric

Ucluelet...is a village, with a population of 1,512 (1986), on the west side of Ucluelet Inlet. The principal industries are tourists, fishing and shipping logs. There are several stores, including a liquor store, a laundromat and a post office (V0R 3A0). A medical clinic is operated in conjunction with the hospital at Tofino. A local broadcast station, CBXO, transmits on a frequency of 540 kHz....The inlet is frequented by pleasure craft and numerous commercial fish boats. (p. 284)

There are generally three choices for cruising boats that visit Ucluelet: You can use either of the two public docks (near stores), pick up a buoy either side of Lyche Island, or stay inside the small boat harbor farther in on the west side. Speed limit in Ucluelet Harbour is 7 knots.

Ucluelet, like Tofino, is a full-service town

West Coast recreation takes many forms

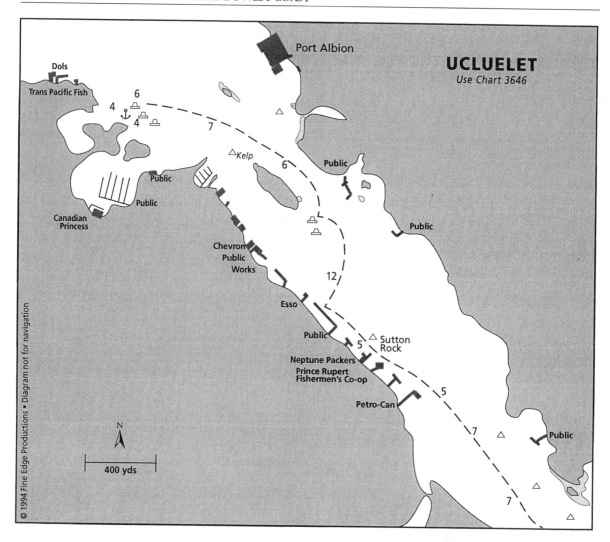

that bustles with activity in the summer. The town, which has a large fishing fleet and a number of fish buyers, seems to be more oriented to boats than Tofino, which draws more of the tourist trade.

Stores are located on the western bluff between the first and second public docks. Banks in Ucluelet are open Tuesday through Saturday (the Tofino bank is open Monday, Wednesday and Friday). Petro Canada, on the west shore, is the first big dock on entering; next to it is the Esso fuel dock. The Chevron fuel dock is just north of the second public wharf, and washers/dryers, showers, and telephones are available.

Summer public bus connections to Port Alberni run twice a day on weekdays and once a day on weekends from Murray's Grocery. Delivery service of groceries to the public dock is also available at Murray's.

A variety of fishing boats and other work boats can be seen in Ucluelet. The large fishing boats with steel "doors" at their sterns are known as draggers. The doors hold their nets open while they drag the bottom for hake and other bottom fish in depths of 200 to 300 fathoms, 20 to 30 miles offshore. When docked, these boats move their gear and lines around frequently, so give them plenty of room.

Cruising boats heading to Toquart Bay, Entrance Inlet or Pipestem Inlet usually find the easiest route is via Newcombe Channel and Macoah Passage.

Anchor in 4 fathoms west and north of the buoys that are located 0.3 mile northwest of Lyche Island. The upper bay is open anchorage with unrestricted swinging room.

Ucluelet to Bamfield

Chart 3671 metric

A sheltered small craft route from Ucluelet to Bamfield, useful in good visibility, passes north of Chrow Islands, between Great Bear Rock and Alley Rock, and across Loudoun Channel through Clarke-Benson Passage; through the Broken Group using Coaster Channel; across Imperial Eagle Channel and through Satellite Passage across Trevor Channel into Bamfield Inlet.

Happy kayaker

Newcombe Channel

Chart 3671 metric

Newcombe Channel leads from Ucluelet Inlet into Loudoun Channel NW of Chrow Islands and Sargison Bank. A rock that dries 0.3 m (1 ft) lies 0.2 mile SSW of Food Islets. The sea sometimes breaks on the NE and SW parts of Sargison Bank. (p. 281)

Because the dangerous underwater rock off Food Islets referred to in *Sailing Directions* is difficult to locate, you should head directly for the light on Chrow Islet after passing Beg Islets. When you are 200 yards off Chrow Islet light, you can turn to a heading of 022° magnetic and head for the entrance to Macoah Passage.

Macoah Passage

Chart 3670 metric

Macoah Passage, on the NW side of Barkley Sound, leads from Newcombe Channel into Toquart Bay. From Newcombe Channel it is entered west of Forbes Island. Local knowledge is required because of drying and shallow depths off the mainland shore and foul ground in the vicinity of the islands. (p. 312)

Macoah Passage, a relatively straight shot to Toquart Bay, should provide little difficulty for a cruising boat. In heavy fog, the mainland shore and offshore islands make good radar targets, and the fairway lies approximately halfway between the two targets. Keep your echo sounder running to warn you if you drift too far to either side. We use a compass heading of 016° magnetic through the passage while favoring the port-hand shore, and we follow the 8- to 10-fathom curve all the way without difficulty.

Toquart Bay

Chart 3670 metric; Snowden Island anchor: 49°01.60' N, 125°19.67' W

Toquart Bay, north of David Channel, is well sheltered and has low shores....

Anchorage can be obtained in the outer part of Toquart Bay, in 25 m (82 ft) with Hermit Islet bearing 153° and the south extremity of Snowden Island bearing 076°. Good anchorage can be obtained in 10 to 20 m (33 to 66 ft) about midway between the north extremity of Snowden Island and the islet close off the north shore, north of it. (p. 312)

Toquart Bay, with a number of log dumps and booming grounds along shore, can be a busy place. A logging road that connects to the Tofino-Port Alberni highway is a favorite put-in place for kayakers heading to the Broken Group. A popular campground and boat launching ramp are located just south of the rock breakwater at the north end of the campground.

Toquart Bay is an easy anchorage for larger vessels. Anchor anywhere (avoiding Pope Rocks) over a wide, flat, 8- to 12-fathom shoal.

Anchor in 8 fathoms on the northeast side of Snowden Island. There are smaller, shal-

lower and more scenic anchorage sites in nearby Entrance Inlet.

Pipestem Inlet
Chart 3670 metric

Pipestem Inlet, on the east side of Toquart Bay, has steep rocky shores rising abruptly to high elevations on its north side; the south side is less steep. The inlet extends 4.5 miles ENE.... Pipestem Inlet is used for commercial production and collection of oyster spat, usually in July. To avoid damage to spat collection gear, proceed with caution at a reduced speed.... Anchorage for small vessels can be obtained 0.1 mile SW of Bazett Island in 22 m (72 ft), mud. (p. 312)

Pipestem Inlet is a narrow, high-sided fjord. It is quiet and calm, but generally too deep for good small boat anchorages. There are many private floats and buoys as part of the oyster operations. Water temperature in Pipestem Inlet can reach over 70°F in the summer months.

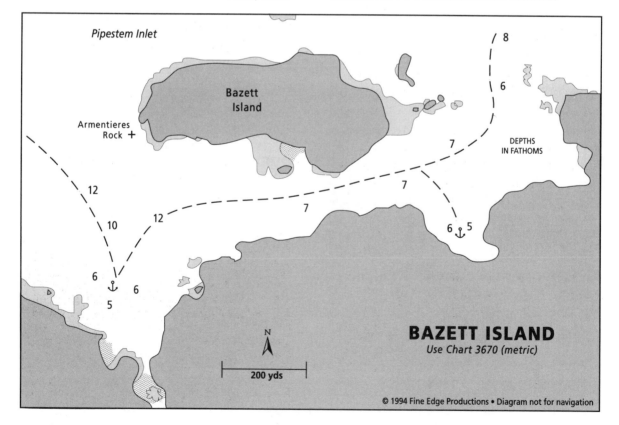

BAZETT ISLAND
Use Chart 3670 (metric)

© 1994 Fine Edge Productions • Diagram not for navigation

Refuge Island

Chart 3670 metric; anchor: 49°01.64' N, 125°18.74' W

The north side of Refuge Island provides well-sheltered anchorage for small craft, close-in. Swinging room is limited. This is a good place to explore the tidelands behind Hillier Island and Lucky Creek on the east.

Anchor in 6 fathoms over a mixed bottom, midway between Refuge Island and the two islets to the north.

Bazett Island (left)

Bazett Island

Chart 3670; anchor; 49°01.05' N, 125°17.73' W

The passage south of Bazett Island has a minimum fairway depth of about 6 fathoms and offers moderate protection. This is a temporary anchorage since afternoon westerlies can create a good chop. The bottom appears to be rocky with uneven holding. Small craft can get close to shore in a small cove on the south side to the west or a very small one to the east.

Anchor in 5 fathoms using a stern tie to shore.

"Cataract Creek Cove"

Chart 3670 metric; anchor: 49°01.18' N, 125°17.04' W

This small unnamed cove off the entrance to Cataract Creek offers moderate shelter; however, the cove is neither as flat nor as shallow as numbers on the chart indicate. Temporary anchorage can be taken in the middle of the is-

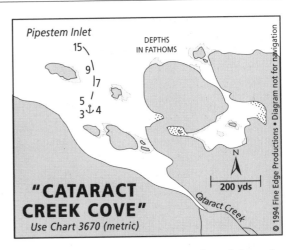

lets. Tidal flats off Cataract Creek and the saltwater lagoon to the east provide interesting possibilities for exploration. The entrance to the lagoon is quite narrow and suitable only for inflatables or sea kayaks. Local knowledge is needed before entering.

Anchor in 5 fathoms over a rock and kelp bottom with questionable holding power.

Entrance Inlet

Chart 3670 metric; anchor: 49°00.14' N, 125°17.70' W

Entrance Inlet...has a rock awash off its east shore, 0.4 mile inside its entrance. Cigarette Cove, at the head of the inlet, is reported to provide sheltered anchorage for small craft. A sport fishing resort with several float cabins is on the west side of the inlet and along the north shore of Cigarette Cove. (p. 312)

Cataract Creek Cove

Tiny, secluded Entrance Inlet offers good shelter from all winds and seas. Anchorage in the

outer cove can be taken on the western side just north of the float house and the fish farm. Avoid any cables that may be associated with the fish farm.

Anchor in 6 fathoms, mud bottom with good holding.

Cigarette Cove

Cigarette Cove

Chart 3670 metric; anchor: 49°00.44' N, 125°17.42' W

The entrance to Cigarette Cove is narrow and shallow, so keep a lookout for rocks. Don't attempt to enter using radar—the entrance is too small and intricate to be safe in conditions of poor visibility. The fairway follows the center of the passage with a minimum depth of 1 to 1.5 fathoms at its north end. A small, private red plastic float marks a starboard hand rock awash on one-third tide or less.

Although Cigarette Cove is small and extremely well sheltered, most of the bay is taken up by the fishing resort. Excellent temporary

Approaching Entrance Inlet

shelter can be found for one or two small boats in the western center of the bay. Swinging room is limited.

Although the shore is covered with lovely old-growth cedar, the noise of the resort's generator and the congestion inside Cigarette Cove make it desirable only for a passing visit or as a refuge in foul weather.

Anchor in 2 to 3 fathoms soft mud with good holding.

"Lyall Point Bight"

Chart 3670 metric; anchor: 48°58.54' N, 125°17.42' W

Lyall Point Bight is what we call the small unnamed bight 1.3 miles east northeast of Lyall

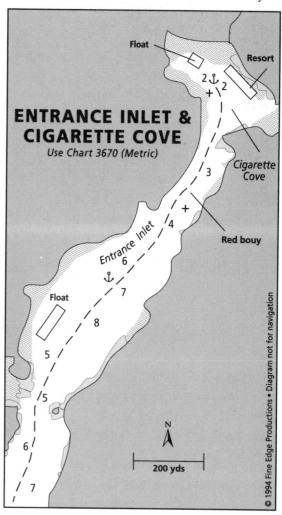

View to the south from "Pinkerton Island Cove"

Point. It offers good protection in stable weather from all but the worst west to northwest winds. It is quiet and free from most winds and seas, and you can land easily on its beaches. Sea birds seem to congregate here, and we have been delighted by the sight of a large squadron of tufted puffins.

Against the flat-looking coastline, this bight

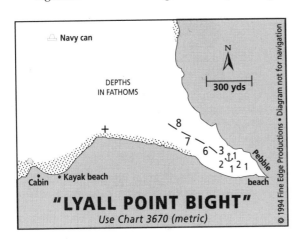

is somewhat difficult to see. To locate its entrance, identify the most southerly of two white and orange Navy tank buoys in Mayne Bay before you enter. There are no hazards, and you can enter in poor visibility. This bight provides excellent anchorage for cruising boats, free of man-made blights.

Anchor in 3 fathoms in the center channel about 100 yards off the drying flat at the head of the bay. The bottom of sand, gravel and mud has good holding.

Pinkerton Islands

Chart: 3670 metric; anchor: 48°57.56' N, 125°16.66' W

Pinkerton Islands, located on the north side of Sechart Channel adjacent to the Vancouver Island mainland, are a miniature version of the Broken Group. These islands are partially developed, being outside the park, but they do offer remoteness and some fine scenery.

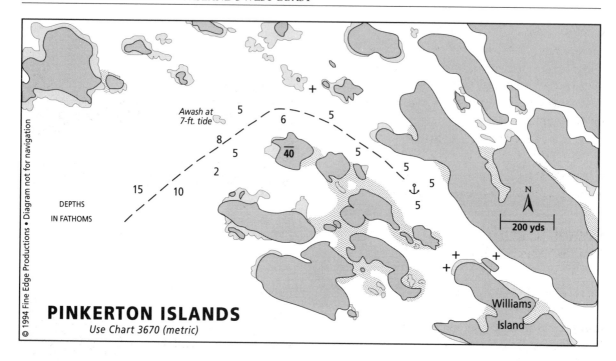

Awash at
7-ft. tide

DEPTHS
IN FATHOMS

© 1994 Fine Edge Productions • Diagram not for navigation

PINKERTON ISLANDS
Use Chart 3670 (metric)

N

200 yds

Williams
Island

A picturesque, almost bombproof anchorage can be taken in the center of the Pinkerton Islands as indicated in the diagram. If you like to take a leisurely row in your dinghy but don't want to wander too far from your boat, this is a great place to anchor. It is intimate and scenic, and the water can be a warm 65°F in summer. With little or no wind, however, bugs can be bothersome. Homesites are found on the inner beaches, out of sight to the north.

The entrance has a dangerous rock you should identify in order to avoid it. Just west of islet (40), the rock is awash on a 7-foot tide. If you enter on less that a 7-foot tide, it is easy to identify. The minimum depth in the fairway, midway between islet (40) and the rock, is 5 fathoms. If you favor islet (40) too closely, you will skirt a 2-fathom shoal.

Once you have passed the entrance rock, turn east over a flat-bottomed channel. For a view, anchor off a "window" between the islets on the south side.

Anchor in 5 fathoms mid-channel. The bottom is mud with very good holding.

Equis Beach and Sechart
Chart: 3670 metric, 3671 metric;
anchor: 48°57.89' N, 125°17.57' W

An easily entered bay offering good protection from all but strong westerlies lies off Equis Beach, just east of Sechart, a once-thriving village and whale processing plant. Black bears roam the beach, and the deserted develop-

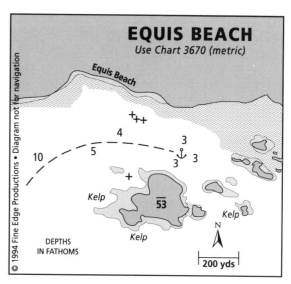

EQUIS BEACH
Use Chart 3670 (metric)

Equis Beach

DEPTHS
IN FATHOMS

Kelp

Kelp

Kelp

N

200 yds

© 1994 Fine Edge Productions • Diagram not for navigation

ments are fast fading into the brush.

Entrance from the west is straightforward. Stay off the reefs next to islet (53) and the submerged rocks near Equis Beach. The bay has a flat bottom and adequate swinging room for several boats.

Anchor in 3 fathoms on the north side of islet (53) in the center of the bay. Setting your anchor can be a little tricky—the bottom is hard sand with kelp, and holding is mediocre.

Canoe Island

Chart 3670 metric; position: 48°57' N, 125°15' W

Although for years the float located at Gibraltar Island served as the *Lady Rose's* main drop-off point for kayakers visiting the Broken Group, the float has been moved to the north side of Canoe Island, not far from the log booming grounds where the boat now stops.

Above: Pinkerton Islands inner basin
Below: Equis Beach from the south

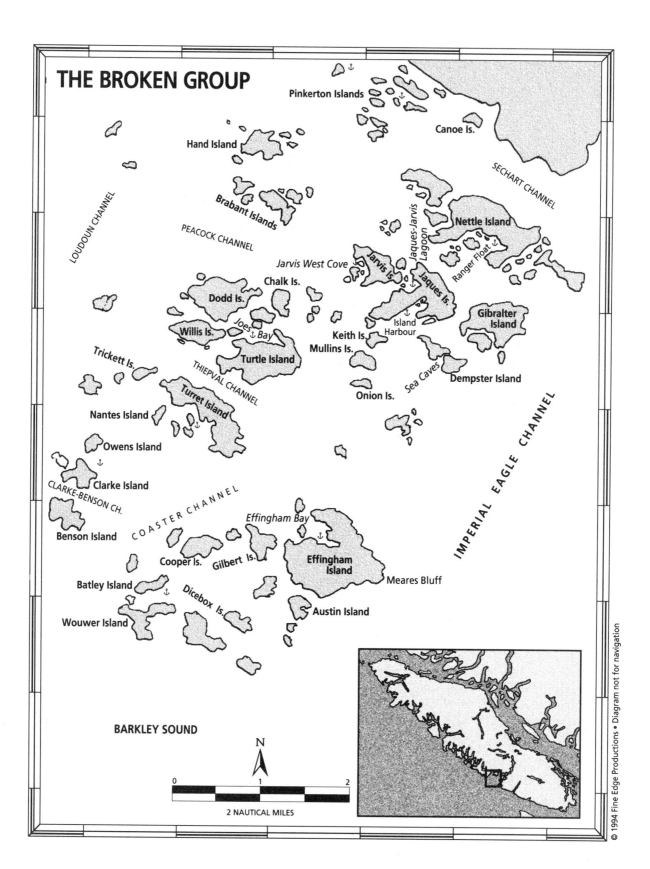

THE BROKEN GROUP

Pinkerton Islands

Canoe Is.

SECHART CHANNEL

Hand Island

LOUDOUN CHANNEL

Brabant Islands

PEACOCK CHANNEL

Jaques-Jarvis Lagoon

Nettle Island

Ranger Float

Jarvis West Cove

Jarvis Is.

Chalk Is.

Dodd Is.

Jaques Is.

Gibralter Island

Willis Is.

Joes Bay

Island Harbour

Keith Is.

Turtle Island

Mullins Is.

THIEPVAL CHANNEL

Sea Caves

Dempster Island

Trickett Is.

Turret Island

Onion Is.

Nantes Island

Owens Island

Clarke Island

CLARKE-BENSON CH.

COASTER CHANNEL

IMPERIAL EAGLE CHANNEL

Benson Island

Effingham Bay

Cooper Is.

Gilbert Is.

Effingham Island

Meares Bluff

Batley Island

Dicebox Is.

Austin Island

Wouwer Island

BARKLEY SOUND

N

0   1   2

2 NAUTICAL MILES

19

The Broken Group – Pacific Rim National Park

Barkley Sound is so large that many early sailing ships mistook it for the Juan de Fuca Strait, some to their destruction. Surrounded by open water in the middle of this sound is a cluster of islands, the Broken Group, which by their unique geometry form a small recreational paradise. The Broken Group, located within the Pacific Rim National Park, has become a mecca for sea kayakers and canoeists. Cruising yachts, as well, find these protected waters a unique and friendly maritime environment.

Archeologists think that at one time 10,000 natives lived in the greater Barkley Sound. These people, known now as the Nuu-chah-nulth, were great seamen; their habitat included every nook and cranny on the sound, including all islands of the Broken Group.

There are more than 100 culturally significant sites in the Broken Group. The list includes native village sites, kitchen middens, canoe runs, fishtraps, shipwrecks, and abandoned mines, examples that span centuries and remind us of a people whose lives and work were tied to the sea.

Needless to say, a number of sensible rules apply in this beautiful national park. Cultural artifacts and features are protected by law, and their removal or disturbance is illegal. Wildlife is protected and should not be disturbed. Camping is allowed only in designated spots, and all trash should be packed out. Take only pictures, be especially careful with fire, and respect the rights of others to a clean, quiet and primitive environment. Park officials are studying the possibility of limiting access during peak periods, and, as at Hot Springs Cove, boaters can help minimize the need for more regulations by showing sensitivity and respect for the area.

Barkley Sound is named after Captain Charles Barkley who, accompanied by his 17-year-old wife, sailed into these waters aboard the *Imperial Eagle* in 1787. (The true name of the ship was *HMS Loudoun,* but she had sailed in disguise under the Austrian flag to avoid paying taxes!) The Barkleys were the first Europeans to arrive in these islands.

Reeks Island, the Broken Group

Effingham Bay

Broken Group
Chart 3670 metric

> *The Broken Group is composed of a large number of comparatively low wooded islands, islets and rocks. Several channels lead through these islands. Sechart Channel, between Hand and Brabant islands, Coaster Channel and the channel between Clarke and Benson islands, are the only channels marked by lights. With the exception of the above-mentioned channels, together with Peacock and Thiepval channels, none of the channels should be attempted without the aid of local knowledge.* (p. 313)

While the outer reefs and islets of the Broken Group protect the inside waters, the aspects of the rugged, exposed coast are maintained and offer some excellent cruising opportunities.

A number of coves within the Broken Group have varying degrees of shelter; by moving around to different coves, a cruising boat can explore the facets of these islands close at hand. Several of the islands have comfortable picnic and camping sites, trails that lead through primitive rain forests, or sandy beaches that invite swimming. Others offer a variety of sea caves, tide pools, reefs, and sea lion colonies.

The only all-weather anchorage for cruising boats is located in Effingham Bay, which can be entered in heavy fog using radar. Although other coves, such as Jaques/Jarvis lagoon, may be more protected, entering them in poor weather is difficult and is not advised.

Effingham Bay
Chart 3670 metric; anchor: 48°52.45' N, 125°18.23' W

> *Effingham Bay, on the NW side of Effingham Island...affords sheltered anchorage with good holding ground, mud, in 14 m (46 ft). The bay is approached from Coaster Channel between Gilbert Island and a rock awash, 0.2 mile north. It is entered south of an islet lying 0.3 mile south of Raymond Island, keeping slightly to the north of mid-channel to avoid a shoal spit extending north from Effingham Island.* (p. 313)

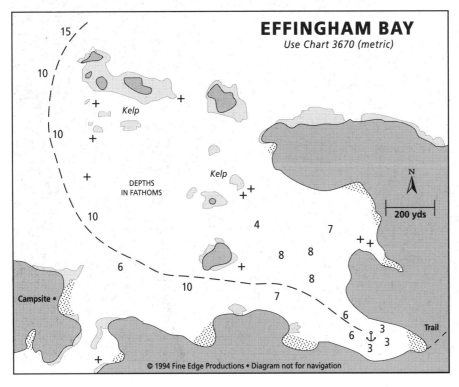

A popular anchorage, Effingham Bay, has room for quite a few boats. The bay is well protected from serious weather and is easily entered from the east through Imperial Eagle Channel or from the west by way of Clarke-Benson Passage and Coaster Channel.

Effingham Island is the only island in the Broken Group that boasts a freshwater lake. An Indian village site is on its eastern shore. A half-mile trail to the village site leads from the head of the nook and proceeds due east to the outer beach. This is an easy to moderately difficult hike that involves some crawling over fallen trees; the walk takes 20 to 30 minutes each way, and rubber boots are recommended. The rain forest on the island is a good example of old growth, and the sizes and varieties of trees are thrilling to behold. The village site can be easily identified by its cleared, flat areas and by the midden of old shells that measures 10 feet deep and over 100 yards long.

Sea cave, Effingham Island

A large sea cave is located 0.3 mile southeast of the village site towards Meares Bluff. The trail peters out well before the cave, and you have to make your way along the beach. You can enter the cave at half tide, but if you want to stay dry, you need to wait until it goes out. Maidenhair ferns grow like potted plants on the walls of the cave, and as is characteristic of many of these islands, a good collection of sculpted driftwood lies on the outer beach.

Effingham Bay is a good place to launch an inflatable boat or kayak to explore the outer islands. Take your camera—the subject matter is endless. Dice Box Island, for instance, is noted for its large sea cave, and Wouwer Island is

Leaving Effingham Bay

known for its sea lion colonies.

The most picturesque anchoring site is deep in the southeast corner of Effingham Bay where the trail for the outer beach starts. The water is fairly deep (7 to 8 fathoms), and the shore is steep-to with a 2-fathom line less than 100 feet from shore. Larger vessels can anchor anywhere in the bay over a flat bottom (except for a few rocky spots). Water temperature in summer holds at about 63°F.

Anchor in 3 fathoms close to the beach; bottom is gravel, mud, shell bottom with good holding.

Nettle Island

Chart 3670 metric; anchor: 48°55.75' N, 125°14.97' W

> *Nettle Island...Prideaux Island, Glen Islet, Reeks Island and Swale Rock form the SW side of Sechart Channel at its east end. A park ranger's float cabin is in the NE corner of a bay on the south side of Nettle Island.* (p. 313)

Nettle Island, in the northeast corner of the Broken Group, offers good protection in all weather. The eastern part of the southern bay, just north of the ranger's float cabin, is easy to enter and has plenty of swinging room for several boats. In this quiet bay you can enjoy hearing the call of visiting loons.

The park warden is frequently on patrol visiting the seven campgrounds within the Broken Group, but if you wish to contact him, you can leave a note on the bulletin board. On the move all the time, rangers keep track of park visitors and are a friendly source of information and history. Please do not tie to the ranger's float, since rangers and kayakers come and go at all hours and need this space.

Nettle Island, like Effingham Bay, is a good secure place to leave your boat while you explore the vicinity, particularly if you want to check out the lagoon between Jarvis and Jaques islands by dinghy before committing your cruising boat. The area around Swale Rock, 1.5 miles east at the junction of Imperial Eagle Channel and Sechart Channel, is known for the best sportfishing in the Broken Group.

Anchor in 3 to 6 fathoms about 100 yards north-northwest of the float. The bottom is mud with good holding. Larger vessels can anchor in the center of the bay in 8 fathoms.

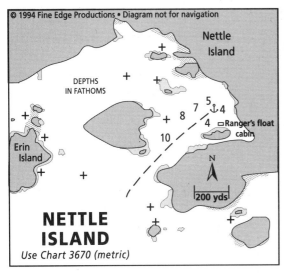

Ranger station, Nettle Island

Jaques/Jarvis Lagoon
Chart 3670 metric; anchor: 48°55.35' N, 125°16.49' W

Jaques/Jarvis Lagoon, one of the quietest anchorages you can find anywhere on Vancouver Island, looks more like a subtropical lake than part of the Pacific Ocean. Curtains of moss hang from the trees, and the water, thick with eel grass, foams along the surface. *Primeval* is the word for this lagoon—at any instant you expect to see lower forms of life emerge before your eyes.

The lagoon is a great place for bird-watchers, since many of the migrating birds that pass through the Broken Group find shelter here. Also worth exploring is a primitive stone fish trap on the west side of the lagoon where natives trapped fish after a high tide.

The lagoon affords extremely good shelter under all conditions. Entering and leaving require careful maneuvering in the right conditions, however, and we do not recommend this lagoon for all cruising boats. At high tide there are three entrances to the lagoon, but only the north entrance can be used by a cruising boat.

The fairway is quite narrow and has a minimum depth of about 3 feet at zero tide. Since it is difficult to see from any direction, most skippers quickly dismiss the idea of entering. If you are interested, reconnoiter the entrance by dinghy before you attempt such a challenge.

At adequate tide levels, small boats can en-

Jaques Island

ter safely during fair weather by proceeding at dead-slow with alert lookouts stationed on the bow. It is surprising how many 40-foot sailboats like to anchor here! If you have a deep keel boat, you should enter (and exit) on the last hour or two of a rising tide; this will allow you to lift off in case you misjudge the fairway and ground your vessel. The current through the short narrows generally runs slowly, and if you see foam drifting on the water, you can use that pattern to detect the faster and deeper channel.

The chart indicates that an underwater rock lies awash at 2 feet on the east side of the entrance, but we did not visually located it on a 6-foot tide. Many boats overcompensate by hugging the west shore and sometimes inadvertently scrape the reef that extends 15 feet or so into the water. It is best to enter on a sunny day when you can clearly see the reef and the bottom. Locate the western edge of the reef (it has a well-defined square corner) and follow it, staying a few feet to the east. The fairway has a relatively flat bottom. Once you enter the lagoon, the water becomes murky and clouded with bits

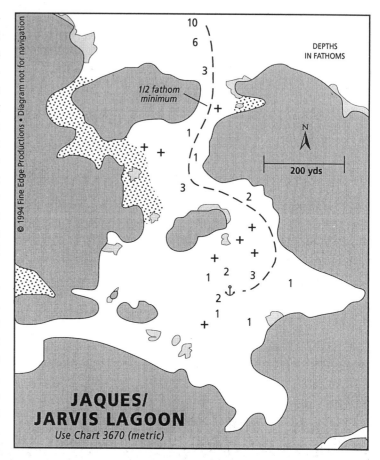

Leaving Jaques/Jarvis Lagoon

of vegetation.

As soon as you pass through the entrance, you come to a 3-fathom patch, a space too small to use for an anchorage, but large enough to allow you to turn east and hug Jaques Island's wall and reef while you pass the cluster of rocks awash just east and southeast of islet (21). Keep these rocks to starboard (some are visible underwater) and follow a right-hand semi-circular route that brings you back to a southwest heading. Several boats can anchor in the center of the bay. Totally landlocked, the lagoon has no hint of swell, seas or wind, and unless a front passes through, you need little if any swinging room.

Anchor in 2 to 3 fathoms near the center of the bay. The bottom is soft mud with good holding.

Landlocked Jaques/Jarvis Lagoon, looking north toward entrance

Island Harbour
Chart 3670 metric

> *Harbour Entrance, between Dempster Island and Gibraltar Island, is the main channel leading from Imperial Eagle Channel to Island Harbour. Eussen Rock, in the centre of the fairway, has 3 m (10 ft) over it and is steep-to.... Island Harbour can also be entered by the passage south of Dempster Island.... Island Harbour...affords well sheltered anchorage for small vessels 20 m (66 ft), about 0.2 mile NE of the east extremity of Keith Island.* (p. 314)

Island Harbour is a natural harbor that affords good shelter to larger vessels in a central and easy-to-reach location. Trading vessels no longer ply these waters, so the harbour now sees mostly kayakers coming through on a north-south passage. This is a good place to stay while you visit the sea caves of Dempster Island.

Cruising boats can find good shelter in the cove on the south side of Jaques Island at a point south of the lagoon mentioned above. A boat can anchor anywhere the water is sufficiently shallow, but the middle nook formed by the three peninsulas on the southeast corner of the island offers the best shelter from afternoon chop.

Anchor in 4 fathoms close in, avoiding the charted rock, over shell and mud bottom. Holding is undetermined.

Dempster Island
Chart 3670 metric

Dempster Island, a small, irregularly shaped island southeast of Jaques Island, has a picturesque and rugged coast. Surrounded by rocks, islets and reefs, it can be explored by dinghy in calm weather. Some of the best sea caves in the Broken Group are located on Dempster's southwest side. You can paddle a dinghy into the southernmost and largest of the caves, but beware of a surge that can surprise you even on a calm day.

Of interest on the north side of the island is a blowhole that spouts and howls when surge or swell moves through. You can hear it from quite a distance when conditions are right.

"Jarvis West Cove"
Chart 3670 metric

Jarvis Island has several islets on its west side that form a narrow cove. The cove we call Jarvis West provides good shelter and generally allows a cruising boat to be alone. The cove is typical of the Broken Group and Pinkerton Islands, a few well-placed islands and islets define a patch of calm water.

Part of the fun of exploring this area is that you can poke your nose in behind some of these islets and find a quiet place to call your own. Many of the nooks and passages between and around the islands have small, sharp rocks that rise suddenly from moderate depths, so beware!

As a fisherman in Sea Otter Cove told us, "In stable weather, you can anchor anywhere and sleep without a problem; in bad weather you won't sleep—anywhere!"

In Joes Bay, 1.5 miles southwest of "Jarvis West Cove," you can find an all-weather anchorage with plenty of room to ride out a major storm.

Joes Bay, looking east

"Joes Bay"

Chart 3670 metric;
anchor: 48°54.93' N,
125°19.43' W

Joes Bay was named after Salal Joe, an old-timer who lived at the southeast corner of the bay even after the Park was established. The larger bay, also called Joes Bay by locals, is formed by Dodd, Willis, Turtle, Walsh and Chalk islands and is the largest, flattest and shallowest anchorage in the Broken Group. You can see remnants of a stone fish trap on the shoal at the southeast corner of Dodd Island.

"JOES BAY"
Use Chart 3670 (metric)

© 1994 Fine Edge Productions • Diagram not for navigation

A cruising boat can enter only from the north or east, but the north entrance is a better choice in foul weather. Both routes contain submerged rocks, as indicated on the charts, so you need to navigate carefully.

The northeast corner of Dodd Island has a reef that extends underwater from shore at most tide levels to an estimated 150 feet. If you favor Dodd Island at this point to avoid the underwater rocks off Chalk Island, be careful not to overcompensate. We have seen bottom paint here! Exit (or enter) between Turtle and Walsh islands by staying mid-channel and avoiding the charted rocks.

The fairway between the two islands has a minimum depth of 3 to 4 fathoms and should not be a problem. Be aware, however, of another reef that extends about 150 feet from Dodd Island towards Walsh Island.

The entire inner bay has a flat bottom. You can anchor on the north side of Turtle Island before you reach the 8-fathom hole or even closer in toward Joes Bay (see chart) if a southeaster is expected. In a blow you have plenty of room to put out scope with a high ratio of rode to depth. The wind may pass through the opening between the islands, but fetch is small and little in the way of seas build up.

Anchor in 4 to 5 fathoms over a mud bottom with good holding.

Turret Island

Chart 3670 metric; anchor: 48°53.96' N, 125°20.74' W

The islands south of Turret Island are part of what is called the Outer Broken Group, where remnants of Pacific swell may be felt, wind blows with greater strength, and the trees take on a more rugged appearance.

Nearly landlocked, this bay has very little fetch and provides a snug retreat. Just a short

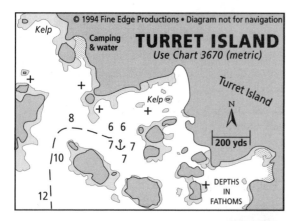

© 1994 Fine Edge Productions • Diagram not for navigation

TURRET ISLAND
Use Chart 3670 (metric)

Kelp

Camping & water

Turret Island

Kelp

Kelp

N

200 yds

8

6 6

7 ⚓ 7

7

10

12

DEPTHS IN FATHOMS

Turret Island cove

dinghy ride from the Turret Island campsite takes you out of sight of the anchorage and around the corner. The reefs and tide pools of the nearby islets offer great exploring.

The islets west of Trickett Island are connected by a large sandbar and are fun to beach comb. Try not to get caught in your dinghy on the north side of the bar at high tide; it's a long row back around to the south side!

Some cruising boats anchor temporarily in front of the Turret Island campsite; however, the cove is quite small, and there is a dangerous rock awash in its center as well as another on its west side. If you wish to be closer to the outside, consider temporary anchorage off the Clarke Island campsite.

Among the islets off the southwest side of Turret Island, east of Nantes Island, there is a well-sheltered anchorage that makes a good

base for exploring the Outer Group. The water is fairly deep (like Effingham Bay), and the best anchorage is on the northeast side of islet (36) in the center of the bay.

Anchor in 7 fathoms over a mixed bottom that is mostly soft mud. You need a soft touch when you set your anchor, but once you set it, holding is good.

Clarke Island

Chart 3670 metric; anchor: 48°53.57' N, 125°22.33' W

Clarke Island and its neighbor, Benson Island, are destinations of choice for kayakers wanting to experience the outside environment. The eastern shores are in the lee of prevailing northwesterlies, but a short walk to windward gives the full view of Pacific swells beating on offlying reefs and rocks.

There is a log structure ashore. Water is sometimes available, and several trails make for good short hikes. In early morning hours you can often see deer searching the white sand beach for food.

Temporary anchorage in stable fair weather can be taken off Clarke Island campsite. Stay about 200 yards offshore to avoid the shoal and several submerged rocks.

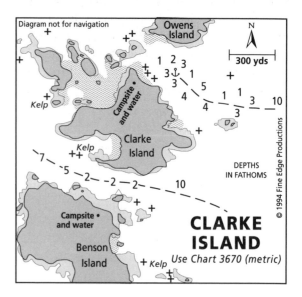

Diagram not for navigation

Owens Island

N

300 yds

1 2 3

3 ⚓ 1

3 1

5

4 1 1 3 10

4 3

Campsite & water

Kelp

Kelp

Clarke Island

DEPTHS IN FATHOMS

7

5

2 — 2 — 2 —

10

Campsite & water

Benson Island

Kelp

CLARKE ISLAND
Use Chart 3670 (metric)

© 1994 Fine Edge Productions

Anchor in 3 fathoms, avoiding the shoals, over a mud-sand bottom with good holding.

Clarke-Benson Passage
Chart 3670 metric; light: 48°53.161' N, 125°22.643' W

The only navigation light on the western edge of the Broken Group is located on an islet off the northeast corner of Benson Island. While this may strike you as an odd place for a navigation light, it marks a strategic passage between Clarke and Benson islands. Although it looks somewhat hazardous, it is on the direct, more comfortable route for small craft crossing from Ucluelet to Bamfield. It is also the shortest way to enter the Broken Group from the north coast.

The passage is rather narrow and shallow, but the route is straight and the bottom is flat with 2 fathoms minimum in the fairway. Using this passage is a case of passing through known and visible hazards, rather than guessing where unmarked rocks might be located.

Benson Island
Chart 3670 metric

Benson Island campsite lies immediately behind the navigation light. The passage between the light and the island is too small and rolly for an anchorage, but some cruising boats find temporary anchorage in the small east-facing cove on Benson Island, 300 yards south-southeast of the navigation light. This spot has more protection than it first appears, but gusty westerlies sometimes curl around in the reverse direction and require a second anchor or a line ashore. I feel it is too exposed for anything but a short lunch stop and do not recommended it. The island is worth exploring, but I prefer to anchor elsewhere and visit it by kayak or motorized dinghy.

Outer Islands
Chart 3670 metric

The islands between Benson and Effingham islands offer some of the finest exploring in the group. No overnight camping is allowed south of Gilbert Island, and only the intrepid poke their noses in this part of the park. Verbeke Reef makes a good resting and observation spot for kayakers. The islet off the west end of Batley Island is a haul-out place from late summer to spring for a large group of sea lions. Wouver Island has two picturesque beaches with picnic sites along its thinnest point. Dice Box Island has two sea caves on its south side. Explore, and you will find your own favorite spots.

While temporary anchorage can be found in stable conditions at a number of places along the outer islands (such as the small coves just east of the shoal between Wouwer and Batley islands), you will gain greater peace of mind if you make your home base in one of the more secure inside coves and visit these outer reaches by motorized dinghy or sea kayak.

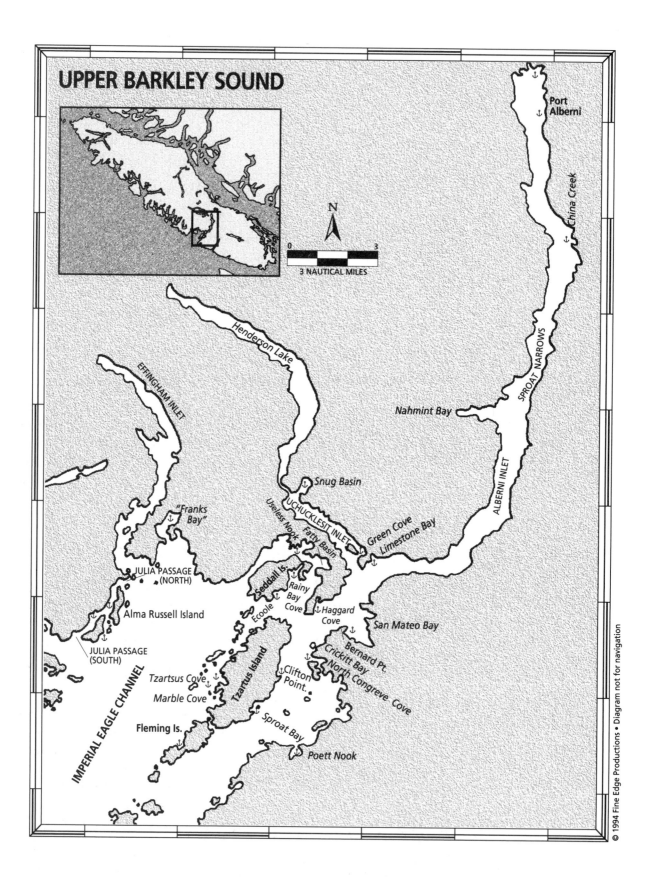

UPPER BARKLEY SOUND

N

0   3

3 NAUTICAL MILES

Port Alberni

China Creek

SPROAT NARROWS

Henderson Lake

EFFINGHAM INLET

Nahmint Bay

ALBERNI INLET

Snug Basin

UCHUCKLESIT INLET

"Franks Bay"

Useless Nook

Fatty Basin

Green Cove

Limestone Bay

JULIA PASSAGE (NORTH)

Seddall Is.

Rainy Bay Cove

Haggard Cove

San Mateo Bay

Alma Russell Island

Ecoole

JULIA PASSAGE (SOUTH)

Bernard Pt.

Crickitt Bay

North Congreve Cove

IMPERIAL EAGLE CHANNEL

Tzartsus Cove

Tzartus Island

Clifton Point.

Marble Cove

Fleming Is.

Sproat Bay

Poett Nook

20

Upper Barkley Sound

The northeast corner of Barkley Sound, known for its excellent sportfishing, has a number of inlets and islands where cruising boats can find secluded anchorages. This area receives far less fog than the outside coast and is a good alternative if coastal fog hangs on for a long stretch. The region also receives very little swell or chop unless heavy storms occur.

Alberni Inlet, which nearly cuts Vancouver Island in half, is a classic, steep-sided fjord, and Port Alberni at its head is a large industrial town with many comforts and conveniences. The highway to Port Alberni gives easy access for trailerable sportfishing boats to several parts of Barkley Sound and Alberni Inlet.

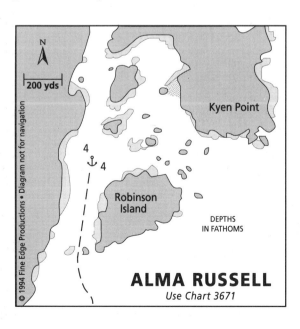

Imperial Eagle Channel
Chart 3671 metric

> *Imperial Eagle Channel is bounded on its SE side by the Deer Group and on its NW side by the Broken Group and a short stretch of Vancouver Island. During south or SW gales, there is a very heavy sea in this channel.*(p. 314)

Imperial Eagle Channel provides access to Upper Barkley Sound. Because of several miles of wide, open fetch, the upper reaches of the channel can generate a good swell or surge from just moderate southerly winds, as well as the gales mentioned in S*ailing Directions*.

Alma Russell Islands
Chart 3671 metric; anchor: 48°57.09' N, 125°12.23' W

A moderately protected and scenic anchorage can be taken inside the bay formed by the two large Alma Russell Islands and small Robinson Island on the south. This anchorage is convenient to good fishing grounds in the area around Swale Rock, but swell develops in strong southwesterlies.

From a distance, the entrance between Robinson Island and the western Alma Russell Island appears to be wide and of easy access. Two submerged rocks, however, make safe entry dependent on tide levels or visibility.

Chart 3671 indicates that the deepest entrance is between two small rocks guarding the bay; the western rock bares on 1-foot tide, the eastern rock at 8 feet. Although we entered on an 8-foot tide, light conditions were such that we were unable to locate these rocks. If you want to give this bay a try, we recommend that you enter at low water when you can see the hazards.

Anchor in 4 fathoms in the middle of the bay. There is plenty of swinging room.

Julia Passage
Chart 3670 metric, 3668 metric; anchor:
48°57.52' N, 125°12.77' W

North entrance, Julia Passage

> *Julia Passage, NW of Alma Russell Islands, offers sheltered anchorage for small craft; local knowledge is required. The north and south entrances to Julia Passage are encumbered with rocks. Float houses are moored along both shores.* (p. 315)

Although its north and south entrances are quite demanding, once you enter Julia Passage, you'll find it has a charm of its own. Its shores are lined with moss-strewn trees; its waters are rich with nutrients that draw animals, birds and sea life. Except for the occasional hum of a motor, absolute calm and quiet reign.

During summer months, a dozen or so float homes scattered about the basin are occupied by friendly, helpful residents who watch over everything with tender loving care and whose stories can keep you entertained for hours. Please help maintain the peaceful setting by observing a no-wake speed limit inside the passage. A great experience for a cruising yacht, Julia Passage epitomizes remote and secluded.

Sportfishing boats coming from the Toquart Bay launching ramp and campground on the way to Effingham Inlet use Julia Passage as a shortcut.

If you are entering from Imperial Eagle Channel, the north entrance—known locally as Canoe Pass—is difficult to see until you are directly upon it. Continue to head west from Harold Islet, and when you are nearly against the shore, the pass opens up. Boats with high masts, antennae or broad high beams may have a problem with the tree limbs. Reconnoitering by dinghy in advance is useful. We had clearance for our 24-foot-high antenna.

The fairway in Canoe Pass is 20 feet wide with a depth of about 4 feet at zero tide. The bottom is gravel and seems to be free of obstructions. You should plan to transit at or near high water slack. Do not attempt to enter in foul weather or limited visibility. Least

Float house, Julia Passage

depth for the entire passage is found in the narrows at the extreme north end. Proceed at dead slow, just maintaining steerage, with a midcourse between the rocks on either side. It's a good idea to have a pole ready to fend off from shore. You'll find no swell or seas here, but a moderate current may flow at times.

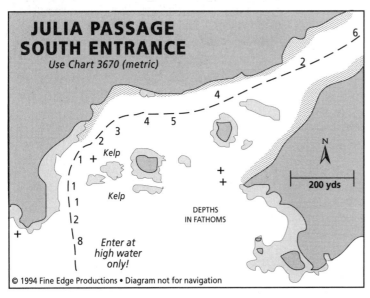

The south entrance is a maze of rocks, both above and below water, which makes precise navigation difficult. Be sure to enter at high water slack when there is good underwater visibility. Do not enter in foul weather. The current at the southern entrance is not strong, but space for maneuvering is quite limited. Small sportfishing boats generally follow close to the west shore or within 50 feet of the eastern shore when they enter and exit.

We found the best route to be the one indicated on the diagram. Stay far west, against the outer edge of a square-shouldered reef that extends from the rocky mainland shore. Ease in slowly on the west side of the mid-channel rocks, where the bottom quickly rises to 2 fathoms. When you are directly west of the two charted rocks, depth is 4 to 6 feet at zero tide. The westernmost charted rock is tooth-shaped and bares about 6 inches on an 8-foot tide.

Kelp on the mid-channel rocks, along the shore reef, and occasionally in the fairway itself helps identify the hazards. The fairway bottom is flat for the most part, but the kelp may trick your echo sounder into believing it is reading the bottom. This can give you a fright when it suddenly indicates 2 feet! After you pass all mid-channel rocks on your starboard and the depth drops to 4 fathoms or more, stay mid-channel until you are in the main basin.

Anchorage, free of all seas and most winds, can be taken at the north end of the main basin, on the northwest side of the first Alma Russell Island. There is also room for a small boat to anchor off the shoal between the two Alma Russell Islands.

Anchor in 3 fathoms off to the side of the fairway at the north end of the main basin, with a soft mud bottom and very good holding.

"Franks Bay" ("Jane Bay")

Chart 3671 metric, 3668 metric; anchor South Cove: 49°00.25' N, 125°08.77' W

Franks Bay, a well-protected anchorage, can be found in the nearly landlocked basin behind Jane Island at the head of Vernon Bay. The *Small Craft Guide,* Vol. 1, says this bay is known locally as Jane Bay.

The waters of the wooded basin are smooth and quiet, but with the exception of its eastern or northern shore, it is too deep for convenient anchorage.

Effingham Lodge, located just inside its entrance on the eastern spit, was planned as a first-class fishing resort. The lodge was never finished and at present remains closed under caretaker's protection. Just east of Effingham Lodge in a small cove an old float shed is designated "Barkley Hilton Float House." You can anchor near the float.

On the far north side of the basin, 200 yards west of the creek outlet, a plaque mounted on a rock outcropping reads:

> Frank's Bay Memorial Marker
> Frank W. Provencal
> Forever in our hearts
> Here in Frank's Bay 1929 to 1984

A hundred yards east of the memorial, you can take temporary anchorage off the grassy meadow in the alluvial fan that was made by the creek.

In southerly weather, the upper Imperial Eagle Channel can develop quite a sea or swell; Jane Island at the entrance to Franks Bay knocks down the chop. The entrance is moderately narrow, but it is quite deep and of little difficulty to small vessels.

South Cove: Anchor in 7 fathoms over mixed bottom in which it is somewhat difficult to set the anchor. Closer in to shore with a stern

Effingham Lodge, Franks Bay

line may be a better option.

North Bay: Anchor in 4 fathoms over a mud and pebble bottom with good holding. To restrict swinging, a second anchor is useful.

Useless Inlet

Charts 3671 metric, 3668 metric; 3646 metric (inset); "Useless Bay" anchor: 48°59.45' N, 125°02.12' W; "Useless Nook" anchor: 48°59.18' N, 125°01.75' W

Useless Inlet, 3 miles ESE from Palmer Point, separates Seddall Island from the mainland; it is accessible only to small craft because its entrance is foul. (p. 315)

Useless Inlet, at the northwest corner of Imperial Eagle Channel, has rather unusual topography. Its entrance is encumbered with above- and below-water rocks that break the seas but make entering difficult. The upper reaches are shallow and about as remote as you can get and still be on saltwater.

Until small-powered vessels entered Useless Inlet, only native canoes ventured within. But nowadays modern cruising yachts can find calm and tranquillity here in this deep, dark inlet.

The entrance reefs off the Seddall Island shore can be hazardous in a heavy southwesterly swell. Heavy kelp on the entrance shoal breaks the seas and swell, but there can be a surge through the narrows that makes navigation diffi-

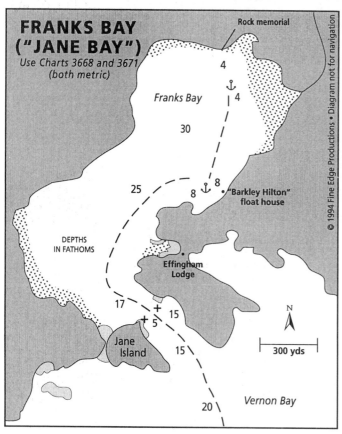

cult. In stormy conditions, the cove in Rainy Bay offers a far safer entrance.

The entrance to Useless Inlet along the far western shore follows an S-shaped course. The key is to favor the west shore and pass on your starboard side all entrance rocks and islets extending from Seddall Island except for the islet close to the western mainland shore. Head slowly for this westernmost islet until you are close aboard. Once you are northwest of the islets, reefs and kelp patches along Seddall Island, a clear channel opens up to the east. Take a jog east around the west islet before you resume a mid-channel course.

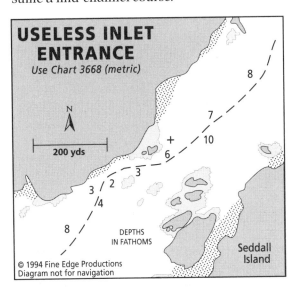

The water in Useless Inlet is warm, and experimental marine farming occurs here. Except for this activity and some logging scars, the inlet is pristine and provides a great exploration opportunity for modern cruising boats.

In the far reaches, where a nook communicates with Fatty Basin by dinghy channel, there is no hint of outside weather. Moisture collects on tree limbs and drips into the perfectly calm inside waters while gales still blow across outside waters.

The narrows into Fatty Basin which has depths of about 1 foot at zero tide is nearly blocked by a small island. On the south side of this unnamed island a dinghy route leads into Fatty Basin. A sign on the shore of the island reads: *No passage for boats beyond this point. Low overhanging cables.* The dinghy passage is full of kelp, and the current is said to reach 4 knots maximum on springs. A second small outlet from Fatty Basin feeds directly into Rainy Bay. Its entrance dries at a tide level of 11 feet. A logging bridge with 13 feet of clearance crosses it. The area around Fatty Basin has been extensively logged.

The Useless Bay anchorage (see inset in Chart 3646 metric) is useful for larger cruising vessels or small boats that don't want the claustrophobia of the inside nook. Caution: The upper part of the bay shoals rapidly.

Useless Nook (see inset in Chart 3646 metric) is located just west of the narrows leading into Fatty Basin. This nook has a small but secure anchorage off to the north side, out of the

Looking into Fatty Basin from "Useless Nook"

current next to an oyster float. This tiny, intimate nook is as secluded as Holmes Inlet Nook in Sydney Inlet.

Useless Bay: Anchor in 4 fathoms over a mixed mud bottom with good holding.

Useless Nook: Anchor in 3 fathoms in a bottom of mud and decaying matter with good holding.

Entrance rocks, Useless Inlet

"Rainy Bay Cove"

vailing chop. Consider it for a lunch stop, but do not leave your boat without a lookout on board.

Anchor in about 3 fathoms mid-channel off the rusting tanks. The bottom is hard, a mixture perhaps of gravel and rocks, and it did not pass our holding test.

Ecoole

Charts 3670 metric, 3668 metric; anchor: 48°58.03' N, 125°03.41' W

> *Ecoole is in a small bay on the SE side of Seddall Island, close within the entrance to Rainy Bay. The wharf and buildings at Ecoole are in ruins (1988).* (p. 315)

Ecoole, a small cove on the south side of Seddall Island, was a major trading post for many years. Now the buildings and tanks are in a state of decay for the most part, and civilization has moved on. The cove is useful only as a stop to fish or rest. An old sign on shore warns: *Danger, no trespassing. Trespassers will be prosecuted.*

Just a shallow, tiny cove, Ecoole offers surprising shelter from pre-

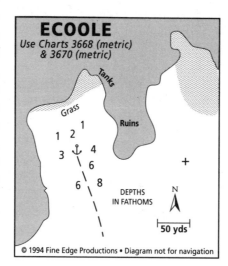

ECOOLE
Use Charts 3668 (metric) & 3670 (metric)

Tanks

Grass

Ruins

1
1 2
3 ⚓ 4
6
6 8

DEPTHS
IN FATHOMS

N

50 yds

© 1994 Fine Edge Productions • Diagram not for navigation

"Rainy Bay Cove"

Charts 3670 metric, 3668 metric; anchor: 48°58.95' N, 125°02.02' W

> *Rainy Bay lies on the north side of Junction Passage. Numerous float cabins of a sport fishing lodge are in the narrow inlet 0.5 mile north of Boyson Islands. A house is on the east shore of Rainy Bay, east of Boyson Islands. Marine farm facilities are in the small bay 0.5 mile NW of Boyson Islands.* (p. 315)

This small cove, deep in the northwest corner of Rainy Bay, has become a popular sportfishing center serving the Junction Passage area. About 14 floats with houses and cabins are located along the western shore. There is little chop here, even in moderate southerlies. The cove, surrounded by trees on all sides, is a pleasant but busy place to stay. Fishermen will give you the scoop on the extraordinary fishing in the vicinity.

Caution: The inner nook shoals rapidly and may have less depth than the chart indicates. A sign on the west entrance shore reads, *Marine watch—all items have been marked. Slow.*

In normal conditions the best anchorage is at the north end of the cove to the west of the shoaling nook. In a strong southwesterly, try anchoring in the lee of the float houses or just inside the western bight near the entrance, avoiding two rocks close to shore.

Anchor in 5 fathoms over a mud bottom with good holding.

Alberni Inlet

Chart 3668 metric; entrance: 48°57' N, 125°01' W

> *Alberni Inlet, a continuation of Trevor Channel, is entered between Chup Point and Mutine Point. The shores on either side are rocky and rugged, rising abruptly from the water's edge to the summits of mountains. At the head of the inlet, in the vicinity of Port Alberni, the land is low and fertile.* (p. 319)

Alberni Inlet is a deep fjord that cuts 40 miles into Vancouver Island from Cape Beale. In 1964 a large tsunami caused by the Anchorage, Alaska, earthquake hit Port Alberni and caused considerable damage. The wave, which hit at night, is said to have had a trough that crested at 8 meters, topping the dikes of the port and flooding part of the city.

The many resorts, fish farms and logging facilities throughout the inlet and Barkley Sound are serviced by the *M.S. Lady Rose,* headquartered at the new Port Alberni Quay. Sea kayakers frequently use the *M.S. Lady Rose* to access the Broken Group from Port Alberni.

Port Alberni is a friendly city of 25,000 people. It offers full services and has several marinas for small craft, as well as large docks and wharves that serve local industries. There are frequent and convenient connections to the East Coast of Vancouver Island.

Marinas for pleasure craft at China Creek, 6 miles south of town, offer most amenities, including fuel, showers and

RAINY BAY & USELESS NOOK
Use Chart 3668 (metric)
DEPTHS IN FATHOMS
© 1994 Fine Edge Productions • Diagram not for navigation

washrooms; China Creek Provincial Park next to the marina has campsites, concessions and a commissary.

Fisherman's Harbour, in the basin close south of Somass Sawmill and just north of Port Alberni Quay (at the foot of Argyle Street), is used extensively by fishing boats and has a floating breakwater. It is close to the downtown commercial area.

The quay houses the offices for *M.S. Lady Rose* as well as the facilities for the Harbour Master, RCMP, fireboat and Fisheries patrol boat. It also contains a number of attractive restaurants and boutiques.

Port Alberni Marina (Clutesi Haven), located on the Somass River 1.5 miles up from town, is popular with both sportfishing as well as cruising boats, and it is close to shopping areas. It has modern amenities and a boat launching ramp. Minimum water depth in the narrow fairway is about 1 to 1.5 fathoms with an overhead cable clearance of 31 meters (see inset on Chart 3668 metric).

Port Alberni Yacht Club at Robbers Passage

Haggard Cove

Chart 3668 metric; entrance: 48°57.75' N, 125°01.43' W

Haggard Cove has cabins of a sport fishing resort around its shore and a wharf with three finger floats which are protected by a rock breakwater across the entrance. (p. 320)

Haggard Cove is a small enclosed bay less than a mile north of Chup Point. The marina located in the cove is a popular sportfishing resort. A substantial rock breakwater offers good protection for small craft during stormy weather.

San Mateo Bay

Chart 3668 metric; Bernard Point float: 48°56.77' N, 125°00.14' W

San Mateo Bay is mainly deep but anchorage for small vessels can be obtained close offshore and at the head of the bay, between Banton Island and the coast south of it, in 26 to 33 m (14 or 18 fm). Care should be taken to avoid the fish pens in this area.... A public float, on the south side of Bernard Point, is not connected to shore and has a depth of 11 m (36 ft) alongside and 46 m (150 ft) of berthing space; it provides sheltered mooring. (p. 320)

San Mateo Bay is no longer one of the most beautiful bays in Barkley Sound. The east side of the bay is filled with fish farms, and the high ridges behind the bay were clear-cut and left with ugly scars. Ritherdon Bay, in the northeast corner of San Mateo Bay, is full of pilings and log booms and is too deep for anchoring.

Bernard Point, a provincial recreation area, has a small detached public float anchored just off its south side; it is available to recreational powerboats and sailboats only. Its location offers good shelter to cruising boats in the area, and it makes a good lunch stop that gives you a chance to stretch your legs on shore. Bernard Point has picturesque rock knolls along its eastern shore. Anchor in 6 fathoms west of the float; the bottom is undermined.

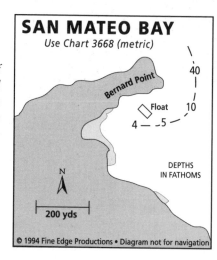

SAN MATEO BAY
Use Chart 3668 (metric)

Bernard Point

40

◇ Float   10

4 — 5 —

N

DEPTHS IN FATHOMS

200 yds

© 1994 Fine Edge Productions • Diagram not for navigation

Champagne on a sunny afternoon

Float, San Mateo Bay

Limestone Bay

Chart 3668 metric, 646 metric (inset);
anchor: 48°59.12' N, 124°58.33' W

*Limestone Bay, to the north of and shel-
tered by Limestone Islet, offers shelter and
anchorage to small craft, especially from
winds blowing down the channel. A public
float, with a depth of 7 m (23 ft) alongside, is
not connected to shore.* (p. 320)

Limestone Bay provides excellent protection
when northerlies whistle down Alberni Inlet.
The bay is easy to enter, and Limestone Islet
has a navigation light on its south side. On entering, keep the quick flashing white light to

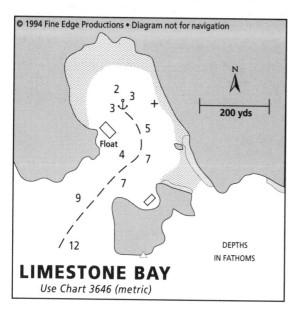

© 1994 Fine Edge Productions • Diagram not for navigation

N

200 yds

Float

DEPTHS
IN FATHOMS

LIMESTONE BAY
Use Chart 3646 (metric)

starboard. A low spit connects the islet to the
mainland. The deep water of Alberni Inlet
quickly shoals to good anchoring depths on the
west side of the islet.

This bay does not afford good protection
from southwesterlies.

The float on the south side of the bay is very
small and is used mainly by sportfishing boats.
It is protected by a log boom breakwater on its
east side, and there is a cabin on shore. A float
house is anchored in a nook in the islet's west
shore. The bay shoals at its head and is full of
eel grass.

Anchor in 3 fathoms at the head of the bay
over muddy, sandy bottom with some sea
grass. Holding is good.

Uchucklesit Inlet

Chart 3646 (inset); entrance: 48°59' N,
125°00' W

*Uchucklesit Inlet, a branch of Alberni Inlet,
is entered between Burrough Point and
Brooksby Point.... Caution.— Numerous
float houses, marine farm facilities and
close to the surface installations are
moored in Uchucklesit Inlet. Mariners
should modify their speed and proceed
with caution because these installation are
vulnerable.* (p. 320)

Uchucklesit Inlet is undergoing development
and offers little interest for the cruising boat.
Green Cove, once a storm refuge, is now a commercial operation. Snug Basin, at the far northwest corner of the inlet, offers all-weather protection and is a good place to wait out a storm.

Green Cove

Chart 3646 metric (inset);
position: 49°59.33' N, 125°58.86' W

*Green Cove, east of Cheeyah Island, affords
well sheltered anchorage in 10 to 20 m (33
to 66 ft), mud and sand bottom. A barge grid
is on the NE side of the cove.* (p. 320)

You can no longer anchor in Green Cove; it is entirely filled with a new log booming operation. In an emergency it might be possible to get protection by tying directly to the log breakwater.

Kildonan, 1.5 miles northwest of Green Cove, is being transformed into an attractive resort complex. Located just west of a picturesque waterfall, it has modern floats, sportfishing boats and kayaks. In addition, many fine homes are being built in its vicinity.

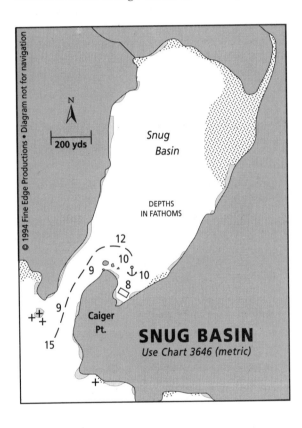

Snug Basin

Chart 3646 metric (inset);
anchor: 49°01.20' N, 125°01.72' W

Snug Basin, on the north side of the head of Uchucklesit Inlet, offers secure anchorage for small craft, mud bottom. Caiger Point has booming grounds, a float and dry land sorting area on its south side; the west entrance point has several houses and a float. (pp. 320-32l)

Snug Basin is a well enough protected anchorage to ride out even the most vigorous storm. It is not a usual cruising destination because of its deep water and nearby development.

The entrance is straightforward and can be easily entered in bad weather. A radar approach can be made with due attention to the booming operation on the south side of Caiger Point and to the rocks south of the west shore.

The entire basin has a flat bottom, and larger boats or those that want unlimited swinging room can anchor farther north, near mid-bay. The surrounding mountains are high, and the fetch is small.

Avoid a below-water rock 20 yards east of the islet on the north side of the peninsula. The mountains have been logged here, but second growth is coming back. Surface water temperatures in the summer remain in the mid-sixties—good for swimming.

Anchor in 8 to 10 fathoms, mud bottom, inside the southeast bight, just north of a float house. Good holding requires that you put out significant anchor rode.

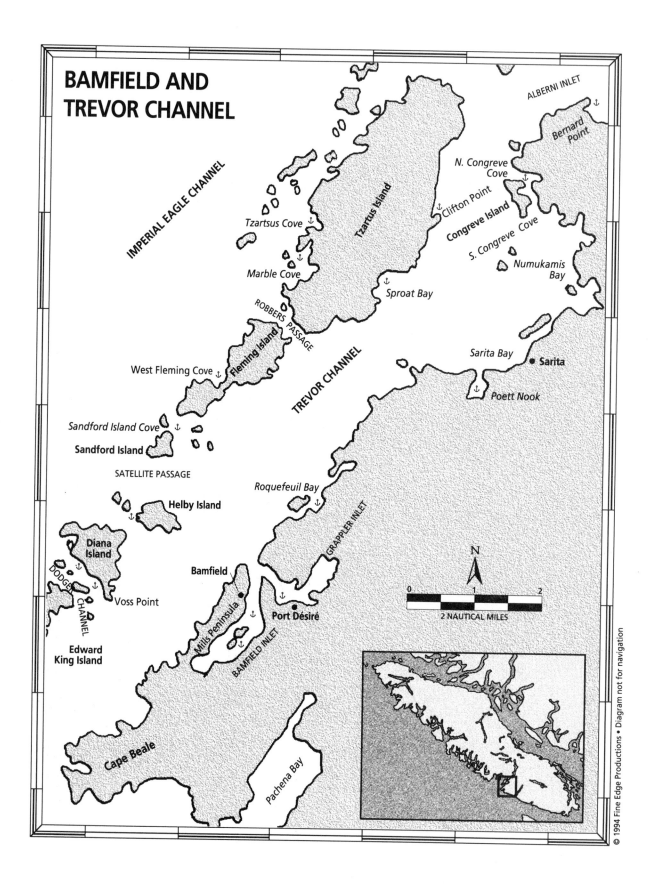

BAMFIELD AND TREVOR CHANNEL

ALBERNI INLET

IMPERIAL EAGLE CHANNEL

Bernard Point

N. Congreve Cove

Clifton Point

Tzartsus Cove

Tzartus Island

Congreve Island

S. Congreve Cove

Numukamis Bay

Marble Cove

ROBBERS PASSAGE

Sproat Bay

Fleming Island

TREVOR CHANNEL

Sarita Bay

Sarita

West Fleming Cove

Poett Nook

Sandford Island Cove

Sandford Island

SATELLITE PASSAGE

Roquefeuil Bay

Helby Island

GRAPPLER INLET

Diana Island

N

DODGE CHANNEL

Bamfield

Voss Point

0   1   2

Edward King Island

Mills Peninsula

Port Désiré

2 NAUTICAL MILES

BAMFIELD INLET

Cape Beale

Pachena Bay

21
Bamfield and Trevor Channel

The southeast side of Barkley Sound, often overlooked by cruising boats, has a number of pleasant destinations of its own. The Vancouver Island shore is somewhat developed, and the anchorages, with the exception of Poett Nook, Bamfield and Grappler Inlets, are uninteresting. The Deer Group of islands, however, offers some outstanding scenery and unusual places to anchor, where you can find excellent fishing and scuba diving.

Bamfield Inlet has the attractive, scenic village of Bamfield, a Port of Entry for boats coming from the U.S. Residents and shopkeepers are friendly, relaxed and easygoing. The eastern side of Bamfield is connected to the island's highway system via dirt road. The western side is free of all but a half dozen cars. A historic boardwalk connects much of the town.

Trevor Channel
Chart 3671 metric; entrance: 48°50' N, 125°10' W

Trevor Channel...leads along the east side of Barkley Sound to Alberni Inlet. The fairway across a sill in its entrance, between Cape Beale and Seapool Rocks, is marked by two sectored lights and has about 25m (82 ft) over it. Inside the fairway is deep and 0.4 mile wide at its narrowest part.... Anchorages.—If it is necessary to anchor in Trevor Channel, Entrance Anchorage is recommended as it is easy access from either Trevor or Imperial Eagle Channels.

Mackenzie Anchorage, Roquefeuil Bay, Christie Bay and Sproat Bay also provide anchorage. Small craft can find shelter in Bamfield Inlet, Poett Nook, the inlet north of Congreve Island, or in the small a bay NW of Clifton Point. (p. 316)

Trevor Channel, on the south side of Barkley Sound against the Vancouver Island mainland, is the protected route from Cape Beale to Bamfield and Alberni inlets. Because of numerous aids to navigation at the entrance of Trevor Channel and its unambiguous radar targets, it is also the safest way to enter Barkley Sound in times of foul weather or limited visibility.

The Deer Group—composed of islands, islets and reefs—forms a northwestern boundary along Trevor Channel. Edward King Island, the

Grappler Inlet, looking out toward Trevor Channel

first major island of the group, cuts the prevailing northwesterly swell, and you can find shelter in its lee. Trevor Channel is busy at all hours, especially with the hundreds of sportfishing boats that scurry to and from their favorite fishing spots. Bamfield Inlet and the village offer sheltered protection in all weather, and you can find most cruising amenities here. As mentioned above, Bamfield is a Port of Entry.

Anchorages inside Trevor Channel tend to be busy and subject to noise and wake. For more scenic and secluded anchorages—but also more exposure—consider those in the Deer Group or along Imperial Eagle Channel. The coves south of Robbers Passage, only 3 miles or so from Bamfield, are especially colorful.

The following descriptions continue around Barkley in a clockwise direction.

Cricket Bay

Chart 3671 metric; position: 48°65.41' N, 125°01.13' W

Cricket Bay, a shallow and foul bay, offers little protection from any weather. It is used by sportfishing boats because of its proximity to the fishing grounds in Junction Passage. There

is a float house on the north side of the reef. We do not have local knowledge of its anchoring potential.

"North Congreve Cove"

Chart 3671 metric; anchor: 48°55.74' N, 125°01.50' W)

Congreve Island is separated from the mainland by a drying channel; between the north side of the island and the mainland is a bight, with depths of 17 m (56 ft) that offer anchorage and shelter for small craft. A sport fishing resort in the bight consists of a large floating lodge and several float houses. (p. 319)

Basketball court, "North Congreve Cove"

Along with Poett Nook at the south end of Numukamis Bay, the channel on the north side of Congreve Island offers small craft the best protection from weather in the northern end of Trevor Channel. We call it North Congreve Cove to differentiate it from South Congreve Cove at the southeast end of the island; this latter cove has a foul bottom and is not recommended.

North Congreve Cove, however, is well sheltered, but it is still rather deep for convenient anchoring. Along its north side, the cove is taken up largely by Barkley Sound Resort; one of the floats is a huge basketball court!

The "drying channel" to the south can be used by kayaks when the tide is right. There are

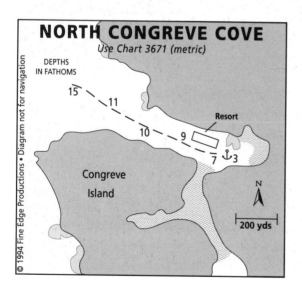

several float houses located along this passage.

Anchor in 8 fathoms off the resort. The bottom is undetermined. Smaller boats can get complete protection behind the resort near an old barge in 3 fathoms.

"South Congreve Cove"

Chart 3671 metric; entrance: 48°55.34' N, 125°01.40' W

South Congreve Cove, open to prevailing chop that comes up Trevor Channel, is suitable only for temporary shelter from strong northerlies. We could not get our anchor to set easily in the rock and kelp bottom, and we do not recommend the cove for overnight anchorage. Cruising boats wanting to fish Junction Passage or Hosie Islands would do better to anchor in Poett Nook.

Clifton Point

Chart 3671 metric; anchor: 48°55.30' N, 125°03.50' W

> *Clifton Point, 1 mile west of Congreve Island, has a dangerous reef 0.1 mile off its SE side. The small cove, close NW of Clifton Point, provides a sheltered anchorage for small craft; a large building is at the head of this cove.* (p. 319)

The small hook behind Clifton Point offers temporary shelter from southwest winds and chop, but because of its maze of floats and buoys, there is room for only one boat. You will need to anchor in deep water near the mouth of the bay. This is a busy place, and it cannot be recommended as an overnight anchorage.

Anchor in 8 fathoms near the floats over an undetermined bottom.

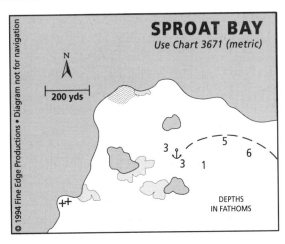

Sproat Bay

Chart 3671 metric; anchor: 48°54.36' N, 125°04.56' W

> *Sproat Bay...has islets and a shoal rock in its north part. Marine farm facilities are in the bay.* (p. 319)

Sproat Bay is busy with floats and a marine farm. A large sign on the northern islet reads, *No Trespassing.* A cruising boat can find temporary shelter in the center of the bay off the marine facilities; however, we do not recommend it.

Anchor in about 4 fathoms over an undetermined bottom.

Sportfishing boats, Poett Nook

Christie Bay and Sarita Bay

Chart 3671 metric

Robbers Passage, Port Alberni Yacht Club

Christie Bay lies between Poett Nook and the SW extremity of Santa Maria Island. The coastal area of the bay, between the east entrance point of Poett Nook and the logging settlement Sarita, is a booming ground. (p. 319)

This part of the mainland coast has been completely taken over in the last 10 years by log booming operations. An A-frame derrick dominates the shore. Large vessels can find shelter here, but Poett Nook, just southwest, is safer and quieter.

Poett Nook

Chart 3671 metric; anchor: 48°52.70' N, 125°03.01' W

Poett Nook, 1 mile east of Nanat Islet, is entered through a straight but narrow channel. A drying ledge, at the south end of the entrance channel where it opens into the basin, extends a short distance from the west shore into the channel and basin. A campground is in the NE corner of the basin and a marina, adjacent to the campground, provides fuel and supplies. The basin affords good anchorage and shelter to small craft. (p. 319)

Although the entrance to Poett Nook is narrow, it is easy to access. The minimum depth in the fairway

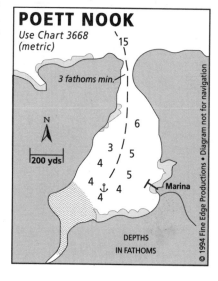

POETT NOOK

Use Chart 3668 (metric)

15

3 fathoms min.

N

200 yds

6

3 5

4

4 5

4 ⚓ 4 — Marina

4

DEPTHS IN FATHOMS

© 1994 Fine Edge Productions • Diagram not for navigation

is about 3 fathoms. Use caution because of the many sportfishing boats zipping about.

Poett Nook is an excellent all-weather anchorage for cruising boats. The marina on the east shore, an active sportfishing center, does not allow boats over 24 feet to tie up.

The mooring fee is 50 cents per foot per day with over 100 spaces available; in August, however, most spaces are already taken. Gasoline is available on a fuel dock. Many Port Alberni residents keep their sportfishing boats here and commute via restricted logging road.

The southwest corner of the bay has room for several cruising boats. Although the bottom is flat without obstructions, it rises sharply on the south side from 4 fathoms to 1 fathom in one boat length!

Anchor in 4 fathoms, keeping far enough off the south shore to provide adequate swinging room. The bottom is a mixture of mud, sand and sea grass with good holding.

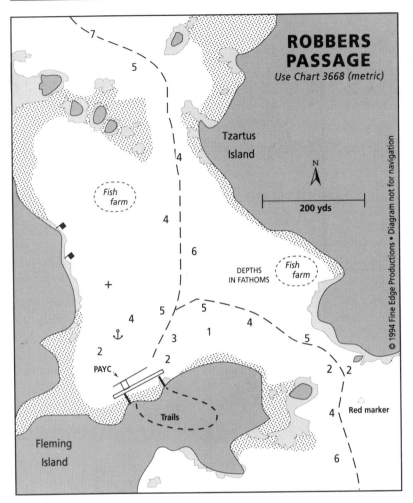

ROBBERS PASSAGE
Use Chart 3668 (metric)

Tzartus Island

N

Fish farm

4

6

DEPTHS IN FATHOMS

Fish farm

5 5 4 5
4 3 1 4
2 2 2 \2
PAYC 2 4\
Trails 4\ Red marker
6

Fleming Island

© 1994 Fine Edge Productions • Diagram not for navigation

200 yds

Robbers Passage

Chart inset 3668 metric; PAYC float:
48°53.58' N, 125°07.02' W

Robbers Passage...separates Fleming Island from Tzartus Island and connects Trevor Channel to Imperial Eagle Channel. It is only suitable for small craft because of numerous drying ledges and rocks in its east and west entrances. Shoal depths of less than 2 m (7 ft) extend NE from Robbers Pass day beacon to the shore on Tzartus Island. (p. 318)

Narrow and scenic, Robbers Passage opens up into a well-sheltered, landlocked cove. Winslow's Lodge, a fish farm, and several smaller cabins and floats are located here.

The Port Alberni Yacht Club has an exten-sive float dock and activity center on the eastern shore of the bay. PAYC operates this facility as an outstation for its club members and guests. The clubhouse has 300 feet of float space. Limited water and power are available. A caretaker's cabin is on shore, as well as picnic sites and several short hiking trails. A nominal fee is charged for use of the facilities, and an honor box is used when caretakers are away. This friendly outpost for cruising boats is one of the most sheltered spots in the Deer Island Group.

To enter from Trevor Channel, take Robbers Pass day beacon to your starboard. The shoal just south of the day beacon is well marked with a kelp patch. A white private float marks the rock awash off the western entrance.

Anchor in 3 to 4 fathoms off PAYC over a mud-sand bottom with good holding. There is room enough for several cruising boats.

Marble Cove

Chart 3668 metric, 3671 metric; anchor:
48°54.76' N, 125°06.69' W

Marble Cove, at the SW end of Tzartus Island, is sheltered by Fry Island and has marine farm facilities in it. (p. 315)

Marble Cove offers moderate protection in fair weather. When a light gale blows up Imperial Eagle Channel causing 1-meter chop with whitecaps, just a gentle rocking motion occurs behind Fry Island. The outer shore of Fry Island has several sea caves that are worth checking out. The coast along Tzartus Island also has sea caves.

A small sportfishing operation on floats is located in the northeast corner of the cove. Marble Cove Camp, located on the south side of the cove, has picnic tables.

The south entrance is deep and easy to enter, but you should avoid the foul ground near Tzartus Island. The north entrance is narrow and shallow with about 2 fathoms minimum in the fairway.

The center of the cove is exposed to the south and a little too deep for anchoring. The best place to anchor is in the northwest corner just above the float cabin and log breakwater.

Anchor in about 5 fathoms, mixed bottom with moderate holding.

"Tzartus Cove"

Chart 3668 metric, 3671 metric;
anchor: 48°55.14' N, 125°06.25' W

An attractive, small unnamed cove that we call it Tzartus Cove is located a half mile northeast of Marble Cove. It is protected from the heavy afternoon chop that sometimes picks up in Imperial Eagle Channel. The cove is undeveloped, scenic, and perhaps the quietest among the Deer Island Group. In many ways, this is a more comfortable place than the more well-known Marble Cove. The water is a cool 56°F, while coves a little farther inland are 10° warmer.

The entrance is unobstructed and the bottom is flat. There are rocks close to either shore and there is a small kelp patch near the eastern shore. The offshore islets are a good base from which to explore, fish or scuba dive.

Tucked up well towards the head of the cove, you will find the water so smooth and clear you can see your anchor.

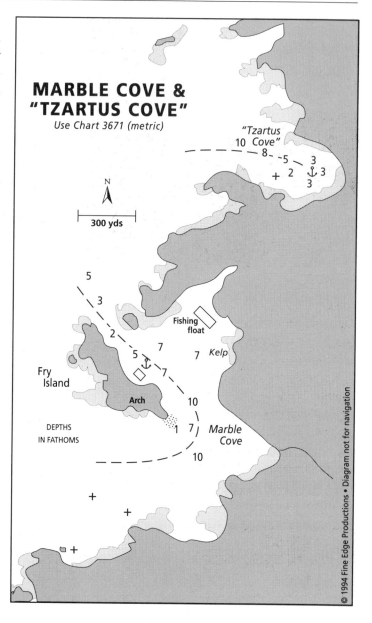

Anchor in 3 fathoms, mid-channel, about 60 yards from the head of the cove. The bottom is mud and sand with good holding.

"West Fleming Cove"

Chart 3668 metric, 3671 metric;
anchor: 48°53.05' N, 125°08.68' W

An unnamed cove on the western shore of Fleming Island offers a conditional, exposed anchorage with an excellent view of the Bro-

Marble Cove

ken Group. It should be used only as a temporary stop in fair weather, however. A sandy beach at the head of the cove offers easy landing. There is a big sea cave on the high bluff on the north entrance. The western side of Fleming Island is a favorite sportfishing area.

The reef on the west side of the cove has extensive kelp beds that smooth out the prevailing swell. These swells heap up on the reef before dissipating, and they can be quite impressive. The fairway bottom is flat, but beware of dangerous rocks and reefs at the head of the cove.

Temporary anchorage can be taken mid-channel in the lee of the kelp-covered reef. The water tends to be murky because of the action of waves on the reef.

Anchor in 4 fathoms over a mixed bottom (gravel and kelp) with moderate holding. An anchor watch is advised.

"Sandford Island Cove"

Chart 3671 metric; anchor: 48°52.42' N, 125°09.84' W

Another small unnamed cove is located among the islets and rocks between Sandford and Fleming islands. It is exposed to winds from all directions, and although it's an interesting anchorage, this is conditional on fair, stable weather. We call it Sandford Island Cove, and it has quite an outside feeling with permanently windswept trees and a superb view of the ocean. It is a great temporary base from which to explore the area, and it offers close access to the excellent fishing grounds of Fleming Island. In these waters scuba divers retrieve many fishing lead weights and lures—and occasionally even a complete fishing pole.

The islets off the northwest end of Sandford Island break prevailing channel swells and chop to nearly a ripple. It is amazing how effective the surrounding islets, rocks and reefs are. In a small cruising boat, you can enter the cove with careful piloting from either the south or north end. In case the swell or weather in Imperial Eagle Channel starts to pick up, the south exit offers an easy 2.5-mile escape route across Satellite Passage and Trevor Channel into Bamfield Inlet.

We anchored east of the islets, just north of the thick trees on Sandford Island. We kept an eye on the glass, the wind and potential sea surge, however, as we enjoyed the windswept view.

Anchor in 3 fathoms, mixed bottom with mediocre holding. An anchor watch is advised.

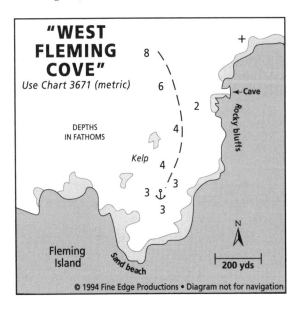

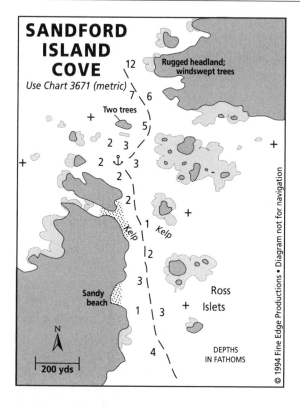

SANDFORD ISLAND COVE

Use Chart 3671 (metric)

Rugged headland; windswept trees

Two trees

Kelp

Kelp

Sandy beach

Ross Islets

N

200 yds

DEPTHS IN FATHOMS

© 1994 Fine Edge Productions • Diagram not for navigation

Helby Island

Chart 3671 metric; 48°51.09' N, 125°10.77' W

The passage between Helby Island and Ohiat Islet is foul, and should not be attempted. (p. 314)

Because of Trevor Channel's great depths and numerous underwater telephone cables that terminate in Bamfield and Port Alberni, there is no anchorage available for cruising boats. Although large vessels can anchor in Entrance Anchorage on the east side of Helby Island, it is too deep for cruising boats. Mackenzie Anchorage, located on the east side of Diana Island, suffers from the same problem. In a small vessel, however, you may find temporary shelter from southwesterlies in the lee of Diana Island, tucked in close to shore. Beware of underwater reefs that extend well out from shore.

The reef on the west side of Helby Island provides temporary shelter under favorable conditions and is an interesting lunch stop. This location has an outstanding reef environ-

ment and is very scenic. A second lunch stop is available just west of the northeast tip of Diana Island. These are both fair-weather stops only, but they can add to your enjoyment in exploring the area.

Dodger Channel

Chart 3671 metric;
NW anchor: 48°50.21' N, 125°11.96' W
SE anchor: 48°50.06' N, 125°11.60' W

We consider Dodger Channel one of the best sites for anchoring, viewing, and experiencing the exposed coast of Barkley Sound before heading for Victoria. While the channel is well sheltered in fair summer weather, it is not a place to be caught in foul weather or stormy conditions.

Edward King Island's outer coast gets the full brunt of the prevailing westerly swells that skirt the outer edge of the Broken Group. Inside Dodger Channel during fair summer weather you can watch these wild proceedings in calm and relative safety.

The west side of the channel has impressive views of swells exploding on the rocks, while the east shore has beautiful, windswept old-growth silver snags. When a swell runs in Trevor Channel, you can hear the whistle buoy loud and clear. The reef to the southeast of Haines Island has a sandy beach with easy landing. Although locals sometimes camp here, the water runs in the chilly 50°F range.

The west entrance to Dodger Channel passes by the south side of Kirby Point, a rugged prominence on which the sea breaks heavily. Thick foam from breakers frequently covers the entrance from Kirby Point to Seppings Island, making it appear more forbidding than it really is. This entrance is deep, but swells diminish in the lee of the reefs as you head in.

Avoid the rocks and reefs off the north and east shores of Seppings Island, and take a mid-channel route favoring the deeper shore of Diana Island.

The south exit is narrow and shallow with only 2 feet in the fairway at zero tide, so if you venture through the south side check the tide tables and station an alert lookout on your bow. Stay mid-channel between the islet to the east and the underwater reef on the west. The south exit can be used as an escape route to Bamfield Inlet (2.5 miles to the east) but only if there is sufficient water across the bar.

You can drop your hook in two places. The northwest site gives you a wild and woolly view to windward; the southeast site is in the lee and seems like a banana belt.

The northwest anchor site is in the lee of the grassy islet close northwest of Haines Island. Since swell is almost completely dissipated here your boat barely rocks.

Anchor in 2.5 fathoms just outside the line of kelp. A stern anchor helps hold you in position in case of a short-term change in wind direction or a surge of current. The bottom of sand and shells with some kelp or sea grass offers good holding.

The southeast anchor site is in a generally calm spot with good shelter from all quarters. The bay has a completely flat, shallow bottom and enough swinging room for several boats.

Anchor in 1.5 to 2 fathoms over a sand, shell and sea grass bottom with good holding.

Roquefeuil Bay

Chart 3671 metric; anchor:
48°51.18' N, 125°06.76' W

Roquefeuil Bay...has low shores, an uneven bottom, and affords fairly sheltered anchorage in a depth of about 17 m (56 ft). A rock which dries 2.4 m (8 ft) and another with 3.6 m (12 ft) over it lie 0.1 and 0.2 mile north of Dixon Island. A rock with 0.1 m awash over it lies 0.1 mile south of Ellis Islet. Marine farm facilities line the east shore of Dixon Island and the cove 0.2 mile east of Dixon Island is boomed off with a float house in it (1988). (p. 316)

Although the area east of Dixon Island in Roquefeuil Bay is completely out of the swell and chop of Trevor Channel and offers shelter for cruising boats, it is not scenic or secluded. The area has been clear-cut, and a marine farm takes up a good part of the bay.

Anchor in 8 fathoms between the fish farm and the mainland shore. The bottom is mixed and rather deep; holding is undetermined.

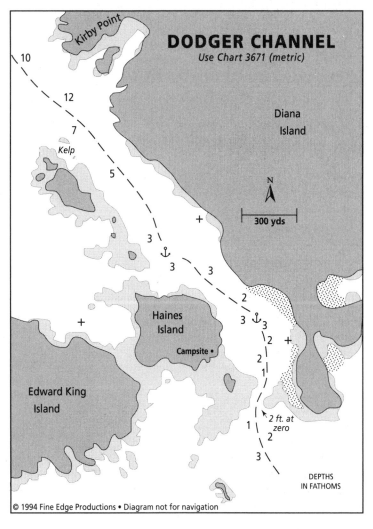

DODGER CHANNEL
Use Chart 3671 (metric)

Kirby Point

Diana Island

10

12

7

Kelp

5

300 yds

N

3

3 3

2

Haines Island

3 3 3

2

Campsite •

2

1

2 ft. at zero

1

2

1

3

Edward King Island

DEPTHS IN FATHOMS

© 1994 Fine Edge Productions • Diagram not for navigation

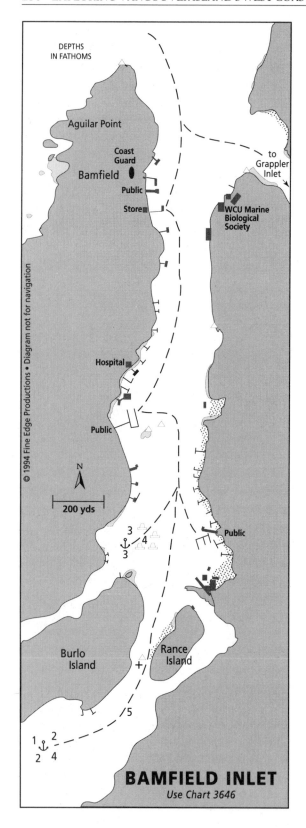

Bamfield Inlet

Chart 3646 metric; anchor: 48°49.83' N, 125°08.33' W

Bamfield Inlet...lies on the east side of Mills Peninsula. Burlo Island and Rance Island, 1 mile south from the entrance, are connected at LW to the west and east sides of the inlet; the passage between them is about 30 m (98 ft) wide with a depth of 3.8 m (12 ft) but has a drying rock and a below-water rock off its Burlo Island shore. (p. 316)

Small vessels can anchor 0.15 mile north of Rance Island; when doing so care must be taken to avoid the submarine cables.... A public wharf close south of the lifesaving station and immediately north of the post office, has a depth of 6.1 m (20 ft) alongside; a float is attached to its south end.... Two public floats, with a common connection to a shore approach structure, are 0.6 mile south of Aguilar Point and close WNW of Bamfield Creek day beacon. These floats are 80 and 57 m (262 and 220 ft) long and have depths of about 4.3 m (14 ft) alongside.... A public wharf, 0.8 mile SSE of Aguilar Point, has a berthing length of 25 m (82 ft) on its outer face. The wharf is approached from shore over a rockfill causeway. Three floats with a common connection are attached on the south side of this wharf. (p. 318)

Bamfield is an attractive, thriving village whose economy is based on fishing, tourism and boating. The people are friendly, self-sufficient and oriented to boats. A Coast Guard heliport and a year-round lifeboat station are located just inside the inlet on the west shore. A Red Cross Outpost Hospital, located 0.4 mile farther south, has its own float. There is a 7-knot, no-wake speed limit in the inlet.

As a Port of Entry, Bamfield receives more than 200 U.S. boats per season. The part-time customs agent, Lorraine, lives in the Coast Guard facility and works part-time in the store next door.

Cruising boats will find repair facilities and a good variety of food, restaurants and lodging.

The west shore of the village is not connected by road to the mainland road system. The east shore village, also a supply center, is connected to Port Alberni by dirt road; the public floats along its shore are congested a good part of the summer season. There are two fueling docks in Bamfield: a Chevron station on the west shore across from the second public dock, and an Esso station, just south of the public dock on the east shore.

The *Lady Rose* calls on Bamfield year-round, stopping on Tuesdays, Thursdays and Saturdays. Leaving Port Alberni at 8 a.m., she arrives in Bamfield between noon and 3 p.m. before returning to Port Alberni. *Lady Rose* ties up at the public wharf in front of the Bamfield Lodge on the west shore and calls at the public wharf on the east shore as well. During the busy summer season, the round-trip is made more frequently. A plane service and a fast water taxi service to Port Alberni are also available.

For exercise, you can follow the lovely boardwalk along the western shoreline or hike to Brady's Beach on Trevor Channel on the northwest corner of Mills Peninsula. At sundown this wide, sandy beach is a particularly good place for shooting photos. The Pacific Rim Trail terminates on the eastern shore.

The substantial buildings on the eastern shore just inside the entrance to Bamfield Inlet belong to Western Canadian University Ma-

Bamfield Coast Guard Station

rine Biological Society, which is engaged in on-going marine environmental studies and education. Regular tours are conducted. At the turn of the century these buildings were the western terminus of the trans-Pacific telegraph cable, and its telegraphers participated in sending the first round-the-world telegraph messages.

Many cruising boats like to take off for Victoria in pre-dawn hours for the last leg of their circumnavigation of Vancouver Island; at the same time dozens of diehard sportfishing boats head out to their favorite fishing spots. Since many of these small, fast boats do not carry running lights, you should make your own vessel as conspicuous as possible for reasons of self-defense.

Bamfield has a number of public docks, but the western shore seems less congested. There are four public mooring buoys just north of Burlo that are fully occupied in the summertime. You can anchor between these buoys and the western shore, staying out of the mid-channel traffic lane. There are also buoys located in Port Désiré in Grappler Inlet.

For a more scenic and less hectic anchorage, continue south through the narrow passage between Burlo Island and Rance Island. The fairway has a least depth of 2 fathoms and an overhead cable with a 56-foot clearance. Pass the red buoy close aboard to avoid the rock just to the southeast.

Anchor in 3 fathoms, mud bottom, southeast of Burlo Island.

Grappler Inlet
Chart 3646 metric

Grappler Inlet is entered about 0.3 mile SE of Aguilar Point and to the north of Grappler Inlet Entrance day beacon.... A public wharf with a float and launching ramp are on the south side of Port Désiré; three private floats are on its north side.... Two public mooring buoys are in Port Désiré. (p. 318)

Brady Beach, Bamfield

Lodging in Bamfield

Port Désiré

Grappler Inlet entrance is a lovely, narrow channel lined with beautiful old growth. The pace in this inlet is much slower than that of Bamfield Inlet.

Port Désiré

Chart 3646 metric; anchor: 48°49.83' N, 125°07.44' W

Port Désiré is a small, quiet and scenic bay in the middle of Grappler Inlet. It is a well-sheltered anchorage.

There is a boat launching ramp on the south shore. The small public float is often crowded with sportfishing boats, and the buoys are generally occupied. Anchor northeast of the public buoys, where there is enough swinging room for several boats.

Anchor in 3 to 4 fathoms over a mud bottom with good holding.

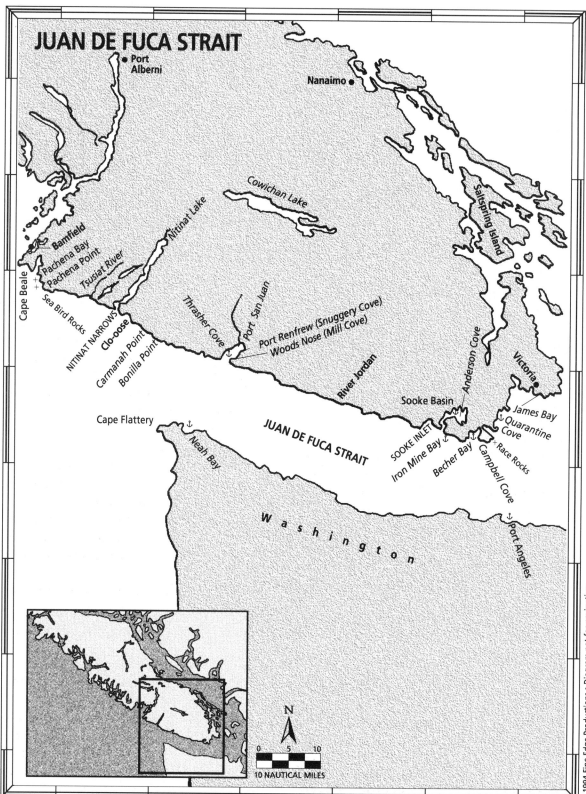

JUAN DE FUCA STRAIT

Port Alberni

Nanaimo

Cowichan Lake

Nitinat Lake

Saltspring Island

Bamfield
Pachena Bay
Pachena Point
Cape Beale
Sea Bird Rocks
Tsusiat River
NITINAT NARROWS
Clo-oose
Carmanah Point
Bonilla Point
Thrasher Cove
Port San Juan

Port Renfrew (Snuggery Cove)
Woods Nose (Mill Cove)

River Jordan

Anderson Cove

Sooke Basin

Victoria
James Bay
Quarantine Cove

SOOKE INLET
Iron Mine Bay
Becher Bay
Campbell Cove
Race Rocks

Cape Flattery

Neah Bay

JUAN DE FUCA STRAIT

Port Angeles

W a s h i n g t o n

N

0   5   10

10 NAUTICAL MILES

22
Juan de Fuca Strait

As you leave Barkley Sound on the last leg of your circumnavigation of Vancouver Island, you and your crew may well have mixed feelings. The protected inside waters of the West Coast's sounds and their beautiful, quiet coves lie behind you, and the Pacific Ocean beckons once more. This time, though, it leads you back through Juan de Fuca Strait to all the activity, commerce and sounds of lower B.C. and Puget Sound, as well as to the comforts and conveniences of "civilization."

Although the stretch between Barkley Sound and the entrance to Juan de Fuca Strait earned the name "Graveyard of the Pacific" in times past, in these days a summer passage should mean little more than a "downhill" run if weather forecasts are good. If you have time to delay your reentry along the way, you can find several nice places to stop. Hopefully you can return another year to explore all those hidden places you missed on this voyage.

Dawn off Cape Beale

Cape Beale to Victoria
Charts 3602 metric, 3606 metric, 3641, 3647 metric

The total run from Bamfield to Victoria is 92 nautical miles, and if you are in a hurry to "head for the barn" you can make it in one long passage. Small cruising boats or those with plenty of time can enjoy the scenery, making stops along the way. Although this long stretch sometimes sends advance fear into a small boat crew, it can be made without a problem in favorable weather.

Once you round Cape Beale, the coast tends more easterly, and within 20 miles you reach Carmanah Point, the north entrance of Juan de Fuca Strait. Due to the shoal waters of Swiftsure Bank, seas can become uncomfortable or even dangerous at times, but as you head farther east the northwest swell gradually decreases.

Juan de Fuca Strait is 53 miles long and 12 miles wide, and it is not unusual for weather to differ decidedly from one end of the strait to the other.

Along the 92-mile stretch, Port San Juan and Sooke Harbour offer good shelter for cruising boats in most summer weather.

In order to clear Carmanah Point and enter the strait before prevailing winds come up, most skippers head out of Barkley Sound for Victoria in the early morning hours after checking the 4 a.m. weather forecast.

If you are caught in the strait when a southerly storm comes up, you can run to Neah Bay on the Washington coast for protection.

Swiftsure Bank

Chart 3602; 48°33' N, 125°00' W

Swiftsure Bank...has a least depth of 34 m (112 ft).... From April 15 to October 31 large numbers of fishing vessels can be encountered inside the 100 m (328 ft) line on La Perouse and Swiftsure Banks in the approach to Juan de Fuca Strait. (pp. 65, 68)

Cape Beale to Carmanah Point

Chart 3602; Cape Beale light: 48°7.20' N, 125°12.85' W

Cape Beale...is a bold, rocky point covered with trees. It is reported to give a poor radar response at 20 miles under normal conditions. Reefs fringe the promontory to a distance of 0.5 mile...Cape Beale Sector light (176) is shown at an elevation of 51 m (167 ft) from a red lantern on a pyramidal tower, 9.7 m (32 ft) high, with white slatwork daymarks on three sides. It has a radio beacon, emergency light and a heliport. The fog signal consists of one blast on two horns every 30 seconds. (p. 285)

As you leave Barkley Sound, give a wide berth to the rocks off Cape Beale before you turn southeast. The combination of prevailing swell and ebb current can cause confused seas and uncomfortable sailing along this section of the coast. In stable weather conditions, this lumpiness quickly smoothes out.

Cape Beale is a sectored light that flashes white and red as indicated on Charts 3671 and 3602.

Pachena Bay

Chart 3602

Pachena Bay, 2.8 miles SE of Cape Beale, is exposed to the heavy swell which is usually present and should not be used as an anchorage. Shelter for small craft can be found inside the Pachena River entrance but local knowledge is required to enter the river. (p. 68)

We have no local knowledge of this area, but we have seen many an adventurous sportfishing boat heading out of Bamfield on calm mornings to try their luck at Pachena Bay.

Seabird Rocks

Chart 3602; light: 48°45.00' N, 125°09.15' W

Seabird Rocks, off the entrance of Pachena Bay, are bare.... Seabird Rocks light (177), on the largest rock, is shown from a white tower with a red band on at the top. (p. 68)

Seabird Rocks, halfway between Cape Beale and Pachena Point, are one of the few obstructions found along this stretch of the coast until you reach Race Rocks near Victoria. A particular hazard to boats that hug the coast in poor visibility, these rocks should be passed a half mile or more to the southwest. Seabird Rocks light flashes white every 4 seconds.

Several species of seabirds nest here in early summer—an interesting place for birdwatching. You are not allowed to land without a permit.

Pachena Point

Chart 3602; light: 48°43.34' N, 125°05.77' W

Pachena Point light (178) is shown at an elevation of 56.4 m (185 ft) from a white tower, 12.2 m (40 ft) high. It is fitted with an

Crossing the bar—Nitinat Narrows

emergency light and has a heliport. A prominent white house with a red roof is close west of the light. The fog signal consists of one blast on a horn every minute.
(p. 68)

Pachena Point light flashes white twice in a period of 7.5 seconds. A short distance off the point, the large white radar dome behind Ucluelet lines up over the Cape Beale light.

If the visibility and weather cooperate, you can close the shore and follow the 20-fathom curve for a close-up view of the changing coastal terrain, and at the same time see Cape Flattery to the southeast across the strait.

Halfway between Darling River and Klanawa River is Tscowis Creek where a 40-foot waterfall drops into the sea. A suspension bridge that crosses the creek is part of the Pacific Rim Trail. On the north side of the creek you can frequently see tents at the campground ashore, as well as a few cabins on the south side. An old rusting barge on shore just above the waterfall provides an additional landmark. Just south of this creek, you can see the first of the many caves that appear along this part of the coast.

Do not confuse Tscowis waterfall with the more obvious and well-known Tsusiat Falls, located 4 miles to the south. At Klanawa River you can see an overhead trolley that hikers must use to cross the river. The trolley is a remnant of the original lifesaving trail built as an escape route for shipwrecked sailors.

Tsusiat River
Chart 3606 metric; way-point: 48°41.15' N, 124°56.05' W

Tsusiat River, 7 miles ESE of Pachena Point, has Tsusiat Falls at its mouth which can be seen for a considerable distance. As the only feature of its kind on this part of the coast it is useful as an aid in fixing position.
(p. 68)

Tsusiat River has a spectacular waterfall about 30 feet wide and 25 feet high that plunges in free fall directly to the sandy beach. This area is a favorite camping spot for hikers of the Pacific Rim Trail, and in summer you can usually see a number of brightly colored tents located at the foot of Tsusiat Falls.

Nitinat Narrows and Nitinat Lake
Chart 3647 metric, 3606 metric;
Nitinat Bar: 48°40.11' N, 124°51.05' W

Nitinat Narrows...entered between Tsuquanah Point and Whyac Point, leads about 1 mile north into Nitinat Lake. Nitinat Bar, with depths of 0.9 m to 2 m (3 to 7 feet), extends across the entrance of the narrows. Saw Tooth Rocks, a local name, lie south of Tsuquanah Point and are the

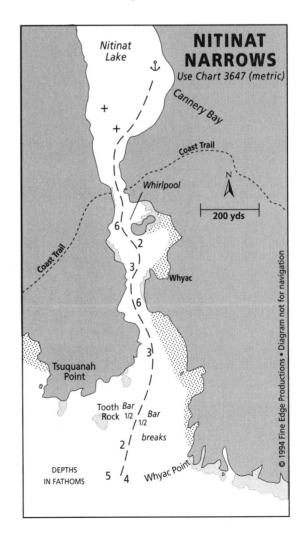

Above: Exiting Nitinat Narrows
Below: As you exit Nitinat Narrows, keep Tooth Rock to your starboard

visible part of the bar. A large 1 m (3 ft) high rock lies on the NW side of the approach.... A short distance within the entrance, the channel narrows to about 30 m (98 ft) and several rocks, covered less than 2 m (6 ft) exist in the fairway. Entry should be attempted only by those in possession of local knowledge. Nitinat Lake is often used as a harbour of refuge by fishing vessels and tugs of moderate draught. Most of the buildings in the Indian Reserve are in ruins. It is reported (1972) that there are numerous deadheads in Nitinat Lake. Nitinat River flows into the north end of Nitinat Lake.

Caution.—Being exposed to the ocean swell, and especially with an ebb tidal stream, the sea on Nitinat Bar at the entrance to Nitinat Narrows becomes very heavy and confused under adverse weather conditions; under these circumstances no vessel should attempt to enter. Even under favourable conditions local knowledge is required for entry. (p. 68)

Three miles south of Tsusiat River, 12-mile-long Nitinat Lake is a rare natural phenomenon. A tidal lake with freshwater on its surface and saltwater below, it is one of the few freshwater lakes on our planet that pours directly into an ocean. The surging water of its narrows have challenged skippers for hundreds of years. In local native dialect, Nitinat means dangerous rushing waters. As the name implies, entering is not recommended for cruising boats.

Nitinat Narrows was the site of Whyac, an impregnable Indian village that prospered with a good dose of local knowledge and canoeing skills. The people were reputed to have been excellent whalers, hunters, warriors and fast paddlers!

Legend has it that three young men who lived in the village in the middle of the narrows took their canoes inland to explore the long waters. After paddling several hours, they glanced back and noticed that the mountains had mysteriously moved, blocking their retreat. Two of the braves were lost in an overnight skirmish with another tribe at the far end of the lake, and as the remaining brave paddled furiously toward home the next morning, the mountains suddenly reopened, letting him escape from Nitinat Lake into the protected narrows.

The surf that breaks over the bar at the shallow entrance has had a notorious reputation for wrecking small boats. The extremely narrow entrance and foul ground surrounding it make it dangerous to approach for even a close look. (See photographs in *Sailing Directions*, page 69.) Any skipper thinking seriously of entering Nitinat should check it out first with a well-powered inflatable.

When we took *Baidarka* over the bar into the fast-flooding narrows, the crew was terrified and the captain and mate had white knuckles. While it was exciting, it was not enjoyable. Here is what we found.

The minimum depth of 2 meters indicated on the chart is closer to 3 feet, adjusted for zero tide. We could see the wavy sand all the way across the bar, and the bottom appeared uncomfortably close to the hull, despite the calm weather.

Incoming water drops 6 to 12 inches vertically across the bar and dances in little wavelets. Past the bar, our echo sounder jumped around like a yo-yo, giving us little steering guidance. The bottom of the narrows is uneven, causing the water to swirl. We could maintain a mid-channel course only with intense concentration.

The very rapid current in the narrows (8 knots at springs) makes aborting the passage through the narrows almost impossible. The narrows are just that—*narrow!* We took advantage of the large clockwise-turning whirlpool on the north side of the unnamed islet just north of Whyac to turn us around so we could beat a hasty retreat. I have been told that if there is another attempt to enter Nitinat it will be with a different crew!

If you wish to explore Nitinat, study Chart 3647, arrive early, explore it with a well-powered inflatable, and, if possible, talk with local sportfishermen who sometimes venture out from deep inside the lake.

"Tooth Rock" and the bare rock close off Tsuquanah Point define the west side of the channel. For a fairway follow a mid-course between these two rocks and the reefs off the eastern shore, favoring the west side.

The two rocks shown on the chart at the north end of the narrows have less than 6 feet over them at zero tide. They can be avoided by favoring the east shore.

A cannery was located on the east shore at the turn of the century just inside the narrows; anchorage can be taken there out of the main current in about 1.5 fathoms. Anchorage can also be taken in Mud Bay, 1 mile farther north in the same depths, taking care to avoid mid-channel shoals.

Canadian Tide and Current Tables, Vol. 5, indicates that *turn to flood* occurs at the higher of the two low water times plus 2 hours, and at the lower of the low water time plus 4 hours and 17 minutes. *Turn to ebb* occurs at high water times plus 2 hours and 15 minutes. Maximum flood and ebb are 8 knots.

Clo-oose

Charts 3602 metric, 3606 metric;
buoy "YJ": 48°38.83' N, 124°49.83' W

> *Clo-oose...is an abandoned village. Light Buoy.—Clo-oose light and whistle buoy "YJ" (179), 1 mile SW of Clo-oose, is a fairway buoy.* (p. 68)

Clo-oose, a small indentation in the coast marked by buoy "YJ," offers minimal protection as a temporary respite from the strait. It is not recommended as an overnight anchorage.

Caution: Inside the inner point near creek outlet, the water shoals rapidly; two uncharted rocks lie off the two houses to the west.

Anchor off the inner point (just off the big sea cave) in 2 fathoms, or anchor in an easterly wind near the reef a half-mile southeast. You need a second anchor to keep your bow into the residual swell. An anchor watch is advised.

Nitinat Lake

CLO-OOSE
Use Charts 3602 & 3606
(both metric)

Tusquanah Point
Whyac
Two old houses
Sea cave
Clo-oose

DEPTHS IN FATHOMS

N

Buoy "YJ"

Kelp

1/2 mi

© 1994 Fine Edge Productions • Diagram not for navigation

Carmanah Point

Chart 3606 metric; light: 48°36.72' N, 124°44.00' W

Carmanah Point (48° 37' N, 124° 45' W) is the NW entrance point to Juan de Fuca Strait.... Carmanah Point light (180) is shown at an elevation of 55.6 m (182 ft) from a white tower with a red lantern, 9 m (30 ft) high. It is fitted with an emergency light, a radiobeacon and has a heliport. The Fog signal consists of three blasts on a horn every minute. (p. 68)

Juan de Fuca Strait separates the SW part of Vancouver Island from the north coast of the State of Washington. The west boundary of the strait is a line between Carmanah Point (B.C.) and Cape Flattery (Washington). Juan de Fuca Strait was discovered in 1592 A.D. by a Greek mariner named Apostolos Valerianos, but commonly known as Juan de Fuca, who was a native of Cephalonia in the service of Spain; in 1787 the strait was rediscovered by Charles William Barkley, an Englishman employed by the Austrian East India Company.

At its east entrance and as far east as Race Rocks, a distance of about 50 miles, the strait is about 12 miles wide, and for a further 30 miles to Whidbey Island, its east boundary, it has a width of about 16 miles. (p. 63)

Welcome to Juan de Fuca Strait! If it's a clear day you can see the flashing light on Cape Flattery to the south.

Bonilla Point

Chart 3606 metric; light: 48°5.74' N, 124°42.98' W

Bonilla Point, about 2 miles SE of Carmanah Point, slopes gradually to the sea; reefs extend about 0.6 mile west and south from it. Inland of the point the mountains attain elevations in excess of 1,000 m (3,280 ft).... Bonilla Point Fisheries light (180.5) is shown at an elevation of 17 m (56 ft) from a tower with a fluorescent orange triangular slatwork daymark. It is seasonal and privately maintained. (p. 68)

Bonilla Point is a private light operated for the fishing fleet. It has a sectored light, as indicated on the chart. The light generally operates only between June 1 and December 7 each season.

Because this part of the coast is lined with chalky bluffs that are pock-marked with large caves, it is a sea kayaker's paradise; haul-out spots abound all along this coast. Several dozen Indian village sites were once located along both the north and south shores of the strait, and the habitants thought nothing of crossing regularly by canoe.

A suspended tram across Walbran Creek and a suspension bridge at Logan Creek make good marks from which to plot your dead-reckoning position.

Snuggery Cove water taxi

Port San Juan

Charts 3647 metric, 3606 metric; entrance buoy "YK": 48°32.08' N, 124°29.02' W

Port San Juan, entered between Owen Point...and San Juan Point, is easily identified from seaward, appearing as a gap between two mountain ranges; it affords the first anchorage on the north shore within the strait. It extends about 3.5 miles inland terminating in a muddy sand beach.

Port San Juan is exposed to SW winds and a heavy sea rolls in when a moderate gale blows from that direction; a swell is nearly always present in the outer part of the inlet. Although it is possible for a

vessel with good ground tackle to ride out a gale if anchored in the most sheltered part of the port, it is recommended that, immediately the approach of a SW gale is indicated, the vessel should weigh and seek shelter in Neah Bay.... San Juan Point light (183.5) is shown from a white tower, with a red band at the top, on the corner of a white rectangular building. The fog signal consists of one blast on a horn every 30 seconds. (pp. 68, 70)

Anchorage can be obtained anywhere in the port in 10 to 16 m (33 to 52 ft), sand bottom. A good small craft anchorage is off the west shore north of Quartertide Rocks, offshore from the mouth of Hobbs Creek. Another good small craft anchorage can be found off the east shore, about 0.4 mile NE of public wharf. (p. 70)

Several bights around the perimeter of Port San Juan offer good protection to small craft, and while these anchorages are not bombproof, they do provide shelter against summer gales if they are chosen with the wind and sea in mind. The prevailing northwest swell diminishes as soon as you enter the bay.

"Thrasher Cove"

Chart 3647 metric;
anchor: 48°33.47' N,
124°28.13' W

A good small craft anchorage is off the west shore north of Quartertide Rocks, offshore from the mouth of Hobbs Creek. (p. 70)

Thrasher Cove, a small indentation on the west shore, hardly shows as a bight on the chart, but it offers modest shelter in pre-

"THRASHER COVE"
Use Chart 3647 (metric)
Water taxi landing
Hobbs Ck
© 1994 Fine Edge Productions • Diagram not for navigation
Kelp
DEPTHS IN FATHOMS
N
200 yds

vailing northwest conditions. You can identify this spot by the sign for the Pacific Rim Trail and by the campers on shore.

This area is where many hikers start their trek of the Pacific Rim Trail. They catch a water taxi across the bay in Snuggery Cove and land on the rock outcropping east of the campsites.

Anchor in 2 fathoms just east of the outlet of Hobbs Creek over a mixed gravel bottom of undetermined holding.

Gordon River

Chart 3647 metric

Gordon River, at the north end of Port San Juan, has a bar across its entrance with a drying spit extending from its east entrance point. In 1979 a depth of 0.4 m (1 ft) could be carried across this bar by keeping close to the west entrance point. Close inside the entrance, anchorage for small craft can be obtained in 4 m (13 ft). (p. 70)

Browns Creek, the eastern tributary to Gordon River, has a large sportfishing marina with private buoys that mark the drying section.

The small anchorage mentioned in *Sailing Directions* may provide good protection to small cruising boats; however, the bar can be crossed only in adequate tide level. In foul weather you should not attempt it. There is easier access to protection across the bay on the east shore.

Anchor in 3 fathoms over a sand-mud bottom near the head of the bay.

Snuggery Cove and Port Renfrew

Chart 3647 metric; anchor:
48°33.32' N, 124°25.11' W

...Another good small craft anchorage can be found off the east shore, about 0.4 mile NE of the public wharf. (p. 70)

A T-shaped public wharf, in

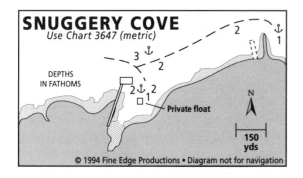

Snuggery Cove, has a berthing face 73 m (240 ft) long and a depth of 4.6 m (15 ft) alongside. (p. 71)

The public wharf in Snuggery Cove has no float. A detached private float fills the inner bay. Port Renfrew, the village just behind Snuggery Cove wharf, is at the end of Highway 14, which leads to Victoria. Limited supplies are available. Fuel has to be delivered via a service truck and jerry-cans from the local garage.

Arrangements for the water taxi to the start of the Pacific Rim Trail can be made at the small hotel. Annually, 6,000 to 8,000 hikers hike the trail from here to Bamfield, taking anywhere from five to seven days.

Anchor in 2 fathoms in the lee of the wharf near the unconnected private float. There is very little swinging room, and the bottom is rocky with kelp.

The rock breakwater north of the wharf offers some protection against westerlies. Anchor

in 1 to 2 fathoms as indicated in the diagram.

In stable weather, there is unlimited room to anchor to the north of the wharf in 4 fathoms.

Woods Nose and "Mill Cove"
Chart 3647 metric; anchor: 48°32.87' N, 124°26.28' W

Woods Nose is a small point fringed by several low islets. (p. 70)

Woods Nose is the name given on the chart to a group of islets on the eastern shore of Port San Juan, a mile southwest of Snuggery Cove. "Mill Cove," the local name for a scenic little cove behind these islets, offers good protection from southeasterlies. A small beach in the cove is not visible until you pass east of Woods Nose. Unless you are cruising by kayak, there is no shelter until you reach Sooke Harbour, another 32 miles.

Tuck behind the reef and kelp that extend northeast of the islet. In prevailing northwesterlies, there is enough swinging room for one or two small cruising boats. In a southwest blow, anchor close up into the kelp behind the islet and put a stern anchor out or run a line ashore. The beach has a good landing spot in case you want to stretch your legs.

Anchor in 2 fathoms over a mixed bottom of sand, rocks, shell and kelp. Holding power is mixed.

Entrance to Snuggery Cove

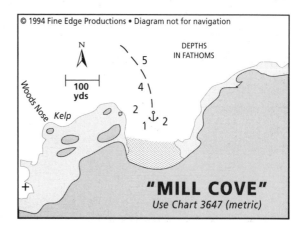

Sooke Inlet

Charts 3430 metric, 3641;
Whiffin Spit light: 48°21.52' N, 123° 42.61' W
Whiffin Spit anchor: 48°21.62' N, 123°43.05' W

Sooke Inlet, the entrance to Sooke Harbour and Sooke Basin, is entered between Parsons Point...and Company Point. Parsons Spit extending offshore from Parsons Point, has drying and sunken rocks on it.... (p. 71)

Sooke Harbour is used extensively by commercial and sports fishing vessels and tugs and barges of the logging industry. The entrance to Sooke Harbour is not visible from small craft until nearly up to Simpson Point, as the entrance is almost closed by Whiffin Spit and Grant Rocks.... (pp. 71, 73)

Whiffin Spit light (188) on the east end of the spit, is shown at an elevation of 6.4 m (21 ft) from a white tower with a green band at the top. A fog signal, operated from the light on request only, consists of one blast on a horn every 30 seconds. Requests to operate the fog signal should be sent to Victoria Coast Guard Radio (VAK) or telephone (604) 642-3431....

Tidal streams run with considerable strength around the extremity of Whiffin Spit, attaining 4 kn during large tides. Slack water, about 20 minutes duration, occurs at or near HW at Sooke....

During the fishing season, vessels are often anchored in the area just north of Whiffin Spit. (p. 73)

Both Sooke Harbour and Sooke Basin offer good, sheltered anchorages. The shallow harbor has a number of drying mud flats, and currents inside are strong. There are three ranges to keep you lined up on course when you enter. For a description of these ranges see *Sailing Directions*, page 73, as well as the noted charts. Be prepared for narrow channels and a lot of traffic in Sooke.

Against the western shore of the bay is Sooke Harbour Marina, as well as fishing

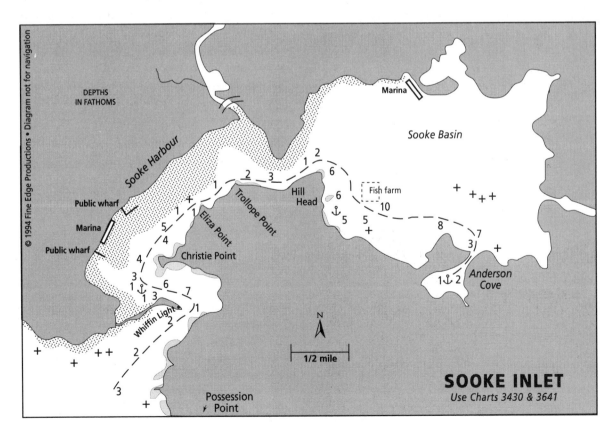

wharves and a public wharf with two finger floats. Because the area is so busy and congested during summer, berthing for cruising boats is hard to find.

A somewhat quiet and well-protected anchorage can be found on a line between the southernmost two dols and the first tree on Whiffin Spit.

Anchor in 1 to 2 fathoms, sand and mud bottom with good holding. If a blow is expected, the best anchorages in south winds are in Sooke Basin.

Sooke Basin

Charts 3430 metric, 3641; anchor: 48°22.35' N, 123°40.77' W

> *Sooke Basin is entered from the NE side of Sooke Harbour, between Trollope Point and Hill Head. The entrance to Sooke Basin requires careful navigation due to the narrow channel and extensive drying areas, created by silting from the Sooke River.... To enter Sooke Basin keep in deep water along the east side of Sooke Harbour heading toward Eliza Point. It is advisable to enter Sooke Basin after LW and during daylight hours when the drying banks are visible.* (p. 73)

Sooke Basin is a large landlocked bay with many beautiful homes nestled along its shores. Most visiting yachts take the easternmost route to enter Sooke Basin and follow the shore very closely—sometimes as close as 60 feet—between Eliza and Trollope Points. Stay just outside the kelp line and pass green buoy "V13" on your port side. Continue to favor the south shore from Trollope Point to Hill Head to avoid Billings Spit. The minimum depth in the fairway is about 10 feet, and the current is strong. Sunny Shores Marina is located on the north shore next to Goodridge Peninsula.

Be careful to avoid the large marine farm east of Hill Head. Its sign reads: *Caution—underwater pipeline in vicinity.*

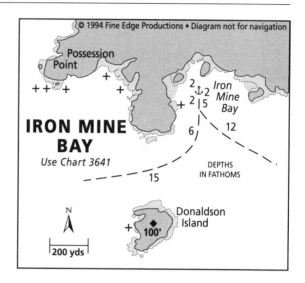

You can find sheltered anchorage south of Hill Head, on the south side of islet (57). Have your binoculars handy—there is abundant bird life in the basin, including murres, double-crested cormorants, loons, swans and gulls.

Anchor in 3 fathoms over a mixed bottom with fair holding. You'll need to do some scouting to find good holding spots just off the homes with private docks.

Anderson Cove

Charts 3430 metric, 3641; anchor: 48°21.72' N, 123°39.29' W

Anderson Cove, located on the far south side of Sooke Basin, is a landlocked bay that offers ex-

Campbell Cove

cellent protection in all weather.

To enter, stay close to the eastern shore through the narrows to avoid a rock located in the middle of the entrance. There is about 3 feet at zero tide in the fairway and the current runs at about 1 knot, but inside the water is calm. Before you anchor, be sure you pinpoint the submerged pilings as well as foul ground near the south shore, and stay clear of the oyster farm.

Anchor in 1 to 2 fathoms in the center of the bay over a mud-shell bottom with good holding.

Iron Mine Bay

Chart 3641; anchor: 48°20.31' N, 123°42.22' W

Iron Mine Bay, a scenic bay north of Secretary (Donaldson) Island, offers good protection from prevailing westerlies. (Chart 3641 shows Donaldson Island, but most locals call it Secretary Island.) It's a good place to stop temporarily if you're waiting for the tides to change in Sooke Harbour or near Race Rocks, but it does not afford shelter in southeasterlies.

Anchor in 3 fathoms on a shelf off the pebble beach. For an overnight anchorage, consider Campbell Cove 4 miles east.

Becher Bay

Charts 3641, 3430 metric

Becher Bay...entered between Alldridge Point and Smyth Head, is open to Juan de Fuca Strait and has numerous sunken and drying rocks within 0.1 mile of its shore; deadheads are likely to be encountered in the bay.... Tidal streams in Becher Bay are particularly strong and close attention should be paid to the charted information concerning them.... Anchorage with good shelter can be obtained in Murder Bay, on the north side of Campbell Cove.... Pacific Lions Marina is on the west side of Becher Bay in Campbell cove and the floats are removed during winter months. Cheanuh Marina, on the north side of Becher Bay...is protected by a floating breakwater. (p. 74)

Becher Bay is another large outpost of sportfishing boats. Cruising boats will find good shelter in Campbell Cove.

Campbell Cove

Charts 3641, 3440 metric, 3430 metric; anchor: 48°19.67' N, 123°37.83' W

Campbell Cove offers good protection in the summer and has easy access. It is an excellent place to stay while you wait for optimum weather or tidal conditions. The large sportfishing marina on the west side of the cove has complete services for sportfishing boats. Out of the traffic, the most protected place to anchor is south of the rock marked by a protruding pipe.

Anchor in 2 fathoms over a hard mud bottom with sea grass and kelp. The bottom is

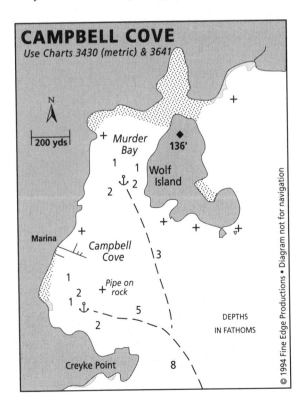

CAMPBELL COVE
Use Charts 3430 (metric) & 3641

N
200 yds
Murder Bay
136'
Wolf Island
1   1
2   2
Marina
Campbell Cove
3
Pipe on rock
1
2
1
5
2
Creyke Point
8
DEPTHS IN FATHOMS

© 1994 Fine Edge Productions • Diagram not for navigation

hard to penetrate but has good holding once your anchor is set.

Murder Bay

Charts 3641, 3440 metric, 3430 metric; anchor: 48°20.00' N, 123°37.68' W

Murder Bay, a shallow, drying bay at the north end of Campbell Cove, offers protection from easterlies if you anchor in the lee of Wolf Island. The bay is congested with private floats and buoys.

Anchor in 1 fathom behind Wolf Island over sand-mud bottom with sea grass and good holding.

Race Rocks

Charts 3641, 3440 metric; Great Race Rock light: 48°17.89' N, 123°31.80' W

Race Rocks...are a group of low, bare rocks.... Other dangers, on which heavy dangerous overfalls and races occur in bad weather, lie within a 0.4 mile radius from Great Race Rock.... Caution.—Wind conditions and/or wave sequences can cause tide-rips, backeddies or tidal currents to suddenly become very dangerous; large swells can develop with little warning. This area should be treated with due caution. (p. 74)

Race Rocks mark the last major obstacle before you turn northeast to Victoria. The navigation light here flashes every ten seconds, and the fog signal is 3 pairs of double blasts followed by 48 seconds of silence. This is a busy sportfishing area, and a lot of small craft traffic converges here. Consult *Canadian Tide Tables*, Vol. 5 for expected tides, currents and times of turning.

Race Passage

Charts 3641, 3440 metric

Race Passage lies between the dangers surrounding Race Rocks and those fringing Bentinck Island; it can be used by small craft in good weather provided they have the power to offset the tidal stream that flows through it. When using this passage, favour the Bentinck Island side keeping just outside the line of kelp, as the outermost danger on the south side of the channel is covered at HW and the strongest eddies are found near it.... Tidal streams in Race Passage attain 6 kn on the flood and 7 kn on the ebb; dangerous tide-rips are formed. Severe tide-rips are often encountered at Christopher Point and in the vicinity of the islands off Church Point....

(pp. 74, 75)

Consult *Canadian Tide Tables*, Vol. 5 for tides, currents and times of turning.

Quarantine Cove

Charts 3641, 3440 metric; William Head light: 48°20.58' N, 123°31.56' W

Quarantine Cove, well protected from westerlies, is a good place to await favorable tides or study weather conditions at Race Passage. It is exposed to easterlies. A penitentiary is located on the south shore, and you may not approach closer than 200 meters.

Anchor in 5 fathoms in mid-bay over mud bottom with good holding.

Victoria

Charts 3641, 3440 metric, 3415 metric; Odgen Point breakwater light: 48°24.82' N, 123°23.55' W

Victoria, the seat of the Provincial Government, has a population of 66,303 (1986) and the Capital Regional District has a population of 264,614. The fort and the foundation of the city were established in 1843 and given the name Fort Albert which shortly afterwards was changed to Fort Victoria.... Ten public finger floats...(close east of Shoal Point), are generally used by the fishing fleet; between May 30 and August 31, when the fishing fleet is at sea, they are used by pleasure craft. (pp. 80, 81)

One of the most beautiful cities anywhere,

Victoria has plenty of old-world charm. It is a friendly port for cruising yachts, and it offers excellent small craft facilities.

The Harbour Master's office and patrol craft monitor Channel 73. Victoria Harbour has a speed limit of 5 knots. Fuel docks are located in the Shoal Point public floats.

First-time visitors should try to moor in James Bay, close to the downtown area.

James Bay

James Bay
Chart 3415 metric

> *James Bay, SE of Laurel Point, has the Provincial Parliament Buildings near its south end and the Empress Hotel near its east end.... Public floats provide facilities for pleasure craft along the east side of James Bay.... Public finger floats, on the east side of James Bay, have depths on the outside of 3.2m (10 ft) and 2 m (7 ft) along the inside of the main float. The floats are used by pleasure craft.* (pp. 80, 81)

In our opinion, the public floats located in James Bay in view of the Empress Hotel, as well as those just north, offer some of the finest city docking anywhere in North America. Within walking distance of the floats, you find restaurants, art galleries, gift shops, museums and provisions. At night, the lights of the Parliament Building and the Empress Hotel backlight the harbor, and musical groups along the quay provide entertainment.

Following a cruise down the wild and pristine West Coast, reentry into urban living can be a shock. Fortunately, Victoria gives you only a mild, genteel jolt into the rhythms of landlubber life.

A nominal fee is charged for tying up in front of the Empress Hotel (stay is limited to two days and rafting is encouraged). Electricity is available (small amperage only—the circuit breaker is located on the quay across from the gangway). Restrooms, showers and laundry facilities, located 100 yards north under the Visitors Center on the lower quay, are open during summer season only.

The custom's wharf is on the east side of Inner Harbour, north of Ship Point Wharf (telephone 604-388-3339). Immediately north of the custom's wharf is a large complex of public floats where long-term moorage is available.

Don't miss the Provincial Museum one block to the south and the British Columbia Maritime Museum a few blocks to the north. The Visitors Center on the quay is a wealth of information on what is going on and how to get there.

Food supplies can be ordered from Williams' View Street Market, one of Victoria's oldest continuous markets, dating from the late 1800s. Located at 749 View St. (telephone: 604-384-0525), their facilities include a deli-restaurant, bakery and cappuccino bar. With advance notice they will flash-freeze meats and deliver your order directly to your boat.

Although there are too many fine restaurants, shops, boutiques and art galleries to list here, we do have to mention several of the places we always head to after we dock: Munro's Books at 1108 Government St. (telephone: 604-382-2464) for the best selection of books on British Columbia, and Murchies, next door, for bulk tea and coffee and treats in their cappuccino bar at 1110 Government St. (telephone: 604-383-3112; 800-663-0400).

Schooner—James Bay

Part III
Appendixes and References

APPENDIX A
Vancouver Island Distances Tables

Distances along the West Coast of Vancouver Island

From *Sailing Directions*, Vol. 1, 15th Edition, 1990; used with permission of CHS.

Location key (with light house bearings as labelled):
- Egg Island Lt. Ho., brg. 065°, 2 miles
- Cape Scott Lt. Ho., brg. 078°, 2 miles
- Outer Cove
- Holberg
- Coal Harbour
- Port Alice
- Winter Harbour
- Kaine Island Lt. Ho., brg. 000°, 1 mile
- Solander Island Lt. Ho., brg. 040°, 2.5 miles
- Kyuquot
- Fair Harbour (Entrance)
- Zeballos
- Tahsis
- Gold River (Muchalat Inlet)
- Estevan Point Lt. Ho., brg. 036°, 3 miles
- Hotsprings Cove
- Tofino
- Amphitrite Point Lt. Ho., brg. 031°, 3 miles
- Ucluelet Inlet (Entrance)
- Toquart Bay
- Port Alberni
- Bamfield
- Cape Beale Lt. Ho., brg. 075°, 1.5 miles
- Carmanah Point Lt. Ho., brg. 021°, 3 miles
- Race Rocks Lt. Ho., brg. 000°, 1.5 miles
- Victoria (Ogden Point)
- Vancouver (Brockton Point)

From	Victoria	Race Rocks	Carmanah Pt	Cape Beale	Bamfield	Port Alberni	Toquart Bay	Ucluelet Inlet	Amphitrite Pt	Tofino	Hotsprings Cove	Estevan Pt	Gold River	Tahsis	Zeballos	Fair Harbour	Kyuquot	Solander Is	Kaine Is	Winter Harbour	Port Alice	Coal Harbour	Holberg	Outer Cove	Cape Scott	Egg Island
Cape Scott																										36
Outer Cove																									10	46
Holberg																								61	69	105
Coal Harbour																							17	46	54	90
Port Alice																						17	33	50	58	94
Winter Harbour																					31	26	42	27	35	71
Kaine Island																				6	29	25	40	21	29	65
Solander Island																			21	27	50	46	61	39	46	82
Kyuquot																		27	48	54	77	73	88	66	73	109
Fair Harbour																	15	39	60	66	89	85	100	78	85	121
Zeballos																44	40	58	79	85	108	104	119	97	104	140
Tahsis															34	58	74	85	79	108	104	119	97	104	133	169
Gold River														#16	#48	#43	°87	°108	°114	°137	°133	°133	°148	°126	°133	169
Estevan Point													34	44	58	70	87	108	114	137	133	133	148	126	133	152
Hotsprings Cove												36	37	52	57	53	70	91	97	114	130	116	131	109	116	166
Tofino											14	50	51	66	71	67	84	105	111	134	130	145	123	130	166	186
Amphitrite Point										27	34	70	71	86	91	87	104	125	131	154	150	165	143	150	186	201
Ucluelet Inlet									23	41	49	85	86	101	106	102	119	140	146	169	165	180	158	165	201	207
Toquart Bay								+6	29	47	55	91	92	107	112	108	125	146	152	175	171	186	164	171	207	217
Port Alberni							13	+16	39	57	65	101	102	117	122	118	135	156	162	185	181	196	174	181	215	250
Bamfield						39	43	49	72	90	98	134	135	150	155	151	168	189	195	218	214	229	207	214	215	221
Cape Beale					6	35	17	19	20	43	61	69	105	106	121	126	122	139	160	166	189	185	200	178	185	215
Carmanah Point				23	29	58	42	38	37	60	78	86	122	123	138	143	139	156	177	183	206	202	217	195	202	238
Race Rocks			53	76	82	111	95	91	90	113	131	139	175	176	191	196	192	209	230	236	259	255	270	248	255	291
Victoria		10	63	86	92	121	105	101	100	123	141	149	185	186	201	206	202	219	230	236	259	265	280	258	265	301
Vancouver	80	87	140	163	169	198	182	178	177	200	218	226	262	263	278	283	279	296	317	323	346	342	357	335	342	378

References
+ Via Felice Channel
° Via Cook Channel and Tahsis Inlet
Via Tahsis Narrows

Principal Distances within the Inside Passage between Vancouver Island and the Mainland

From *Sailing Directions*, Vol. 1, 15th Edition, 1990; used with permission of CHS.

Inset chart (northern points)

Column headings (diagonal): Blinkhorn Peninsula · Beaver Cove · Alert Bay · Port McNeill · Sointula · Pulteney Point

From	distances (nearest → farthest)
Sointula	5
Port McNeill	4½, 7½
Alert Bay	6, 6, 9
Beaver Cove	5, 10, 10, 14
Blinkhorn Peninsula	3, 7, 12, 12, 15

Main chart

Diagonal headings (top → bottom): Pine Island Lt. Ho. (Entrance) [Cape Scott Lt. Ho.; brg. 050°, 1 mile] · Bull Harbour (Entrance) [Cape Caution Light; brg. 150°, 1.3 miles] [Cape Caution Light; brg. 078°, 2.2 miles] · Port Hardy · Alison Harbour · Blunden Harbour · Pulteney Point · Blinkhorn Peninsula · Broken Islands (See Note 4) · Kelsey Bay · Port Neville (Entrance) · Stuart Island (Settlement) (See Note 3) · Seymour Narrows · Campbell River · Comox · Powell River · Blubber Bay · Pender Harbour (Entrance) (See Note 2) · Halfmoon Bay · Northwest Bay · Nanoose Bay (Richards Point) · Nanaimo · Vancouver (Brockton Point) · New Westminster (See Note 1) · Victoria (Ogden Point)

From	distances (as read, left → right)
Bull Harbour (Entrance)	32
Port Hardy	30, 12
Alison Harbour	11, 20, 22
Blunden Harbour	22, 20, 43, 32
Pulteney Point	21, 21, 9, 39, 16
Blinkhorn Peninsula	16, 14, 29, 20, 49, 27
Broken Islands	18, 30, 17, 34, 31, 55, 42
Kelsey Bay	15, 33, 45, 33, 50, 46, 87, 58
Port Neville	19, 34, 52, 64, 51, 69, 65, 89, 76
Stuart Island	8, 27, 42, 60, 72, 59, 77, 73, 97, 85
Seymour Narrows	7, 15, 34, 49, 67, 79, 66, 84, 80, 104, 91
Campbell River	36, 43, 50, 69, 85, 103, 115, 102, 119, 115, 139, 127
Comox	41, 34, 41, 49, 68, 83, 101, 113, 100, 117, 114, 138, 125
Powell River	8, 33, 43, 50, 57, 76, 91, 109, 121, 108, 126, 122, 146, 133
Blubber Bay	33, 41, 54, 75, 82, 90, 109, 124, 142, 154, 141, 158, 155, 179, 167
Pender Harbour	21, 31, 39, 39, 74, 81, 88, 107, 123, 141, 153, 140, 157, 153, 177, 165
Halfmoon Bay	5, 18, 29, 37, 42, 72, 78, 86, 105, 120, 138, 150, 137, 154, 151, 175, 162
Northwest Bay	25, 26, 42, 53, 61, 64, 96, 102, 110, 129, 144, 162, 174, 161, 179, 174, 199, 186
Nanoose Bay (Richards Point)	11, 35, 35, 52, 62, 70, 74, 105, 112, 120, 138, 154, 172, 184, 171, 188, 184, 208, 196
Nanaimo	18, 21, 37, 41, 37, 58, 66, 75, 101, 108, 116, 134, 150, 168, 180, 167, 184, 180, 204, 192
Vancouver (Brockton Point)	12, 18, 25, 46, 46, 48, 69, 77, 85, 112, 118, 126, 145, 160, 178, 190, 177, 194, 191, 215, 202
New Westminster	13, 20, 21, 30, 52, 52, 54, 75, 83, 91, 118, 125, 132, 151, 166, 184, 196, 183, 201, 197, 221, 208
Victoria (Ogden Point) — Vancouver row	34, 40, 46, 35, 48, 70, 70, 79, 99, 107, 109, 142, 148, 156, 175, 190, 208, 220, 207, 225, 221, 245, 232
New Westminster	40, 46, 53, 59, 54, 65, 87, 88, 94, 114, 122, 126, 157, 164, 171, 190, 205, 223, 235, 222, 240, 236, 260, 248
Victoria (Ogden Point)	72, 73, 76, 81, 88, 85, 95, 117, 118, 122, 143, 151, 156, 186, 193, 200, 219, 234, 252, 264, 251, 269, 265, 289, 277

Distances in Juan de Fuca Strait, Admiralty Inlet, Puget Sound and the S.E. Part of the Strait of Georgia

From *Sailing Directions*, Vol. 1, 15th Edition, 1990; used with permission of CHS.

From \ To	Vancouver, B.C. (Brockton Point)	Nanaimo, B.C.	New Westminster, Wash.	Blaine, Wash.	Bellingham, Wash.	Anacortes, Wash.	Olympia, Wash.	Tacoma, Wash.	Bremerton, Wash.	Seattle, Wash.	Eagle Harbour, Wash.	Everett, Wash. (See Note 3)	Port Gamble, Wash.	Port Ludlow, Wash.	Port Townsend, Wash.	Point Wilson Lt. Ho.	Victoria, B.C. (Ogden Point)	Port Angeles, Wash.	Race Rocks Lt. Ho.	Sooke Harbour, B.C.	Port Renfrew, B.C.	Noah Bay, Wash.
Nanaimo, B.C.	34																					
New Westminster, Wash.	40	46																				
Blaine, Wash.	47	53	47																			
Bellingham, Wash.	70	74	70	37																		
Anacortes, Wash.	68	74	69	35	16																	
Olympia, Wash.	173	178	172	139	124	110																
Tacoma, Wash.	149	154	148	115	100	86	34															
Bremerton, Wash.	138	143	137	104	89	75	50	29														
Seattle, Wash.	129	134	128	95	80	66	50	25	14													
Eagle Harbour, Wash.	129	134	128	95	80	66	50	25	13	8												
Everett, Wash. (See Note 3)	111	116	111	78	63	49	73	49	38	29	29											
Port Gamble, Wash.	110	115	109	76	61	47	79	55	44	34	34	28										
Port Ludlow, Wash.	105	110	104	71	56	42	76	52	41	32	32	25	10									
Port Townsend, Wash.	92	97	91	58	43	29	84	60	49	40	40	34	21	16								
Point Wilson Lt. Ho.	89	94	88	55	40	26	84	60	49	40	40	34	21	16	3							
Victoria, B.C. (Ogden Point)	80	85	79	53	49	35	115	91	80	71	71	65	52	47	34	31						
Port Angeles, Wash.	92	100	91	65	55	42	113	89	78	69	69	63	50	45	32	29	19					
Race Rocks Lt. Ho.	87	92	87	60	55	41	117	93	82	73	73	67	54	49	36	33	10	12				
Sooke Harbour, B.C.	97	102	97	70	65	51	128	103	92	83	83	77	64	59	46	43	20	21	10			
Port Renfrew, B.C.	131	136	131	104	99	85	161	137	126	117	117	111	98	93	80	77	54	54	44	36		
Noah Bay, Wash.	130	135	130	103	98	84	160	136	125	116	116	110	97	92	79	76	53	54	43	35	14	
Cape Flattery, Wash. (Tatoosh Id. Lt. Ho.)	138	143	138	111	106	92	168	144	133	124	124	118	105	100	87	84	61	61	51	43	16	10

Notes on label bearings as shown on chart:
Point Wilson Lt. Ho. brg. 225°, 1 mile; Race Rocks Lt. Ho. brg. 000°, 1.5 miles; Noah Bay, Wash. brg. 140°, 3.5 miles; Sooke Harbour, B.C. (Entrance).

APPENDIX B
Key VHF Radio Channels

Emergency
16—Calling and Distress
22A—U.S. Coast Guard
06 Ship-to-ship safety
Search & Rescue Telephone Numbers
1-800-742-1313 or 604-388-1543; 604-363-2333; 604-666-4301

Weather Channels
WX-1—Alert Bay, Comox
WX-2—Alberni, Nootka
WX-3—Victoria
WX-4—Tofino
21 B—Vancouver, Victoria, Alert Bay

Marine Telephone Operators
01 Kyuquot
23 Courtenay, Vancouver, Estevan Point, Jordan River
24 Port Hardy, East Thurlow Island, Tofino
25 Vancouver, Port Angeles
27 Bamfield, Campbell River, Winter Harbour, Victoria
28 Ucluelet
64 Ganges, Campbell River
85 West Vancouver, Sechelt, Alert Bay
87 Nanaimo, Brooks Peninsula, Pachena Point
88 Vancouver

Canadian Marinas & Yacht Clubs
68 South of Campbell River
73 North of Campbell River

Ship-to-Ship
68, 69, 72, 78

Vessel Traffic Services
71 Vancouver (north of Strait of Georgia)
74 Tofino (West Coast
14 Seattle (Juan de Fuca Strait)

APPENDIX C
Summer Sea Reports

The U.S. *Navy Marine Climatic Atlas*—as well as summaries presented in Canadian *Sailing Directions*—indicate what you might expect when you cross Queen Charlotte Sound. The mean and maximum significant wave heights for combined sea and swell at the west entrance to Queen Charlotte Sound, 60 miles northwest of Cape Scott, are 1.7 to 3.8 meters (6 to 13 feet) for June through August—half those recorded for the other three seasons of the year. Maximum waves indicated—13 feet—are generally associated with low pressure gales that occur during summer months for a day or two every two to six weeks.

According to the *Climatic Atlas,* during August, short seas—as opposed to longer swells—are 4 feet or less off Vancouver Island 90 percent of the time. (This percentage is identical to that given for August off the coasts of Southern California and Baja California, while the August figures for most of the coast of Central and Northern California are 4 feet or less only 70 percent of the time.)

APPENDIX D
West Coast Wind Reports

The following wind reports show percentages of wind speeds for May through September for typical West Coast areas:

Herbert Island
(North of Goletas Channel near Pine Island where Queen Charlotte Straits meet Queen Charlotte Sound)

May, winds less that 20 knots 88% 20 to 33 knots 8% winds greater than 34 knots 3 %
June, winds less than 20 knots 94 %, 20 to 33 knots 6 %.
July, winds less than 20 knots 97%, 20 to 33 knots 3 %.
August, winds less than 20 knots 97%, 20 to 33 knots 3%.
September, winds less than 20 knots 94 %, 20 to 33 knots 5 %, winds greater than 34 knots 1 %.

Solander Island
Off Cape Cook on Brooks Peninsula

May, winds less than 20 knots 57%, 20 to 30 knots 32 %, winds greater than 34 knots 10%.
June, winds less than 20 knots 55%, 20 to 30 knots 37%, winds greater than 34 knots 7%.
July, winds less than 20 knots 66%, 20 to 30 knots 30%, winds greater than 34 knots 3%.
August ,winds less than 20 knots 57%, 20 to 30 knots 36%, winds greater than 34 knots 6%.
September, winds less than 20 knots 69%, 20 to 30 knots 26%, winds greater than 34 knots 5 %.

Estevan Point
Approximate center of West Coast Vancouver Island

May, winds less than 20 knots 84%, 20 to 30 knots 14%, winds greater than 34 knots 2 %.
June, winds less than 20 knots 86%, 20 to 30 knots 13%, winds greater than 34 knots 1%.
July, winds less than 20 knots 87%, 20 to 30 knots 12%, winds greater than 34 knots nil.
August, winds less than 20 knots 92%, 20 to 30 knots 7 %, winds greater than 34 knots nil.
September, winds less than 20 knots 90%, 20 to 30 knots 9 %, winds greater than 34 knots 1%.

Race Rocks
East end Juan de Fuca Strait, 10 miles south west of Victoria

May, winds less than 20 knots 80%, 20 to 30 knots 19%, winds greater than 34 knots 1%.
June, winds less than 20 knots 76%, 20 to 30 knots 23%, winds greater than 34 knots 1%.
July, winds less than 20 knots 73%, 20 to 30 knots 26%, winds greater than 34 knots 1%.
August, winds less than 20 knots 82%, 20 to 30% 17%, winds greater than 34 knots 1%.
September, winds less than 20 knots 92%, 20 to 30 knots 7%, winds greater than 34 knots 1%.

APPENDIX E
Frequency of Fog

Frequency of fog reported in all observations:

Location	May	June	July	Aug.	Sept.
Cape Scott	12.3%	14.7%	19.3%	24.7%	20.0%
Estevan Point	10.3%	12.8%	14.8%	21.4%	18.4%
Spring Island (3 mi. SW of Walters Cove)	10.6%	11.5%	11.6%	16.5%	15.2%
Tofino	14.1%	18.1%	21.8	29.8%	26.8%

APPENDIX F
Duration of Daylight

Typical duration of daylight at 50° North, northern third of Vancouver Island:

June 15
(Pacific Daylight Time at 120° W)

Nautical (morning)	twilight	0301
Civil	twilight	0406
Sunrise		0450
Sunset		2111
Civil	twilight	2155
Nautical (evening)	twilight	2301

Hours of daylight : 16 hours, 21 minutes
Hours of daylight and civil twilight: 17 hours, 49 minutes
Hours of daylight and nautical twilight: 20 hours

August 15
(Pacific Daylight Time at 120° W)

Nautical (morning)	twilight	0426
Civi	twilight	0512
Sunrise		0548
Sunset		2020
Civil	twilight	2056
Nautical (evening)	twilight	2141

Hours of daylight: 14 hours, 32 minutes
Hours of daylight and civil twilight: 15 hours, 44 minutes
Hours of daylight and nautical twilight: 17 hours, 15 minutes

Notes on Duration of Daylight Tables

1. Civil twilight is defined as that time when the sun is six degrees below the nominal horizon. At this time, the horizon is clearly visible, as are the brightest stars.

2. Nautical twilight is defined as that time when the sun is twelve degrees below the nominal horizon. At this time, the horizon is barely visible or fading from view.

3. Factors of local terrain, fog or moonlight can influence usable daylight or twilight hours.

4. See the Nautical Almanac for the formula to interpolate for exact times for various Latitudes and Longitudes.

APPENDIX G
Procedures Used in Gathering Local Knowledge

1. Coves, bays or bights which seemed to offer full or limited protection from different weather situations were identified and visited by our boat.

2. Routes were sketched and photographed.

3. Perusal of a possible anchor site was made with a dual frequency recording echo sounder to identify major underwater obstacles and to check the depth and flatness of the bottom over the expected swinging area. These depths were recorded on the sketches.

4. Once an anchor site was selected, a sample anchor test was made of the bottom by using a small "lunch hook" attached to light line and six feet of chain.

5. The response of the anchor to the bottom was noted (i.e. soft or hard mud, sand, gravel, rocky, etc.).

6. Additional line was let out to fully set the anchor.

7. A pull-down with the engine in reverse was made against the anchor to test holding power of the bottom

8. Upon retrieving the anchor, I inspected the residue on its flukes to verify bottom material.

9. Discussions were held with local residents and fishermen about anchorages, names, etc., and their comments were noted on the sketches.

10. A rough draft of the manuscript was submitted to local residents for their review.

11. The information gathered from our procedures, or that submitted by local residents, was consolidated and edited and became the local knowledge we have presented in our diagrams and text.

APPENDIX H
First Nations Tribal Councils

Nuu-chah-nulth Tribal Council Band

Ahousaht
General Delivery
Ahousaht, B.C. V0R 1A0
604-670-9563 or 670-9531
Fax 604-670-9696

Ditidaht
P.O. Box 340
Port Alberni, B.C. V9Y 7M8
Operator Nitinaht Raven
N692932 (0711)
604-745-3333

Ehattesaht
P.O. Box 716
Campbell River, B.C. V9W 6J3
604-287-4353
Fax 604-287-2330

Hesquiaht
P.O. Box 2000
Tofino, B.C. V0R 2Z0
Operator Hesquiaht Boat Basin 98077
604-724-8570

Kyuquot
General Delivery
Kyuquot, B.C. V0P 1J0
604-332-5259
Fax 332-5210

Muchalaht/Mowachaht
P.O. Box 459
Gold River, B.C. V0P 1G0
604-283-2532 or 283-7522
Fax 604-283-2335

Nuchatlaht
P.O. Box 40
Zeballos, B.C. V0R 2A0
604-724-8609
Fax 604-761-2060

Opetchesaht
P.O. Box 211
Port Alberni, B.C. V9Y 7M7
604-724-1225
Fax 604-724-1232

Sheshaht
P.O. Box 1218
Port Alberni, B.C. V9Y 7M1
604-724-1225
Fax 604-724-4385

Tla-o-qui-aht
P.O. Box 18
Tofino, B.C. V0R 2Z0
604-725-3233
Fax 604-725-4233

Toquaht
P.O. Box 759
Ucluelet, B.C. V0R 3A0
604-726-4230 or 726-7223 or 726-7764
Fax 604-726-4403

Uchucklesaht
P.O. Box 157
Port Alberni, B.C. V9Y 7M7
604-724-1832

Ucluelet
P.O. Box 699
Ucluelet, B.C. V0R 3A0
604-726-7342
Fax 604-726-7552

Ohiaht
P.O. Box 70
Bamfield, B.C. V0R1B0
604-728-3414
Fax 604-728-3452

Oclucji Band Office
604-724-8609

Other Tribal Councils

Quatsino Band
P.O. Box 100
Coal Harbour, B.C. V0N 1K0
604-949-6245

GWA; Sala-nakwax-da'xw Band
P.O. Box 998
Port Hardy, B.C. V0N 2P0
604-949-8343

Kwakiutl Band Council
P.O. Box 1440
Port Hardy, B.C. V0N 2P0
604-949-6102

Bibliography

Blier, Richard K., *Island Adventures, An Outdoors Guide to Vancouver Island.* Victoria: Orca Book Publishers, 1991.

Blier, Richard K., *More Island Adventures, An Outdoors Guide to Vancouver Island.* Vol. 2, Victoria: Orca Book Publishers, 1993.

Chappell, John, *Cruising Beyond Desolation Sound.* Vancouver: Naikoon Marine, rev. ed. 1987.

Chettleburgh, Peter, *An Explorer's Guide: Marine Parks of British Columbia.* Vancouver: Special Interests Publications, Maclean Hunter, 1985.

Dawson, Will, *Coastal Cruising.* Vancouver: Mitchell Press, 1959.

Denton, V. L., *The Far West Coast,* Toronto: J. M. Dent & Sons Ltd., Canada, 1924.

Drushka, Ken, *Against Wind and Weather, The History of Towboating in British Columbia.* Vancouver: Douglas & McIntyre Ltd., 1991.

Efrat, Barbara S. and Langlois, W. J. (editors), *Nu·tka· Captain Cook and the Spanish Explorers on the Coast,* Sound Heritage, Vol. VII, No 1. Victoria: Aural History Provincial Archives of British Columbia, 1978.

Graham, Donald, *Keepers of the Light, A History of British Columbia's Lighthouses and Their Keepers.* Madeira Park: Harbour Publishing, 1990.

Hemingway-Douglass, Réanne, *Cape Horn, One Man's Dream, One Woman's Nightmare.* Bishop: Fine Edge Productions, 1994.

Hill, Beth, *The Remarkable World of Frances Barkley, 1769-1845.* Sidney: Gray's Publishing Limited, 1978.

Ince, John and Köttner, Hedi, *Sea Kayaking Canada's West Coast.* Vancouver: Raxas Books, Inc., 1982.

Jewitt, John R., *White Slaves of the Nootka,* Surrey: Heritage House Publishing Company Ltd., 1987.

Jones, Laurie, *Nootka Sound Explored, a Westcoast History.* Campbell River: Ptarmigan Press, 1991.

Minister of Supply and Services, *Marine Weather Hazards Manual, a guide to local forecasts and conditions,* 2nd Edition. Vancouver: Environment Canada, 1990.

Moziño, José Mariano, *Noticias de Nutka, An Account of Nootka Sound in 1792,* translated and edited by Iris H. Wilson Engstrand, Seattle: University of Washington Press, 1991.

Nicholson, George, *Vancouver Island's West Coast 1762-1962.* Vancouver: George Nicholson's Books, 1965.

Northwest Boat Travel, Volume 13, Number 2. Anacortes: Anderson Publishing Company, 1990.

Obee, Bruce, *The Pacific Rim Explorer.* North Vancouver: Whitecap Books, 1986.

Peterson, Lester R., *The Cape Scott Story.* Vancouver: Mitchell Press Ltd., 1974.

Renner, Jeff, *Northwest Marine Weather, From the Columbia River to Cape Scott.* Seattle: The Mountaineers, 1993.

Rue, Roger L., *Circumnavigating Vancouver Island, a Cruising Guide.* Seattle: Evergreen Pacific Marine Publications, 1982.

Sailing Directions British Columbia Coast (South Portion). Ottawa: Department of Fisheries and Oceans, Communications Directorate for the Canadian Hydrographic Service, Vol. 1, Fifteenth Edition, 1990.

Small Craft Guide, British Columbia. Department of Fisheries and Oceans, Institute of Ocean Sciences, Sidney, B.C., Vol. 1, Seventh Edition, 1989

Small Craft Guide, British Columbia. Department of Fisheries and Oceans, Institute of Ocean Sciences, Sidney, B.C., Vol. 2, Eighth Edition, 1990.

Snively, Gloria, *Exploring the Seashore in British Columbia, Washington and Oregon, A Guide to Shorebirds and Intertidal Plants and Animals.* West Vancouver: Gordon Soules Book Publishers Ltd., 1978.

Snowden, Mary Ann, *Island Paddling, A Paddler's Guide to the Gulf Islands & Barkley Sound.* Victoria: Orca Book Publishers, 1990.

Stewart, Hilary (annotated and illustrated by), *The Adventures and Sufferings of John R. Jewitt, Captive of Maquinna.* Vancouver: Douglas & McIntyre, 1987.

Stooke, Philip, *Landmarks and Legends of the North Island.* Port Hardy: North Island Gazette Ltd., 1978

Thomson, Richard E., *Oceanography of the British Columbia Coast.* Ottawa: Department of Fisheries and Oceans, 1981.

U.S. Navy Marine Climatic Atlas, Vol. VIII, prepared by Crutcher, H.M. & Davis, O.M., Naval Weather Service Command, 1969.

Walbran, Captain John T.B.C., *Coast Names 1592-1906 to which are added a few names in adjacent United States Territory their Origin and History.* Vancouver: Published for VPL by J.J. Douglas Ltd., 1971.

Washburne, Randel, *The Coastal Kayaker, Kayak Camping on the Alaska and B.C. Coast.* Chester, Connecticut: Globe Pequot Press, 1983.

Watmough, Don, *Cruising Guide to the West Coast of Vancouver Island, Cape Scott to Sooke including Barkley Sound.* Seattle: Evergreen Pacific Publishing, 1984; reprinted 1993.

Index

Author's Experience

Over the past 25 years Don Douglass and his wife, Réanne, have sailed from 59°N to 54°S latitude, logging over 100,000 miles of offshore cruising. They consider their explorations of Vancouver Island's West Coast by diesel trawler and sea kayak to be some of their most satisfying experiences.

Don, who was raised in a sailing family, has a B.S. in engineering from California Polytechnic University and an M.B.A. from Claremont Graduate School. He has taught outdoor survival and mountaineering classes and written guidebooks on ski touring and mountain biking.

The Douglasses make an annual trip to Alaska where they share the *Baidarka* with their daughter and son-in-law. When they are not cruising in the Northwest, the Douglasses make their home in the mountains of the Eastern Sierra Nevada.

Cape Horn, One Man's Dream, One Woman's Nightmare, by Réanne Hemingway-Douglass, describes the couple's experience of pitchpoling 800 miles west-northwest of Cape Horn in their William Garden-designed ketch. ISBN 0-938665-29-4

New for *Exploring...Cruising Guide Series:*

Exploring the Inside Passage to Alaska, by Don & Réanne Douglass. Up-to-date local knowledge from the San Juan Islands to Glacier Bay. Features 120 detailed diagrams and 350 GPS way-points. ISBN 0-938665-33-2. (Publication date: late 1994)

For information, please check your favorite nautical book dealer or send an SASE to Fine Edge Productions, Route 2, Box 303, Bishop, California 93514.

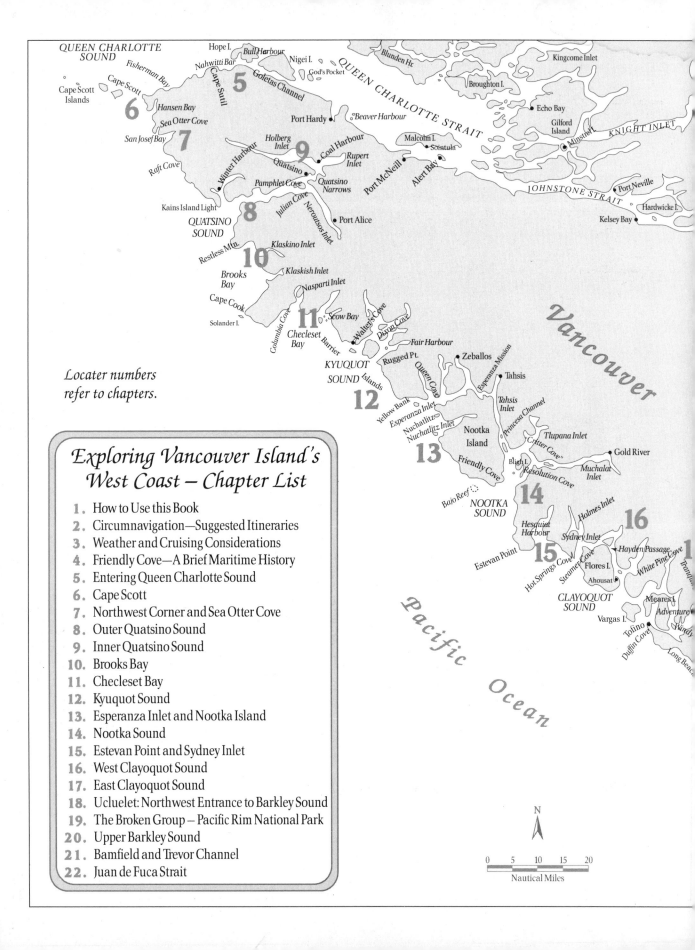

QUEEN CHARLOTTE SOUND

Fisherman Bay
Cape Scott Islands
Cape Scott Islands
Cape Scott
Hansen Bay
Sea Otter Cove
San Josef Bay
Raft Cove
Kains Island Light

Hope I.
Bull Harbour
Nigei I.
Nahwitti Bar
Cape Sutil
God's Pocket
Goletas Channel

5
6
7
8
9
10
11
12
13
14
15
16

Port Hardy
Beaver Harbour

QUEEN CHARLOTTE STRAIT

Blunden Hr.
Kingcome Inlet
Broughton I.
Echo Bay
Gilford Island
Malcolm I.
Soistula
Rupert Inlet
Coal Harbour
Holberg Inlet
Quatsino
Pamphlet Cove
Quatsino Narrows
Port McNeill
Alert Bay
Julian Cove
Neroutsos Inlet
Port Alice

QUATSINO SOUND

Restless Mtn.
Klaskino Inlet
Brooks Bay
Klaskish Inlet
Cape Cook
Nasparti Inlet
Solander I.
Columbia Cove
Scow Bay
Walters Cove
Dixon Cove
Checleset Bay
Barrier
Fair Harbour
Zeballos

KYUQUOT SOUND Islands

Rugged Pt.
Queen Cove
Esperanza Mission
Tahsis
Yellow Bank
Esperanza Inlet
Nuchatlitz
Nuchatlitz Inlet
Tahsis Inlet
Princesa Channel
Tlupana Inlet
Gold River
Nootka Island
"Critter Cove"
Muchalat Inlet
Friendly Cove
Bligh I.
Resolution Cove
Bajo Reef

NOOTKA SOUND

Hesquiat Harbour
Holmes Inlet
Sydney Inlet
Hayden Passage
Estevan Point
Hot Springs Cove
Steamer Cove
Flores I.
White Pine Cove
Ahousat
Meares I.
Adventure

CLAYOQUOT SOUND

Vargas I.
Tofino
Duffin Cove
Long Beach
Windy

Vancouver

JOHNSTONE STRAIT
Port Neville
Hardwicke I.
Kelsey Bay

KNIGHT INLET
Minstrel

Pacific Ocean

Locater numbers refer to chapters.

Exploring Vancouver Island's West Coast – Chapter List

N

0   5   10   15   20
Nautical Miles